CONTINGENT FUTURE PERSONS

Theology and Medicine

VOLUME 8

CONTINGENT FUTURE PERSONS

On the Ethics of Deciding Who Will Live,
or Not, in the Future

Edited by

NICK FOTION

Department of Philosophy, Emory University,
Atlanta, Georgia, U.S.A.

and

JAN C. HELLER

Center for Ethics in Health Care, Saint Joseph's Health System,
Atlanta, Georgia, U.S.A.

KLUWER ACADEMIC PUBLISHERS

DORDRECHT / BOSTON / LONDON

A C.I.P. Catalogue record for this book is available from the Library of Congress

ISBN 0-7923-4707-2   1001557292

Published by Kluwer Academic Publishers,
P.O. Box 17, 3300 AA Dordrecht, The Netherlands.

Sold and distributed in the U.S.A. and Canada
by Kluwer Academic Publishers,
101 Philip Drive, Norwell, MA 02061, U.S.A.

In all other countries, sold and distributed
by Kluwer Academic Publishers,
P.O. Box 322, 3300 AH Dordrecht, The Netherlands.

Printed on acid-free paper

Printed in the Netherlands

TABLE OF CONTENTS

JAN C. HELLER

PREFACE

How ought we evaluate the individual and collective actions on which the existence, numbers and identities of future people depend? In the briefest of terms, this question poses what is addressed here as the problem of contingent future persons, and as such it poses relatively novel challenges for philosophical and theological ethicists. For though it may be counter-intuitive, it seems that those contingent future persons who are actually brought into existence by such actions cannot benefit from or be harmed by these actions in any conventional sense of the terms.

This intriguing problem was defined almost three decades ago by Jan Narveson [2], and to date its implications have been explored most exhaustively by Derek Parfit [3] and David Heyd [1]. Nevertheless, as yet there is simply no consensus on how we ought to evaluate such actions or, indeed, on whether we can. Still, the pursuit of a solution to the problem has been interestingly employed by moral philosophers to press the limits of ethics and to urge a reconsideration of the nature and source of value at its most fundamental level. It is thus proving to be a very fruitful investigation, with far-reaching theoretical and practical implications.

To date, however, almost no theological ethicists or moral theologians have taken up the challenges of the problem of contingent future persons. It should thus come as no surprise that most of the contributors to a volume in the Theology and Medicine series are philosophers. One purpose of this volume, then, is to introduce the problem to theologically interested readers. A second is to advance the investigation of the problem itself, both philosophically and theologically. We will judge the volume a success to the extent that it fulfills these two purposes.

From the start, this volume has been a collaborative effort. For their work and scholarship, we gratefully acknowledge the contributors to the volume. We also thank the General Editor of the Theology and Medicine series, Earl E. Shelp, for his generous support. And last we want to thank our secretaries, Mrs. Pat Redford, in the Department of Philosophy at Emory University, and Ms. Joan Frost, at Saint Joseph's Health System, for their good-humored help and efficiency.

BIBLIOGRAPHY

1. Heyd, D.: 1992, *Genethics: Moral Issues in the Creation of People*, University of California Press, Berkeley, CA.
2. Narveson, J.: 1967, "Utilitarianism and New Generations," *Mind* 76, pp. 62-72.
3. Parfit, D.: 1984, *Reasons and Persons*, Clarendon Press, Oxford.

Nick Fotion and Jan C. Heller (eds.), Contingent Future Persons, vii.
© 1997 *Kluwer Academic Publishers. Printed in the Netherlands.*

INTRODUCTION

This volume raises and discusses a variety of questions about future persons from a variety of viewpoints. The overarching question discussed is: What is the ethical relationship between future persons and those of us who are here now? Many thinkers express this relationship in terms of rights. Do some or all future persons have certain rights charged against us? Do these future persons, for example, have rights pertaining to the environment such that we must act *now* to protect it for them *then*? Do they have a right to be created? More than that, do they have a right to be created in a condition of good health and, even beyond that, a right to be created in a better condition than we had when we were born? And just how strong are these rights? Are these rights absolute (with no exceptions), almost absolute or merely ones that can be rebutted with any number of good reasons?

Many other thinkers express the relationship between us and future generations in terms of duties. These people ask: Do we have duties to care for the environment for the benefit of future persons and perhaps even for the benefit of the various animals and plants found on our planet? Do we have duties to procreate, and to procreate in such a way that future persons are healthy? If indeed we do have such duties, what about their strength? Are they so strong as to require us to make immense sacrifices for future people? Or are these duties rather weak so we are only required to be somewhat sensitive to the needs of these people?

Let us assume for the moment that we have duties of some sort to future people. This is an assumption we might very well accept, especially when we focus on our relationships to those who will be born within our family and ethnic group. We think that we need to do whatever we can so that they will be able to live a good life as we would have liked to have had, and perhaps have had. Initially, doing these things seems perfectly correct and unproblematic. But a problem faces us almost immediately when we realize that future people do not represent just one, two or three generations the way we do; but an indefinite number. There are the future people who will appear on earth within the next few years, within fifty, one hundred, one-hundred and fifty years, two hundred years and so on. If we have duties to each of these groups of future people, it would seem as if we would have to undergo process of discounting ourselves. It is a bit like a couple with a dozen children. Duties toward making each child happy keeps them from doing things for themselves, especially if the family's financial resources are severely limited. Would, then, having duties to all those future people mean that we must make sacrifices for their benefit; sacrifices, some would say, so onerous as to be counterintuitive?

1

Nick Fotion and Jan C. Heller (eds.), Contingent Future Persons, 1-8.
© 1997 *Kluwer Academic Publishers. Printed in the Netherlands.*

Perhaps we need not make quite so many sacrifices. Maybe we don't have to cut the human population level back from over five billion (what it is now) to below one billion; and don't have to cut our energy consumption back to one fifth of what it is now. Instead of discounting ourselves, maybe we should discount future people. Even if we continue to insist that we have duties to them (and/or that these future people have rights), those duties might be less because we don't know how many of them there will be, what they will be like, what their needs and wants will be, what technologies will be available to make them have good or bad lives and, overlapping all these reasons, can't predict distant future events with any precision. So, even though we may have duties to future people, these duties may be less than those we have to ourselves for a variety or combination of reasons. But how much less? Just how much discounting should we do? These are not easy questions to answer.

The discounting problem is only the beginning. Other problems press upon us once we begin thinking about future people. Unfortunately, there is no obvious way to package them, largely because they overlap so much. Perhaps the best way is to follow David Heyd ([1] pp. 95-96). He clusters these problems under the headings of existence, number and identity (or quality).

Problems of existence have to do with whether we have duties to create the next generation and the one following that. Did Mary's parents have a duty to create her or, putting it another way, did she have a right to be created? Does it even make sense to talk about duties and rights here since Mary's parents had no idea that they were creating her, as against some other child? After all, had they delayed their sexual encounter for even a few minutes, a totally different child would likely have been created.

Even if Mary's parents had no duty to create her, and Mary no right to be created, did her parents have a duty to create some child or other? But even if they had such a duty, is this duty *to* the future child itself or to the society? Many argue that we have duties to reproduce since humanity, and the ethnic and/or racial group we belong to, need to replenish themselves. It might even be argued that the parents have duties to themselves. Beyond that, however, does it make sense to say we have a duty to some indefinite future child as well, where, in effect, we are directly concerned with the benefit of this yet to be conceived creature?

Or is there no duty here at all? Perhaps having or not having a child is not a matter of duty (or some right), but something personal. Beyond just wanting the pleasures associated with sex, many people desire offspring. They want children because they enjoy them and, perhaps, because they see these creatures as ways to be immortalized through their genes. Whatever the reason(s), it can be and has been argued that ethics plays no role in driving the creation of babies.

Even if individuals, and individual couples, have no duty to future persons to create them, perhaps the society has such a duty. So perhaps the society has a duty to encourage many but not necessarily all of its members to bring future people into existence. If it does, it might carry out its duty by employing tax policies favoring families laden with children, giving families direct subsidies, giving mothers-to-be and the resulting children free medical care, praising and honoring mothers who have many children and so on. But, again, the question is: Is it just so much rhetoric to say we have duties owed to future people? Are these duties really owed to these people (even before they are conceived), or is the society's replenishment policy driving the process? Or is it both?

Problems dealing with number, Heyd's second heading, have to do with just how many humans we should create. Is it better to create more people, even if the life they lead isn't too good, simply because we do more overall good by having many people around? Might not the total good be greater with many people living a life barely above the level of a worthwhile life, than to have fewer people on the planet with most of them living a very good life? Derek Parfit calls this the Repugnant Conclusion because he and many others find it repugnant to suppose that the former kind of life on earth is better than the latter ([3] pp. 388-389). More generally, number problems when dealing with future people have to do with just how many humans can live optimally on this planet (or elsewhere). These problems also raise questions about an optimal life for non-human animals. How many of these creatures can live on this planet while we, at the same time, continue to reproduce to the point where there are not just six billion of us here but, perhaps, ten, fifteen or more? Do more of us necessarily mean that there will be fewer non-human animals on this planet? Or can, at least to some extent, technology allow us to multiply without harming them too severely?

Problems of identity (quality), falling under Heyd's third heading, are intertwined with those of existence and quantity. If we have duties to create future persons in whatever numbers, do we have duties as well to create them in a healthy and happy state? It would seem so. Yet what if parents create a child who they know will be genetically deformed? From the point of view of the child, it might well wish to live with the deformity if the only choice its parents had was to create it with its deformity or create a totally different child. They could have chosen the latter option simply by waiting to reproduce at a time when, let us say, the mother was no longer ill and thus could create a normal child. Isn't it true that what is good for the deformed child is that it be conceived with its deformity rather than not be conceived? Putting it differently, that child could not be harmed by its parents insofar as it is born deformed because it could never be normal. Harm, as we usually speak of it, compares a normal state of a person to a later inferior state. To harm someone is to degrade his or her status. But the deformed child is not harmed in this way when it is allowed to be conceived. Rather it is given life.

There are other quality of life problems in dealing with future people. Because we have so little control over what happens in the future, it could be argued that our duties to these people do not extend to bringing about good lives for them. Rather, those duties merely demand that we place them in an environment that guarantees them a minimal life. The rest is up to them. Is that the extent of our duties, or do our duties demand more from us?

The articles that follow deal with most of these problems and a few more. The first and second articles, by R. M. Hare and Michael Lockwood respectively, focus on when potentiality counts, that is, at what point can we start counting the interests of a person. These articles deal with a variation of the existence problem. Hare argues that we can start counting even before conception. We can do so not because gametes, embryos and even fetuses have interests as such. Rather possible and actual people have interests in a developed state. Among the interests they have is that their gametes, embryo and fetus be treated properly. Thus a healthy and happy Harriet benefited from the fact that her mother helped conceive her and that, later, she did not abort her. Within limits, an early or late abortion, for Hare, would have been equally harmful to Harriet. Time, as such, is not important. Hare would add that what is good for Harriet is equally good for others who are similarly situated, even if those others, like Harry, were aborted. It would have been equally good for Harry to have developed into an adult and to have lived a healthy and happy life like Harriet.

Michael Lockwood is in deep disagreement with Hare. Whereas Hare talks about the (actual) interests of possible people, some of whom might never exist, Lockwood does not. Instead he talks about possible people having only possible (not real) interests. Not having real interests, it makes no sense for Lockwood to say that we can harm or benefit possible people. Thus we have no duty to create Andrew who exists not even as a glimmer in his father's eye. In contrast, Hare would say we do have a duty to create some as yet to be specified possible person (whom we will call Andrew or Andrea) if we can reasonably expect that the child born will have a good life. For Lockwood creating children is not a duty-bound activity but is, as he says, supererogatory.

(These two articles in this volume are the only ones not directly commissioned for it. They first appeared in *Bioethics* in 1988. Hare's article is in response to another Lockwood article [2]. We did not feel it was necessary to reprint that article as well, since the relevant issues for this volume discussed in that earlier article are amply discussed by Hare and by Lockwood himself in the articles reproduced here.)

Our third article, by Cynthia Cohen, does not address the question: Do we have duties to create babies? but the related question: Do we have a duty knowingly not to create babies who will have serious disabilities? Her answer is "Yes." The "wrongful life" standard, she observes, claims that a child harmed by the means used to create him or her (such as *in vitro* fertilization) has no grounds for complaint, since but for its use that child would not exist—and existence is better than nonexistence. Cohen argues that this standard confuses posthumous nonexistence with preconception nonexistence. To remedy this, it must be expanded to take into account that death is worse than not being conceived. Thus, while we wrong the living child who has serious, but not devastating, disabilities by letting him or her die, we do not wrong the same possible child when we do not create him or her in the first place. That possible child has no interest in being born.

Ingmar Persson is the first of our writers to explicitly bring to the discussion the frequently made distinction between person-affecting and impersonal values. Person-affecting values are those that apply only to so-called actual people—those who exist already or who will come to exist quite apart from the choices their parents make about their existence (e.g., those created "by accident"). Advocates of various forms of the person-affecting doctrine argue that contingent future persons (those who we actually choose to create or not create) do not count in the moral calculus. Only actual persons count. Persson goes against this doctrine by arguing that persons can be helped by being created and, conversely, harmed by not being created. So Persson's stance is basically an impersonal one since value attaches to persons whether they are actual or contingent. In this regard his position is close to Hare's.

Persson also deals with Parfit's Repugnant Conclusion mentioned above. He is loath to admit that it is better to choose a world with a very large number of people who live a life barely worth living as compared to one with fewer people who live a life really worth living. It may seem otherwise if the good life (of more pleasures than pain) is measured simply on a quantitative scale. But when quality of life is taken into account, Persson thinks that the earth populated with fewer people should be chosen over the one with more.

In contrast to Persson, David Heyd is a defender of the person-affecting view. Indeed, he argues that value talk makes no sense unless there are persons (humans) on the scene. But his main concern in his article is not to present a philosophical defense of his views. Rather, it is to show that the Jewish tradition, as found in *Genesis*, can best be interpreted as person-affecting. He argues that the Jewish idea of God is that of a creator who, in creating humans in His image, commands them to be creative (i.e., to multiply). Evidently the Jewish religion is person-affecting both on the level of God and humanity. In part this means that God creates humans and the rest of the universe for God. In turn, humans (choose) to create other humans for humans and, in doing so, they make value judgments possible.

Jan Heller's article investigates many of the problems under discussion in this volume from a Christian perspective. He argues that Christianity is compatible with the person-affecting view in the sense that it conceives of God as an agent (and thus a "person" in at least this sense), and that the world with humans in it is created primarily for God's benefit. Here he is claiming that Christianity is close to what Heyd claims for Judaism. But there is agreement even beyond this point since Heller claims that Christianity is person-affecting on the human level as well. Christianity puts too much emphasis on the importance of the human person (individually and collectively) for it to be otherwise. But as a result of its person-affecting stance, Christianity places no direct constraints on Christians to choose this or that contingent future person. This means that Christianity cannot accommodate a view like Hare's (Persson's and, below, Fotion's) that is concerned with the welfare of future contingent persons directly (i.e., as such, or in and of themselves). Indirectly, of course, concern may be shown. Thus, if a contingent future person is likely to be born with serious defects, we might not choose to conceive that person because doing so would harm either or both the family and the community. However, according to the person-affecting view, because we cannot harm an entity who does not yet exist, it makes no sense to say that we should not to conceive it because of the harm we might do to it. Nor, if it is likely to be healthy, does it make sense to say that we *should* conceive it.

In his article, Nick Fotion returns the discussion to the Repugnant Conclusion. However he takes a different tack from that taken by Persson to avoid that conclusion's seemingly unpleasant consequences. He does not appeal to qualitative considerations. Working from within an impersonal rather than a person-affecting approach, he argues that when we take into account the costs of moving from a world like ours with a population near six billion to one with 50 billion *and* the costs of actually living there, the (overall) costs are too high. We would likely, he says, prefer states more like the ones we have now—or perhaps ones with an even smaller population base. He grants that a total utilitarian theory like his cannot make specific population recommendations about these matters. Given our present knowledge, and perhaps even future knowledge, this theory cannot tell us what sort of population base is ideal. However, this is not to say that other theories can do much better. In the end, his point is that the Repugnant Conclusion "Argument" does not damage the utilitarian position so much as some of its opponents would suppose.

Clark Wolf sees problems with utilitarianism beyond the Repugnant Conclusion. He argues that utilitarians do not fully appreciate the difference between the positive injunction to promote happiness and the negative one to prevent unhappiness. The two parts of utilitarian theory are, as it were, *not* like two sides of one coin. Avoiding unhappiness (misery) is a more serious injunction than doing good. In his modified utilitarian stance Wolf argues that we have obligations not to cause people to exist who would be miserable but no obligations to cause people to exist who would have a good life. With respect to future contingent people who would be miserable, Wolf thus sides with the impersonalists. We can take their interests into account. However, on the side of doing good, he sides with the person-affecting theorists in not taking the interests of future contingent persons into account. Wolf thinks that his theory, being partly utilitarian and partly obligational (deontological), best explains many of the problems facing those who worry about what population policies we should adopt.

In his article, Avner de-Shalit deals with population issues by focusing on the environment. He argues for sensitivity to environmental issues from what he calls a shallow ecological point of view. Such a point of view does not recommend radical changes in our life style as does the Dark Green approach. Nor does it recommend, again as the Dark Greens do, that we focus attention on the environment as a whole (e.g., on duties we have to animals, plants and rivers). Rather, shallow ecological thinking is anthropocentric. It argues that more can be done to save the environment, and the people who are a part of it, if we present our ecological recommendations as if they were ones aimed to help human beings. In part this is because the "shallow" approach asks people to make changes in their lives that they can both understand and be sympathetic with. In contrast, people react against the extreme claims and demands of the Deep Ecologists. About all that Deep Ecology sympathizers tend to accomplish is to make themselves feel righteous. de-Shalit's particular way of expressing these thoughts is to emphasize the importance of the notion of community which, for him, encompasses not just those living now but future people. Our sense of community will help us care for ourselves and those we will create at least for several generations to come.

Compared to de-Shalit, Lukas Meyer looks at many of the issues under discussion in this volume somewhat more narrowly. Instead of being concerned with environmental issues writ large, he focuses on people and the communities they live in. He argues that rights alone cannot account for the relationships we have to future people. Future people do not even have a right to insist that we reproduce. Appealing only to rights theory, we could simply stop reproducing. So duties must also be invoked to supplement the failure of rights theory. But as a person-affecting theorist, Meyer does not say that our duties are owed to contingent future people. Instead, some of the most important of these duties are partly owed to those who have preceded us. Our predecessors have built governments, libraries, museums, schools, centers of worship, businesses and other institutions with the intent of making them available for us and for those who follow us. They have also invested energy and treasure in scientific research (e.g., genetics and atomic theory) and many large engineering projects (e.g., buildings, dams, roads and bridges). We owe it to our predecessors to keep at least some of these long-range institutions and projects in place.

Robert Elliot agrees with Meyer that the concept of rights cannot be applied to contingent future people. However, he adds, nor can justice. For Elliot contingent future people cannot be harmed by not being made existent since, in their non-existent state, they have no point of view at all. There are no good and bad states of affairs against which the non-existent person can, as it were, say to himself that he is better off not existing than existing. Elliot spends a considerable amount of time in his article attacking Persson, whom Elliot takes to be arguing that rights concepts can apply to contingent future persons. He also attacks de-Shalit who, via the notion of community, argues that the concepts of rights and justice do apply to these persons and to environmental issues generally.

In her article, Carol Tauer changes the subject somewhat, although, like our other writers, she is still concerned with the questions of existence, number and identity of future persons. Specifically, she wonders about the moral status of the preimplanted embryo. Still more specifically, she wonders if it makes a difference whether the embryo in an IVF procedure is a "spare" embryo or one engineered deliberately for purposes of conducting research. In dealing with this question she asks about the status of that embryo. Is it a full fledged actual person? A developing person? Or is it merely a possible person? Her answer is that it makes no difference when it comes to dealing with the "spare" vs. dedicated-for-research embryo question. No matter what theory about the status of the embryo one holds, there are no good reasons for allowing research on spare embryos but forbidding it on the ones dedicated for research. It is either allowable to do research on both kinds of embryos; or it is not allowable on either.

Tauer also worries about the disparity between research into and the clinical application of IVF technology. She wonders if enough research has been done with high-tech versions of this technology, and especially with how this lack of research harms women. Given these worries, she suggests that rather than back off on IVF research we ought to back off on (some) clinical uses of IVF technology.

In his article, William George deals with the problems of contingent future persons mainly through the cognitional theory of the theologian Bernard Lonergan. Various processes and concepts in our thinking can, for Lonergan (and George), take on a heuristic character. This means that these processes and concepts are developed to aid us deal with whatever problems face us. The heuristic character of our thinking keeps us open minded, aware of complexities and down to earth. In this light, the various problems of contingent future persons need to be seen not only as abstract and theoretical but also as practical. The concept of contingent future person itself is heuristic insofar as it provokes moral reflection. Given Lonergan's (and George's) understanding of human intelligence as that which seeks or anticipates meaning and value, contingent future persons, and harm or benefit to those persons, are meaningful concepts. For armed with our best accumulated understanding of benefit or harm, we may anticipate the future and thus act now to affect (or block) the emergence, as well as the conditions of emergence, of new persons. This, in turn, suggests that George' position is closer to the person-affecting rather than the impersonal approach. However, it should be noted that his Lonerganian orientation allows him to say that he is backing away from such dichotomies as impersonal/person affecting. Such dichotomies have the demerit, he thinks, of closing off our intellectual options.

As one reads this article it is worth pondering the following question: To what extent do differences in theory (e.g., person-affecting vs. impersonal) make a difference in reproductive practices and population policies? Note that Lockwood says that though he differs with Hare theoretically he doubts that his moral views differ significantly from Hare's. Heller as well observes that although person-affecting views do not take account of the welfare of future contingent people directly, they do so indirectly. From what he and some other of our other writers suggest, this may mean, once again, that theoretical differences do not always lead to yawning differences in practices and policies.

BIBLIOGRAPHY

1.   Heyd, D.: 1992, *Genethics: Moral Issues in the Creation of People*, University of California Press, Berkeley, CA.
2.   Lockwood, M.: 1988, "Warnock Versus Powell (and Harradine): When Does Potentiality Count?" *Bioethics*, Vol. 2, No. 3, pp. 187-213.
3.   Parfit, D.: 1984, *Reasons and Persons*, Clarendon Press, Oxford.

WHEN DOES POTENTIALITY COUNT?
A COMMENT ON LOCKWOOD[1]

Michael Lockwood has put us all in his debt by writing a paper which is both highly original, and clear enough for it to be possible to see where it goes wrong. Very few philosophers writing on this topic have achieved as much. His paper falls into two halves. In the first he explores the problem of what it is morally permissible to do to embryos, and raises difficulties for some widely canvassed solutions. In the second he proposes his own solution, which calls in aid a metaphysical manoeuvre of some sophistication, involving the criterion of personal identity (a contentious question among philosophers). I shall argue, however, that in his exploration he has been bamboozled by the misleading ways in which the problem has usually been posed, and that therefore he has sought the solution in the wrong place, and the manoeuvre, though elegant, is unhelpful.

It will be clearest to start with two apparently simple but actually fundamental logical points about tenses and moods. In two almost adjacent passages on his pages 199 and 200 [8], Lockwood says:

> A potential for X generates an interest only where there is some individual for whom the development of the potential for X constitutes a *benefit*.

and

> Faced with a fourteen day old human embryo, with the potential for developing into a human person, the question we must ask is: Does there now exist any individual for whom the development of this potential would constitute a direct benefit?

There are two important changes here which Lockwood does not appear to have noticed: from 'there is' to 'Does there now exist?' and from 'constitutes' to 'would constitute'. The second of these is clearly correct, for two reasons. First, if what we are speaking of is potential, it cannot be the case that the development of the potential constitutes a benefit *now*. If the benefit were present now, it would be actual not potential; the potential is the possibility (*potentia* is derived from *posse*) that its development will, or would under favourable conditions, occur in the future.

Secondly, the benefits that Lockwood is thinking of are those referred to in the preceding paragraph, and listed on p. 197: 'the ability to converse, self-reflective awareness, the power of rational deliberation and so forth'. These, he says, 'give

9

Nick Fotion and Jan C. Heller (eds.), Contingent Future Persons, 9-18.

normal human life its special worth'. To them we could add some benefits that are not specifically human, such as companionship with others, a vigorous and active life, and so on. Embryos cannot *now* have these benefits, as Lockwood would no doubt agree; they are benefits that the person into whom the embryo would under favourable conditions turn would have. But it is important to notice that what I have just said about the embryo could also be truly said about the foetus or even the neonate. None of these entities can have any of these benefits *now*, even if equipped with a brain. This creates difficulties for Lockwood's solution. For that consists in making a distinction between embryos on the one hand and foetuses with brains and infants on the other. The former, he says, cannot have interests, but the latter can. But if the first passage cited is taken as it stands, none of them can have interests.

So we have at least to recast Lockwood's first sentence cited above to read:

> A potential for X generates an interest only where there is some individual for whom the development of the potential would constitute a benefit.

But we have next to ask whether the step is legitimate from 'there is' to 'Does there now exist?'. 'There is' is often tenseless, like the 'There is an x such that' of quantificational logic. In expressions like 'There is an x such that Fx', the 'Fx' may or may not contain a tense, but the 'There is an x such that' does not have to contain one as well. This is evident in ordinary language too: it is perfectly natural to say (in August) 'There are three dates in October on which it will be possible for you to give your talk'. To say 'There will be three dates...' would be incorrect, because it would imply that at some future time unspecified there will *still* be three dates, which is not the meaning intended. The timetable may fill up.

We have to ask, therefore, whether in the first passage cited the 'there is' is tensed or tenseless. It would seem that in order to make the statement true it has to be tenseless. For it is possible for there to be an individual who *would* benefit, even though that individual (the individual who will enjoy the benefits listed by Lockwood and the ones we have added to his list) does not now exist. Let us suppose that we are talking about this individual even before there is the corresponding embryo--say when it is only a gleam in its parents' eyes. Suppose that they are rich and have no child, and (having read the parable of the rich fool in St Luke 12) are worried about who will benefit from their wealth after they are dead. They may still comfort themselves by saying 'But there is someone who would benefit, namely the child that we hope to have'.

This point appears to have escaped the attention of many who write on this subject, and so it will be worth rubbing it in. The potentiality of the embryo to develop into someone who can enjoy the listed benefits (let us say for short 'into a grown person') is important just because, if it does, that grown person will benefit. The benefit is not to the embryo. Nor is it to the foetus or even the neonate. The preservation of embryos, foetuses and neonates is important just because if they are preserved they will turn into grown people who will benefit from existing (not indeed because bare existence in itself is a benefit, but because in normal circumstances those who exist can have *other* benefits like those listed).

This is clear if we consider cases where the possibility of development into such a grown person is removed. Lockwood himself mentions some of these in relation to the embryo (chromosomal abnormality, or no womb available, p. 191). But foetuses and infants too can be in this predicament for the first of these reasons or others. I do not believe that Lockwood thinks we have a duty to preserve inevitably doomed foetuses and infants (for example anencephalic ones). He must surely therefore agree that where the possibility of development into a grown person is removed the duty to preserve, which arises just because of this possibility, is removed too. That he thinks this about embryos is indicated by his saying that the 'passing comment' of the Tate Committee 'strikes at the heart of their argument' p. 192. But how can he consistently think it about embryos but not about foetuses and infants? What such examples show is that in all these cases it is in the main (I shall discuss other factors below) the interest of the possible future grown person into whom they might turn that imposes on us, in normal cases, a duty to preserve them.

Some will now object that merely possible people cannot have interests. I have answered this objection at length elsewhere [3] [4], so here I can be brief. The answer can be put dramatically by asking Lockwood to suppose that he is a presently existing human adult (as he is), but one who came into being through IVF (as actually he did not). Suppose also that, at some stage in the medical procedures, the surgeons were faced with the question, Shall we implant this embryo or that other embryo (which would have turned, not into Lockwood, but into someone else)?

On these suppositions, Lockwood can certainly be glad and grateful that they implanted the embryo that turned into him, and not the other one, assuming that they could not implant both (see his p. 202). When they were making the decision, both embryos had the potential to turn, given a favourable environment, into adult humans; but only one of them had the potential to turn into this individual, namely Michael Lockwood. Although, if the other had been implanted and come to birth, that neonate too might have been *called* 'Michael Lockwood', it would have been a different Michael Lockwood. The present existing Michael Lockwood has every reason to be thankful that the surgeons implanted the embryo that turned into him, instead of experimenting on it. So the choice that they made undoubtedly conferred a benefit on him.

So if at that time they asked, 'Is there (tenseless) an individual for whom the development of this potential would constitute a direct benefit?', they could truly answer 'Yes'. And the important point is that the answer would still, at the time they asked the question, have been 'Yes' even if, later, they had decided not to implant the embryo but to experiment on it. For even so, it *was* the case that they could truly say to each other 'There is (tenseless) an individual for whom the development of this potential would constitute a direct benefit'. For here, now, we have supposed, is the existing individual Michael Lockwood, large as life, talking to us; and *ab esse in posse valet illatio*. That he now exists shows that it was at that time possible that he should now exist. Even if they had later removed that possibility by starting an experiment on him, it was still true *before* the experiment started that he *could* exist. The embryo still had the potential; and this potential, it might be argued, imposed on them a duty at least to consider the interest of the person whom they *could* bring into existence.

People find it hard to accept this point, because they are confused by some objections which I must now consider.

1. It is alleged that only existing people can have interests. This is plainly false, as the example just given shows. It was in Lockwood's interest that they should implant the embryo that turned into him, although he did not at that time exist.

2. It is also alleged that people who cannot be identified cannot have interests. This would mean that very few people in the future after at most a few years can have interests, because which identifiable individuals are born depends on actions which are not yet decided on, including actions of procreating those individuals. Which individuals are born depends on when we copulate, and that is still a matter of choice; and so, indeed, is whether we copulate at all ([10] 351 ff.). But the allegation is in any case false. The person who will occupy my carrel at the library next may be now unidentifiable, but it is in his interest that I should leave it tidy.

3. It is also claimed that if people who might be born have interests (in particular an interest in being procreated) this could impose on us a duty to procreate all the people we possibly could procreate, and this is held to be absurd. But the argument is fallacious. All procreation is choice (even if the choice is random), because procreating one person entails not procreating another.

Even if they worked at it as hard as they could, a single couple could not (allowing for a few twins) produce many more children on average than one every nine months; but there are many other children they could alternatively have had if they had copulated on different nights. And even the interests of the maximum number of children they could have do not impose on them a duty to have them all. For if they had them all, they might all starve, and that would not be in their interests. The maximum duty that is imposed is to do the best impartially for all the possible people there might be; and this can only be done by having an optimal family planning or population policy, which in turn means excluding some possible people (if only by abstinence). The best policy will be the one which produces that set of people, of all the possible sets, which will have in sum the best life. I have discussed elsewhere in more detail how we should address the problem of balancing quality of life against quantity [7]).

4. It is also objected that if the interests of possible people have to be considered when deciding what we may do to embryos, the same will be true of gametes, certainly in pairs, but perhaps even singly. For, after all, the now existing individual Michael Lockwood has reason to be glad that, and has benefited from the fact that, the gametes which led to his production were not destroyed either singly or conjointly. For if they had been, he would not have existed. This conclusion also is held to be absurd ([8], pp. 197 f.).

But it is not. From the present point of view, contraception and abortion really are on a par, though there may be other reasons for preferring contraception. Both are wrong, though defeasibly so, in that they involve the prevention of somebody coming into existence in whose interest it almost certainly was to exist. But, given that parents cannot have a duty to produce all the children they could produce, they have to choose when to copulate, and how often to do so without contraception; and this choice results in the production of some of these people and the exclusion of others.

It is true that Lockwood has reason to be glad that the gametes which produced him were not destroyed. But some gametes (innumerably many indeed) are inevitably destroyed, and whichever are destroyed might have survived if others had not. If some other sperm had succeeded in fertilizing the ovum, to the exclusion of the sperm which contributed the genes for Lockwood, then somebody else would have had as much reason, ceteris paribus, to be glad to exist as Lockwood has now. Lockwood's parents did not have a duty to secure that he in particular was born; at the most they had a duty to secure that some child was. And perhaps not even that, if enough children are being born anyway to produce the optimum size of population. The same is true of the surgeons deciding which embryo to implant. Given that they have more embryos than they can implant, they have at the most a duty (given the consent of the parents), to implant so many as can, after developing into children, find a place in a family of optimum size. And what that size is, is a question on which the present discussion has little bearing.

The upshot of the discussion is that contraception, abstinence, the destruction of embryos, abortion and even infanticide ought to be controlled, not by the interests of gametes, embryos, foetuses or infants, but by the interests of possible future developed people who there might otherwise be, and that the number of these ought to be decided on by finding the right population and family planning policy. Gametes and embryos do not as such have interests. The developed people they might turn into, or be instrumental in producing, do indeed have interests, and these have to be balanced against one another within the limits of what we can do; but the mere existence of the present gamete or embryo or foetus or even neonate provides no reason why it should have precedence over the others, beyond two relatively weak reasons which I shall be considering in a moment.

5. Lockwood says ([8], pp. 198-199) that it strikes him as preposterous to suggest that there is 'nothing intrinsically wrong with ending the life of a perfectly normal healthy newborn infant, or that infanticide is intrinsically no worse than deliberately preventing conception'. It is not clear what he means by 'intrinsically'; but whatever he means, the 'preposterous' conclusion does not follow from the position I have been maintaining. I have just said that both infanticide and contraception are pro tanto wrong (intrinsically wrong, if Lockwood wishes). They are wrong because they prevent the existence of a grown person who has an interest in existing. And, though from this point of view contraception and infanticide may be equally wrong, their wrongness is, as I said, defeasible: and there are in most cases reasons why contraception is less wrong.

Lockwood himself alludes to one of these reasons on p. 199: 'fertilized egg, embryo, foetus and newborn baby are as it were, successively further down the track towards realizing their potential for worthwhile life'. Another, which Lockwood does not mention, is that infants, unlike ova (whether fertilized or unfertilized) and sperms, are normally already objects of affection, and killing them inflicts grief on those who have come to love them (even if they have decided that all things considered their child, say because of some severe defect, ought to be allowed to die or even be killed in order that another may take its place). I have argued elsewhere [1]) that in such cases the interest of the possible future healthy child ought to take precedence over that of the existing severely handicapped child. A third reason is that, in spite of what some writers have claimed, infants, unlike gametes or even embryos, almost certainly do have some pleasures and desires (for example in or for their mothers' milk); and infanticide frustrates these. These desires cannot weigh much in the balance against the desires of a grown person that might come into existence if the infant did not; but they are something that the infant has and gametes and embryos do not have.

The considerations I have mentioned may account for the intuition to which, in any case, Lockwood says he is not going to appeal ([10], p. 199). The dilemma in which he seeks to place us ([10], p. 197), only in order to extricate us from it by his preferred solution, might not arise at all if we realized that intuitions are not a secure guide in out-of-the-way cases. It will be worth digressing in order to explain why. As I have argued elsewhere [1], there are at least two different levels of moral thinking which need to be distinguished, the intuitive and the critical. The intuitive level, at which we apply learnt moral responses, is, if we have learnt good ones, adequate for the ordinary run of cases (which, indeed, is why they are good ones). But cases in which infanticide or experimentation on embryos are in question are never ordinary ones, and in them our intuitions cannot be relied on to give the right answer.

Probably the best intuitions to have are ones which forbid infanticide but allow contraception. The stages in between are not catered for by these, and therefore we have to think about them more critically. That the intuition which forbids infanticide ought to be overridden in cases like that which I have described, does not entail that it is not the best intuition to have for all but the most abnormal cases. So it is perfectly possible for someone to have both these good intuitions, but to say that infanticide is in abnormal cases justified, and contraception in abnormal cases unjustified (say where the human race is in danger of extinction).

The reason why these are the best intuitions to have for the ordinary run of cases are not hard to find. It would nearly always be wrong to kill infants, and people would be badly educated morally if they could even contemplate it without horror. If we had been brought up that way, a lot of grown people would not come into existence who would have been glad to exist, and this would be a very bad thing. On the other hand, an intuition which in general permits contraception is probably better than the one it has recently replaced, which forbade it, because on the whole people who limit their families by contraception have good reasons (even good *moral* reasons) for doing so; it would be worse if they were prevented from limiting them.

True, we *could* have had (like some other cultures) an intuition that allowed infanticide as a means of family limitation. But our own culture sets a great deal of store by the loving care we give to infants (rightly, because infants treated in that way are much more likely when they grow up to be glad to be alive); and we cannot simultaneously cultivate this loving attitude and be ready to kill infants whenever we find it convenient. Only in extreme cases such as I have described are the two attitudes compatible; cases, that is, where the child is so handicapped that parents think it would be better to give the love to another future and more fortunate child, if one is not going to have them both to love. The reasons for thinking contraception less wrong than infanticide are therefore, though in general good reasons, defeasible, as many people already recognise. Some people may still disagree with the opinion that infanticide in rare cases is justified; but it is certainly not 'preposterous'.

I do not understand what Lockwood means by saying that the first of the reasons that, following him, I have for preferring contraception to infanticide 'is not...a reason which speaks to the individual possessor of potential'. Certainly the grown person Michael Lockwood, who is nearer to realization at the stage of the embryo than at the stage of the gametes, is an individual; and we hope he still has potential for further development. The gametes, the embryo, the foetus and the infant are all individual gametes, etc., and they all have, as they get 'further down the track' the potential for either producing or turning into the individual Michael Lockwood.

Lockwood has been misled by the ways in which the problem has so often been posed. If what I have said so far is correct, what makes the moral difference is what the consequences of different treatments of embryos will be for the people into whom they might turn. Once we see this, it becomes clear that writers on this topic have been on a wild goose chase when they have disputed at such length the question of the stage at which individual human life or personhood, or the like, begins. On this point I agree with Mary Warnock [3]. For *whenever* my life as the individual Richard Hare began, anything that would have interfered with my developing into the grown person that I now am would have been against my interest, and therefore *pro tanto* wrong, though possibly right given certain other assumptions. It would have made no difference at all whether the interference took place before or after I became that human individual; so we need not waste any more ink on the question of when this was.

Nor is this a question that need concern legislators. They need to concern themselves, rather, as legislators always should, with the consequences of their legislation. And on these, as I have argued elsewhere, the contentions I have been making shed a great deal of light [5]. For if the legislators want to do what they ought through their legislation--that is, bring about the consequences that they ought to bring about--they have to concern themselves with the interests of those whom their legislation will affect. And the chief of these are the people that will come into existence if one kind of law is passed, but will not if another kind is passed. And the more restrictive the legislation is, the less embryos there will in practice be, and therefore the less grown people there will be that those embryos turn into.

This is for three main reasons. The first is that IVF could not have been invented, and cannot now be improved, without experiments on embryos, and therefore, just as in the past, if there had been a complete legal ban on experimentation, at least all the people who have been produced by IVF would not have existed, so those in the future whose existence improved methods might make possible will not exist if a ban prevents the improvement. And even with a less restrictive law, the restrictions would impede research and therefore prevent some of them coming into existence.

Secondly, the many grown people who fail to come into existence because of chromosomal abnormalities, but who might come into existence if ways were discovered by research on embryos of detecting and even correcting these abnormalities, will have their existence precluded by a ban. It is of course possible to take the view that detection is enough, and that defective embryos or foetuses or infants should be allowed to die or even be killed, so that people can be born who do not have the defects. But the people who take such a view are not the same people as are most vocal in favour of a ban on experimentation.

Thirdly, this reduction in the number of people produced would not be compensated for by any increase in the number of embryos saved from the experimenter. For if it were illegal to do the experiments, those embryos would not be produced in the first place. A ban on the production of 'spare' embryos would have the same effect. But if spare embryos *are* produced in the course of infertility treatment by IVF, in order to insure against the loss of some, those spare embryos would not, it is true, be experimented on if the law prevented it; but they would (if they were really spare) perish all the same, so that the law would make no difference to the people they would otherwise have turned into. All this I have argued in greater detail in the paper referred to.

From the point of view of securing the existence of grown people, it is not necessary to put any ban on embryo experimentation. If we ask, what the law on embryo experimentation ought to be, the answer will be found by asking, first, how the law should limit experiments on humans in general (and for that matter on other animals) so that those which ought not to be done are not done. This is a question of balancing the expectation of good through the advancement of research against the expectation of harm to the experimental subject. But in practice firm guidelines and firm intuitions (see above) need to be developed to guide those (for example ethics committees) deciding individual cases.

Such guidelines should no doubt be restrictive when they are dealing with ordinary adults, and even more so in the case of children who can give consent only by proxy [9]. When it comes to foetuses, embryos and gametes, however, the harm to be expected from destructive experimentation diminishes successively to vanishing point. This is because (assuming that any possible suffering can be avoided by anaesthesia if necessary) no harm is in these cases done to the subject as such by destroying it, but only to the person that it might turn into; and this may be compensated for by the bringing into being of some other person. Experimentation not involving destruction but only damage is of course another matter; that should be strictly regulated and even banned, in the interests of the person who might survive to be born damaged.

This is most evident in the case of gametes; to destroy a sperm in an experiment makes in practice no difference at all to the number of people that there are going to be, except in very contrived cases. To destroy an ovum is a little more likely to make a difference, but not much. To destroy an embryo *in vitro*, again, makes little difference, for the reasons I have given; but an embryo *in vivo* is another matter. When we come to the foetus and, even more, the infant, which is, as Lockwood puts it 'further down the track', much more harm is done if it is destroyed, because it takes a lot of time and effort to get to the same stage again (to say nothing of the other reasons I gave earlier).

The best law, therefore, would, it seems to me, grade the harms done by experimentation from zero in the case of sperms to a very high figure in the case of viable infants (one that would forbid all but negligible harm), and balance these against the good expected from experiments. Lockwood is quite wrong to say that 'From a purely practical standpoint . . . one cannot apply different cut-off points to different lines of research'. This is exactly what all ethics committees do, or ought to; they ask how much good the research is likely to do, and balance this against the expected harm to the subject. *Some* harm may be done by experiments at any stage except possibly the sperm; and ethics committees should estimate its magnitude and probability.

In any case, it does not look as if the cut-off point suggested by Lockwood (the point at which the embryo gets a brain), has much to recommend it. Harm may be done if the embryos or gametes are destroyed even before this point, but in general less harm, the earlier in development the experiment occurs. There are exceptions, already mentioned: one would not, for example, be doing *any* harm by experimenting, at any stage in its development, on an embryo that was doomed in any case by chromosomal abnormalities.

But Lockwood is wrong to look for a cut-off point at all; he does so only because he (like the Tate Committee, and many others apparently) thinks that the potential that should protect the embryo is something that in some mystical way inheres in it right now (like the soul?); whereas, properly understood, its potential lies in the fact that if it prospers there will, in consequence, in the future, grow up an ordinary grown human person who can enjoy all the blessings that Lockwood lists. It is this fact on which the morality of experimentation, and of legislation about it, depends. The duties of surgeons, experimenters and lawmakers derive from the fact that their actions may further, or may impede, the coming into being of these people.

Department of Philosophy
University of Florida

NOTES

[1] This article originally appeared in 1988 in *Bioethics* 2, No. 3. It is reprinted with permission of the author.

BIBLIOGRAPHY

1.   Hare, R. M.: 1974, 'The Abnormal Child: Moral Dilemmas of Doctors and Parents', *Documentation in Medical Ethics* 3. Reprinted as 'Survival of the Weakest' in *Moral Problems in Medicine*, S. Gorovitz, (ed.), 1st ed. only (Englewood Cliffs, Prentice-Hall, 1976). Also reprinted in R. M. Hare's *Essays on Bioethics*, Clarendon Press, Oxford, 1993, pp. 185-191.
2.   Hare, R. M.: 1981, *Moral Thinking: its Levels, Method and Point*, Oxford University Press, Oxford.
3.   Hare, R. M.: 1987, 'An Ambiguity in Warnock', *Bioethics*, 175-178.
4.   Hare, R. M.: 1987, 'In Vitro Fertilization and the Warnock Report', in *The Ethics of Human Design*, R. Chadwick, (ed.), Croom Helm, London. Reprinted in R. M. Hare, *Essays on Bioethics*, Clarendon Press, Oxford, 1993, pp. 98-117.
5.   Hare, R. M.: 1987, 'Embryo Experimentation: Public Policy in a Pluralist Society', *Bioethics News* 7 (Oct.), 32-43 and Proc. of the Conference *IVF: The Current Debate*, July 1987, Centre for Human Bioethics: Monash University 1987, pp. 106-123. Reprinted in R. M. Hare, *Essays on Bioethics*, Clarendon Press, Oxford, 1993, pp. 118-130.
6.   Hare, R. M.: 1989, 'A Kantian Approach to Abortion', in *Right Conduct: Theories and Applications*, 2nd. ed., M. D. Bayles and K. Henley (eds.), Random House, New York, pp. 147-157. Reprinted in R. M. Hare, *Essays on Bioethics*, Clarendon Press, Oxford, 1993, pp. 168-184.
7.   Hare, R. M.: 1988, 'Possible People', *Bioethics* 2, 279-293. Reprinted in R. M. Hare, *Essays on Bioethics*, Clarendon Press, Oxford, 1993, pp. 67-83.
8.   Lockwood, M.: 1988, 'Warnock Versus Powell (and Harradine): When Does Potentiality Count?' *Bioethics* 2, 187-213.
9.   Nicholson, R. H.: 1986, *Medical Research with Children: Ethics, Law and Practice* (Report of Institute of Medical Ethics working group, Oxford University Press, Oxford).
10.   Parfit, D.: 1984, *Reasons and Persons*, Oxford University Press, Oxford.

I must express my thanks for the very great help I received from all my colleagues at the Centre for Human Bioethics at Monash during an invigorating three months stay there; and also to Michael Lockwood himself, and to John Hare, for helpful discussion.

MICHAEL LOCKWOOD

HARE ON POTENTIALITY: A REJOINDER[1]

In his reply to my article in the preceding issue of *Bioethics* [3], Richard Hare [2] makes some valuable distinctions, which ease the task of pinpointing the differences between us. But let me stress that these differences are largely *theoretical* ones. On most issues of practical policy, I suspect that he and I would find ourselves broadly in agreement, as far as our conclusions were concerned. And although our *arguments* would differ somewhat, I would certainly attach substantial weight to most of the considerations that he mentions.

Let me begin, as does Hare, with the principle stated on p. 199 of my article, according to which

> (1) A potential for X generates an interest only where there is some individual for whom the development of the potential for X constitutes a *benefit*.

I stand by this principle. But, as Hare notes, it calls for further clarification. In the first place, it may reasonably be asked (as Hare does ask) whether the 'there is' is to be understood in a tensed or tenseless fashion. My answer is that it is to be understood tenselessly. Why, then, do I, on the next page, speak as follows?

> Faced with a fourteen day old human embryo, with the potential for developing into a human person, the question we must ask is: Does there now exist any individual for whom the development of this potential would constitute a benefit.

The answer is that if there *now* exists an individual for whom the development of the potential would constitute a benefit, then *a fortiori* there *is*, tenselessly, such an individual. My point is that if there isn't, now, any such individual, because development of the embryo has not yet proceeded to the point where such an individual comes into existence, then it is open to us so to act as to prevent there ever being any individual whose interests are (directly) adversely affected by the non-development of this potential.

That, at any rate, is what follows, assuming that 'individual' is glossed as '*actual* (past, present or future) individual'; and that is how I intended it to be understood, in the passages Hare quotes. (I shall say something about possible individuals in a moment.)

Nick Fotion and Jan C. Heller (eds.), Contingent Future Persons, 19-26.
© *1997 Kluwer Academic Publishers. Printed in the Netherlands.*

Finally, no significance should be attached to the shift from 'constitute', in the first passage, to 'would constitute', in the second; '*would* constitute' is what is meant in both cases. Suppose that we do, *now*, have an individual with the potential for those things that give human life its special worth (and incidentally, I gladly add companionship and a vigorous and active life to my list). The benefit, as Hare says, does not exist now, but is a possible *future* benefit. That, as again Hare points out, is *why* 'constitutes', in the first passage, must be understood as 'would constitute'. But this generates a further source of ambiguity, inasmuch as 'would' is what logicians call a *modal operator*, and the *scope* of the operator has to be made clear. Thus there are two ways of construing (1):

> (1a) A potential for X generates an interest only where there is (tenselessly) an (actual) individual who would benefit from the development of the potential for X,

and

> (1b) A potential for X generates an interest only where the development of the potential for X would result in there being an (actual) individual who benefited from it.

(For the technically-minded, it is a question of whether the scope of the quantifier 'there is' includes that of 'would' (1a) or vice versa (1b).)

As I understand it, the first of Hare's arguments, designed to show that I am committed to giving gametes and early embryos the same status as (late) foetuses and neonates, relies on interpreting (1) along the lines of (1b). For, to be sure, it is true equally of gametes, embryos a few hours or days old, 24-week foetuses and newborn babies, that the development of the corresponding potential for a normal human life would result in there being an individual who benefited from it.

But (1b) is not what I meant by (1). What I meant was (1a). And with respect to that principle, assuming that my account of personal identity is correct, gametes and early embryos are not on a par with late foetuses and neonates. For, as I pointed out just now, destruction of a pair of gametes or an early embryo will prevent there ever being an actual individual with a direct interest in the development of the potential for a normal human life. At a later stage, however, again assuming my account of personal identity, it is too late to prevent this. With the onset of brain life, the individual who stands to benefit from the development of this potential already exists, even though not as yet capable of enjoying these benefits. Hence, late abortion or infanticide, of normal foetuses or neonates, runs directly contrary to the interests of the very same *actual* individuals who, were it not for their being killed, would in due course be able to live a normal human life.

Incidentally, it seems to me that talk of 'possible individuals', in this context, really amounts to nothing more than quantifying over individuals within the scope of a 'would'. Thus understood, I have no particular quarrel with this way of talking.

What I balk at, however, is the idea that we can ascribe, to merely possible individuals, *actual* interests. Possible individuals, if one wants to talk that way, can, surely, only have *possible* interests.

This brings me to Hare's second argument. Hare points out, quite correctly, that I, enjoying as I am the benefits of a normal human life, have a strong retrospective interest in the potential inherent in the embryo, or gametes, that gave rise to me having been allowed to develop. I have reason, therefore, to be glad that my parents did not use contraceptives or have me aborted. Suppose someone had said, shortly after the conception of the embryo from which I developed:

> (2) The potential for a normal human life inherent in this embryo generates an interest in this potential being realised.

It might seem that, knowing what we now know, we must, even on the basis of (1a), the intended interpretation of (1), evaluate this assertion as true. Let us assume (*pace* Aristotle on future contingents) that we can regard statements relating to the future as true, both subsequently and when uttered, if and only if what is asserted comes to pass. Then, when this assertion is made, say in August 1943, it is true that there *will be*, and hence true, tenselessly, that there *is*, an individual who stands to benefit by the realisation of the potential for a normal human life: namely, the future, but nevertheless actual, Michael Lockwood. And isn't this consideration an embarrassment for my position?

It seems to me that, properly regarded, it is not. To be sure, the potential inherent in that newly-fertilised ovum generates (tenselessly) an interest in the corresponding potential being realised, *on the assumption that it will in fact give rise to an individual who stands to benefit or lose out according as this potential is or is not properly realised.* Thus, someone who, in August 1943, thought that the embryo almost certainly *would* develop—not only to the point where, according to me, a human life begins, but into infancy and beyond—could have regarded himself as acting contrary to the interests of an actual, albeit future, individual, if he had given my mother some noxious substance which caused me to be born crippled or mentally retarded. He could then have thought of himself as acting contrary to the interests of an actual future individual. But he could not have so thought, assuming that he accepted my theory of personal identity, if what he had done was to administer a substance which caused a very early miscarriage, before the onset of brain life. For his having done that would have been logically inconsistent with the very assumption upon which the truth of (2) is predicated: namely that I am an actual individual, that I did in fact, somewhere between conception and birth, come into existence.

What is true, therefore, is that it *is* in my interests that my parents did not use contraceptives and that nothing was done to prevent the embryo implanting in the uterine wall, and so forth. It is not, however, true that, had any of those things happened, they would have run counter to interests that I, under those circumstances, would have had. For under those circumstances, *I* would never have existed, and *a fortiori* would not have had any interests at all.

Am I then alleging what Hare (p. 218) holds to be 'plainly false', namely (P) that 'only existing people can have interests'? Well, that depends on whether 'existing' is to be understood in a tensed or tenseless fashion. I am certainly not denying what Hare asserts by way of trying to show that (P) is 'plainly false'. If you now tell me that I am actually the product of a hitherto undisclosed, pioneering experiment in IVF carried out by an Oxford research team in 1943, then I would be bound to agree with Hare that 'It was in *Lockwood's* interest that they should implant the embryo that turned into him, although *he* did not at that time exist'. For what is certainly false is the principle (S) that an action, carried out at time t, can be in, or contrary to, the interests of an individual X, only if X exists at t. (That much is amply demonstrated by the example just given, concerning the administration of a noxious substance prior to the point at which an individual comes into existence, which subsequently causes the individual to be born handicapped, and to suffer in consequence.) On the other hand, I do subscribe to the weaker principle (W) that an action can be in, or contrary to, the interests of an individual X, only if X exists at some time or other. And I have no doubt that Hare would reject (W) as well; he wants to say, as I do not, that an action that prevents X from coming into existence runs contrary to the actual interests that a possible but *non*actual individual has in existing. What Hare says about its having been in my interests that the embryo that turned into me was implanted is, however, perfectly consistent with (W)—and hence not to the point here—since what he is envisaging is a possible world in which I *do* subsequently come into existence, and am glad to be alive and so forth.

It should be emphasised, by the way, that it is precisely because I subscribe to (W), and also think that it makes an important difference, morally, whether or not an action runs contrary to actual interests, that it matters, from my point of view, when a human life begins. And that in turn is why personal identity matters, since my life surely began at the earliest point at which there existed an individual identical with me now. According to Hare,

> *whenever* my life as the individual Richard Hare began, anything that would have interfered with my developing into the grown person that I now am would have been against my interest.... It would have made no difference at all whether the interference took place before or after I became that human individual...([2], p. 222).

If one accepts (W), this is simply not true. As things stand, Hare has a strong retrospective interest in having developed into the grown person that he now is. Moreover, the infant that Hare once was *had*, I want to say, a strong prospective interest in developing further, seeing that the kind of life Hare has enjoyed constitutes a great benefit, and the infant and the later Hare *are one and the same individual*. But there would have been no such (actual) interest, had the process of development been interfered with, so as to cut it short before Richard Hare came into existence. Consequently, such interference would not have been against any actual interest, on Hare's part, in developing, or having developed, into the grown person that he now is. That is to say, it would not have run contrary to an interest, on Hare's part, that obtained within the possible world in which the envisaged interference took place. The key point here is that it is only the individual that itself stands to enjoy the benefits of personhood that can have this direct interest in the process of development being allowed to continue. Consequently, if one accepts (W), it becomes important to know when such an individual arrives on the scene.

Some philosophers, incidentally (though not Hare), would jib at the suggestion that continued development can be in the *interests* of the foetus, after the dawning of brain life, or the newborn infant, seeing that late foetuses and newborn infants lack any desires which can be furthered by such development. But that seems to me perverse. We can perfectly well say of an infant that it is in its interests that it get a good education, without having to find any current desire, on its part, that education would help to satisfy. It is enough, surely, that personhood and education are both great benefits, the value of which, if one receives them, one will subsequently come to appreciate.

Hare remarks ([2], p. 217) that, had people contemplated experimenting on the embryo from which I derived (before the onset of brain life), 'the embryo still had the potential; and this potential, it might be argued, imposed on them a duty at least to consider the interest of the person whom that *could* bring into existence'. Well, I would quibble slightly about the wording of this, since it implies that there is an actual interest, even where there is only a possible individual. But that quibble aside, I don't disagree with what Hare is saying here. Suppose we have a group of doctors, simultaneously engaged in medical research and fertility treatment; and they have, in their laboratory, a newly-created embryo, a healthy-looking specimen. On the one hand, there is some interesting and potentially valuable research they could do on the embryo, which would, however, result in its rapid demise. On the other hand, there is a woman, one of their patients, unable to produce ova of her own, who is eager to have this embryo transferred to her uterus. If it is so transferred, the chances that it will implant and grow into a healthy child are excellent. What is more, the woman and her husband will be loving parents, capable of providing the child with the best possible start in life. Leaving aside the interests of the would-be parents, and duties to the woman arising from the fact that she's their patient, are the doctors entitled simply to ignore the fact that, if transferred to this woman's womb, there is a substantial probability that it will give rise to a human being that has a happy and rewarding life? Hare would say: of course not; and I agree with him. That is something the doctors clearly ought to consider.

More generally, I agree with Hare that the fact that, were one to have a child, it could reasonably be expected to have a happy and rewarding life, is a perfectly good, prima facie reason for having one. Where we mainly differ, I think, is as regards what has come to be known, in the philosophical literature, as *replaceability*. In an earlier article, Hare considers the question whether it is permissible to abort a defective foetus or kill a defective newborn infant, with the intention of 'replacing' it with another normal child: having another, normal child that would not otherwise have been conceived. Call this second child 'Andrew'. (We are to imagine that the parents have already decided to have only one, or only one more, child.) Now it is not Hare's *conclusions* that I want to take issue with, but with something that Hare says, by way of justification of his conclusions:

> I do not think that the harm you are doing to the foetus or the unsuccessfully operated upon newborn infant by killing them is greater than that which you are doing to Andrew by stopping him from being conceived. ([1], p. 369)

Of course, if the defect is sufficiently great, one may not be harming the foetus or newborn infant at all, by killing it; since life with such a defect may be worse than being dead. But that isn't Hare's point. He thinks that Andrew's moral claim on life, *qua* merely potential individual, is, *a priori*, as weighty as that of the actually existing individual that we are contemplating killing. And this implies that, even if the 'replacement' child one is contemplating bringing into existence is likely to lead a life only *marginally* superior to that of the foetus or neonate one is thinking of killing, then, in the absence of other relevant considerations, the right thing to do is still to kill the existing individual and replace it with an Andrew.

That, crucially, is where I disagree with Hare. *I* think that the obligation one has towards an actual individual, not to prevent its potentiality for a worthwhile human life from being realised, is far stronger than any obligation one has to bring into existence, or not to prevent from coming into existence, an otherwise merely possible individual with a similar potentiality. This I take to be the basis of our commonsense assumption that having children at all is largely supererogatory. Indeed, for reasons I have already explained at length, it seems to me thoroughly misleading to speak of 'harming' Andrew, by one's failure even to conceive him. That is not to deny that we can all feel grateful to our parents for bringing us into existence, or that it is a noble and laudable thing to bring new worthwhile life into being. What Hare and I disagree about is how far we are entitled to sacrifice, to that or some other desirable end, the potential for worthwhile life of individuals whose actuality is already an established fact.

Let me, finally, say something about intuitions, and the extent to which it is reasonable to rely on them in one's moral theorising. Though I would certainly not describe myself as an 'intuitionist', I do not entirely share Hare's views on this matter. Hare thinks that the moral intuitions people have are largely to be accounted for on the basis that they have high *acceptance utility*: that is to say, they are intuitions the possession of which is likely, under normal circumstances, to cause people to act in a way that yields good consequences. This, in turn, implies that such intuitions may well prove unreliable, when applied to very unusual circumstances. (There is something rather Darwinian about this; intuitions are likely to have high utility with respect to the sorts of predicament in response to which they have developed, just as species are likely to be well adapted to deal with the sorts of environments in which they have evolved. But just as species may behave in highly maladaptive ways, when placed in alien environments, so our moral intuitions may let us down badly when faced with unusual situations.)

Now I don't deny that this may be *one* reason why we have the intuitions we do. But I don't think it's the only one (nor, of course, does Hare); and I'm not convinced even that it's the main one. Often, it seems to me, the presence of a moral intuition is an indication that there is, so to speak, an argument in the offing. We may not be able to articulate the argument, but it is nevertheless operative, if only in a confused and largely subconscious form, in our thinking. It seems to me a striking fact about our moral intuitions, a fact to which Hare's moral psychology perhaps does insufficient justice, that we have powerful intuitions, not merely about how it is appropriate to act, in actual or imaginary situations, but also about the reasons for so doing. And this seems to me to be true of the intuition I cite in my article, regarding the difference between deliberate failure to conceive and infanticide. Not only do most people have this intuition, but I think one would find also that they have a strong intuition that the sorts of consideration Hare advances ([2], pp. 220-1) by way of explaining why we have this intuition—why, indeed, it is a good intuition to have—are not, in fact, the main or fundamental reasons why they think this way, that they somehow fail to get to the heart of the matter. What I am inclined to believe here is that there *is* an argument underlying people's thinking, on this point, a good argument; and that what I have been saying is largely an articulation of this argument. (That would explain why most nonphilosophers think, contrary to Hare and Warnock, that it *is*, after all, relevant to ask when a human life begins.)

In general, I would not wish simply to disregard people's moral intuitions, even with respect to highly unusual, artificial or fantastic cases. In morals, as elsewhere, something may strike one, intuitively, as correct, essentially because it *is* correct, even if the reason why it is correct and, by the same token, why, ultimately, it strikes one as correct, may need considerable reflection to uncover.

But in the end, I agree with Hare that it is the argument itself, rather than the intuition, that counts. A great many moral intuitions—some of them almost universally held—are, without doubt, based on unsound arguments, on self-serving arguments, on simple prejudice, or on unthinking parroting of other people's attitudes. And wherever there is good reason to think that this is the case—as I am convinced it is, for example, in regard to the attitudes most people have towards the treatment of nonhuman animals—the moral theorist should be wholly undeterred if his conclusions end up flying in the face of what most people intuitively believe.

That said, however, moral arguments, it seems to me, need moral premises. As in any area of thought, it cannot, on pain of an infinite regress, be possible to find arguments to justify all of one's convictions. Thus, even John Stuart Mill, who is highly critical of 'intuitive moralists', concedes that

> Questions of ultimate ends are not amenable to direct proof.
> Whatever can be proved to be good must be so by being shown to

be a means to something admitted to be good without proof ([4], p. 34).

At some point—and here again the situation in ethics is no different from that which obtains in the sciences and elsewhere—we shall be forced to fall back on judgements which seem to us clearly correct, in spite of the fact that we cannot justify them: in short, moral intuitions. Once again, Hare would disagree. For he believes that a substantive moral theory can be derived simply from the logic of moral discourse, so that the only intuitions to which one need ultimately appeal are, in effect, linguistic intuitions. This is an heroic endeavour; but to explain Hare's strategy and to say why, ingenious though it is, it does not, in my view, ultimately succeed, is beyond the scope of this article.

NOTES

[1] This article originally appeared in 1988 in *Bioethics* 2, No. 4. It is reprinted with permission of the author and publisher, Blackwell Publishers Ltd., Oxford.

BIBLIOGRAPHY

1.   Hare, R. M.: 1976, 'Survival of the Weakest', in S. Gorovitz (ed.), *Moral Problems in Medicine* Prentice-Hall, Englewood Cliffs, NJ, pp. 364-9.
2.   Hare, R. M.: 1988, 'When Does Potentiality Count? A Comment on Michael Lockwood's Paper', *Bioethics* 2, 214-26.
3.   Lockwood, M.: 1988, 'Warnock versus Powell (and Harradine): When Does Potentiality Count?', *Bioethics* 2, 187-213.
4.   Mill, J.S.: 1969, *Utilitarianism* (first published 1861), in James M. Smith and Ernest Sosa (eds), *Mill's Utilitarianism*, Wadsworth, Belmont CA, pp. 31-88.

CYNTHIA B. COHEN

THE MORALITY OF KNOWINGLY CONCEIVING CHILDREN WITH SERIOUS CONDITIONS: AN EXPANDED "WRONGFUL LIFE" STANDARD

> Now the man knew his wife Eve, and she conceived and bore
> Cain, saying, "I have produced a man with the help of the Lord"
> (*Genesis* 4:1).

The notion that it could be wrong to have a child seems strange to us, for it challenges many of our basic beliefs about the significance of procreation. Children are gifts of God whom we count as a blessing. As we gain greater control over our powers of reproduction and learn more than ever before about children whom we could bring into the world, however, the question of whether we ought to "produce a man" pushes its way to the fore. By isolating our genes and detecting their connections with certain diseases, we can predict with varying degrees of certainty whether our offspring will be affected by specific genetic conditions. And by merging sperm and egg in a glass dish, we can examine the resulting preembryo before implantation and learn whether it bears a deleterious condition of concern. Thus, prospective parents today face agonizing decisions about whether to conceive children or whether to avoid conception for the sake of children whom they will never know. They are caught in a conflict between the desire and call to have a child and the troubling thought that they might give a life to a child that could be viewed as "wrongful." The notion that it could be wrong to have a child startles us and creates difficult new ethical and theological questions.

Suppose you learn that you are subfertile and have little chance of conceiving a child, but that you might conceive a child using *in vitro* fertilization (IVF). Suppose also that there is reliable evidence that using IVF invariably creates a serious, but not devastating, condition in the children born of it. For the sake of argument, let us presume that IVF is associated with the lack of two limbs in children born of it. Suppose, in addition, that you and your spouse have moral objections to abortion and would not terminate a pregnancy should you learn that the zygote or fetus was seriously affected. While you have no moral objections to using IVF, you do have moral qualms about knowingly conceiving a child with a serious condition. If you were to decide to use IVF to bring a child who would be missing two limbs into the world, would this choice be morally wrong?

The answer concerns whether to actualize possible people—that is, people who do not exist, but who could. These theoretical future persons constitute an enormously large hypothetical group about whom we cannot know much. Still, we can know something about some of these non-existing persons based on extrapolations from what we know about what does exist. We can know, for

Nick Fotion and Jan C. Heller (eds.), Contingent Future Persons, 27-40.
© 1997 *Kluwer Academic Publishers. Printed in the Netherlands.*

instance, that the wealth of possible children includes a class of babies who could be created with the help of IVF. We can know what some members of this class of IVF babies are like in certain respects. Since several embryos are usually created when IVF is carried out for a couple, several of these possible babies have genes derived from you and one other person. They possess such other characteristics as having grandparents who are your parents and your spouse's parents, living in your house on your street, hearing the kind of music you favor, being conceived in a Petri dish on a certain date at a certain time, and not having two limbs. These are your possible children.

Possible children are conceptual constructs. We can develop a notion of them and attribute certain features to them, but whether or not they become actual depends on our actions. In asking whether it would be morally wrong for you to conceive and bring into existence one of these possible children, we are asking whether these children would have what has been termed, "lives worth living" [1]. Or would their lives, under the rubric of the "wrongful life" standard be worse than ...what? The "wrongful life" standard is usually taken to require that their lives must be worse than death. On this standard, it would not be wrong to bring one of your possible children into the world, for surely living without two limbs is not worse than being dead. Even so, it does seem wrong for you knowingly to conceive and bring to birth one of these possible children because of the import for the child of missing two limbs in our society. Is there some way of revising the "wrongful life" standard to explain why it would wrong knowingly to procreate children who would suffer serious, but not devastating, conditions?

THE "NO HARM" VIEW AND ITS DIFFICULTIES

Let us first consider in some detail the position of those who maintain that you would do no harm to these children should you choose to bring them into the world knowing that they will have a serious condition. They claim that it is, in almost all cases, better to exist than not. Since children brought into the world by such measures would not be alive but for the use of these techniques, resorting to them to produce children can do them no harm, except in rare cases ([2],[10],[15],[16], [17], pp. 75-76, 110-11, 122-23, 152, 169-70). Children brought into the world with serious deficits as a result of the very means used for their procreation, therefore, have no grounds for complaint, since they cannot be harmed by being born. Their existence is necessarily better than their nonexistence. They will lead a tolerable, worthwhile life, even though they are missing two limbs. Your choice to conceive a child with a serious condition would not be wrong according to the "No Harm" argument, for that child will have a life that is better than death.

While it is true that the child has a serious condition, the only way in which to prevent this, they maintain, would have been to prevent the child from existing at all ([12], pp. 358-59, 362-63, 371-72). If you had chosen to have a child by means of artificial insemination of a surrogate, for instance, you would, in all likelihood, have avoided having a child with missing limbs. But then, Parfit points out, you would have produced a different child and this surely would not have been better for the child whom you did produce, for you would have denied her a worthwhile life.

Brock illustrates the difficulty with a slightly altered case that he takes from Parfit [1]. A woman is told by her physician that she should not attempt to become pregnant now because she has a condition that is highly likely to result in mental retardation in her child. If she takes medication for a month and then becomes pregnant, there is every reason to expect that she will have a child without this condition. The woman, who is impatient, becomes pregnant now and gives birth to a child who is mildly retarded. On a common sense moral view, Brock argues, she acts wrongly and in particular wrongs her child "by not preventing its handicap for such a morally trivial reason."

Yet the woman's decision is not so easily shown to be wrong as common sense morality would suppose, Brock declares. He uses an argument derived from Parfit to explain this.

The difficulty is that it would *not* be better for the person with the handicap to have had it prevented since that can only be done by preventing him from ever having existed at all; preventing the handicap would deny the individual a worthwhile, although handicapped life. The handicap could be prevented either by conceiving at a different time and/or under different circumstances, in which case a different child would be conceived, or by terminating the pregnancy, in which case this child never comes into existence and a different child may or may not be conceived instead. None of these possible means of preventing the handicap would be better for the child with the handicap—all would deny him or her a worthwhile life…. How could making her child better off by giving it a life worth living, albeit a life with a significant handicap, wrong it ([1] pp. 270-71)?

On this view, if the woman had decided not to become pregnant, or if you decide not to conceive a possible child by means of IVF, the resulting child is denied "a worthwhile life." The only way of avoiding the serious condition that the child incurs is for the woman and also for you to conceive at a different time. But then each of you would conceive a different child, as Parfit observes. Preventing the condition in the child would prevent the very existence of the child. The child is "better off" being brought into the world, even with a serious condition, than not existing at all.

This "No Harm" argument implies that you would have damaged the interests of the child by not conceiving him or her, for you would have removed that child's only chance of existing and having a life worth living. Hare takes the view that possible children have an interest in existing to its logical conclusion when discussing contraception and abortion. He maintains that:

From the present point of view, contraception and abortion really are on a par, though there may be other reasons for preferring contraception. Both are wrong, though defeasibly so, in that they involve the prevention of somebody coming into existence in whose interest it almost certainly was to exist. But, given that parents cannot have a duty to produce all the children they would produce, they have to choose when to copulate, and how often to do so without contraception; and this choice results in the production of some of these people and the exclusion of others ([6], p. 90).

Some possible children, according to Hare, are excluded from this world because couples have intercourse only intermittently. Although it is wrong to deny their interest in existing, we are excused from fulfilling our obligation to meet that interest by our limited reproductive abilities. If we had the capacity, we would be obliged to bring into the world many more possible children with an interest in existing than we currently do, this position implies.

The view that possible children, in almost all instances, are denied a worthwhile existence when their conception is prevented means that it is in the interests of those possible children who could be born of IVF to be brought into the world, even though they are missing two limbs. The upshot of the "No Harm" view is that if you should proceed with procreation using IVF, knowing that any child you conceive would necessarily lack two limbs, you would do no harm to that child.

Now this is a rather odd argument. It is odd for at least two reasons. First, it suggests that if you do not bring a possible child into the world, you will somehow injure or wrong that child. For you to decide against using IVF to conceive a possible child or for the woman in the Brock/Parfit example to have decided against becoming pregnant when she did, would be, in Brock's terms, to "deny the individual a worthwhile, although handicapped life." Second, the argument maintains that once you have knowingly conceived and produced a child with a serious, but not devastating, condition, having done so cannot be assessed as having harmed the child. Both of these claims are odd.

The first claim is odd because the possible child before conception is just that— only a hypothetical child. The "No Harm" argument seems to hypostatize the mere possibility of bringing children into the world by picturing possible children as pre-existing persons with an interest in entering this world. Had you not used IVF to help your possible child make the transition into this world, you would have thwarted his or her interest in existing on this argument.

But your possible child is not waiting in a spectral world of nonexistence, eager to enter this world, but with "no way of being born" ([17], pp. 75-76) except by means of IVF. There are many possible children whom you could conceive by using IVF. There are all those whom you could have conceived if the sperm being used had been obtained from the millions available a second earlier or later or if the procedure had been performed in a different month with a different oocyte. Indeed, were we to accept Hare's view, we would face the intriguing possibility that there are even larger numbers of children whom those who are fertile are obliged to bring into the world. These are the children they could produce by using IVF and other new reproductive technologies to overcome their natural reproductive limits. This would provide a way to meet the interest of these possible children in existing.

Conceiving one possible child entails not conceiving several others, as Hare points out ([6], p. 89). This does not, however, wrong the wealth of possible children whom you might otherwise have conceived. Although there may be second Beethovens or good fathers among them, it is neither good nor bad for them that they are not actualized. Before birth, possible children do not need to be brought into this world and are not injured when this is deliberately prevented. Thus, the enormous number of possible children whom you do not conceive by means of IVF are not wronged by not being brought into existence. You do not have to justify your decision to them, for possible children have no right to be conceived and born.

The second claim, that you have done no harm to the child because you now have a child who lives a worthwhile life, is odd because it justifies your act *after the fact*, that is, when you have a living child. The point of decision about whether to procreate, however, comes *before the fact* of conception and birth. The question at that point is whether it would be wrong for you to use IVF, knowing that this would bring into the world one of your possible children who will be missing two limbs. It is not satisfactory to respond with a *fait accompli*, saying, "But I have produced a child lacking two limbs and this child has a worthwhile life, so I have done nothing wrong." This is the gist of what occurs in the Brock/Parfit case. Now that the child is here with a serious condition, we are reluctant to say that being alive is not a good thing for him or her. *Yet whether the child ought to have been conceived is the very question at issue. Once the child has been born, the moral landscape changes, and the question is different.*

This is because what we owe to existing children differs from what we owe to possible children. Our answer to the question of whether we ought to retain already born children in existence is vastly different from our answer to the question of whether we ought to conceive possible children and bring them into existence in the first place. While we consider it morally necessary, in most instances, to keep children alive, even when they have very serious conditions, we do not consider it morally necessary to conceive them in the first place when we know that they would be born with those same very serious conditions. We can decide against bringing possible children with grave illnesses into the world without moral onus. The situation changes, however, once possible children are conceived and born. Even though they may suffer a serious condition and need extra care from their families and communities, we owe it to them, except in rare cases, to keep them in existence. Consequently, it is important to raise the question whether it would be wrong knowingly to have a child with a serious condition *before conception*, rather than *after birth.*

THE "WRONGFUL LIFE" STANDARD
AND TWO KINDS OF NONEXISTENCE

What is it about already existing children that calls us to keep them alive? A significant moral factor that pushes us toward preserving their lives is that the alternative for them is death. And we attribute serious disvalue to their deaths, even though we may believe in an after-life. Indeed, we view death as so bad that advocates of the "wrongful life" standard maintain that we are obligated to keep children alive unless they have devastating illness that makes their lives worse than death. If their condition is so grave that it meets this standard, it is not obligatory to do everything possible to keep them alive.

The "wrongful life" standard is explained in greater detail by Feinberg:

Surely in most cases of suffering and impairment we think of death as even worse. This is shown by the widespread human tendency to "cling to life at all costs." And even for severe genetic handicaps and inherited maladies, most competent persons who suffer from them will not express regret that they were born in the first place.... In the most extreme cases, however, I think it is rational to prefer not to have come into existence at all, and while I cannot prove this judgment, I am confident that most people will agree that it is at least plausible. I have in mind some of the more severely victimized sufferers from brain malformation, spina bifida, Tay-Sachs disease, polycystic kidney disease, Lesch-Nyhan syndrome, and those who, from whatever cause, are born blind and deaf, permanently incontinent, severely retarded, and in chronic pain or near-total paralysis, with life-expectancies of only a few years. ([4], p. 159)

Here Feinberg considers the only form of nonexistence available to those who are already living—death—and, applying the "wrongful life" standard, argues that in some instances being alive is worse than death. If living children suffer devastating diseases that render their lives worse than death, we would be justified in not preventing them from dying, on this standard. But if they suffer less severe conditions, death would not be worse than life, and it would be ethically questionable not to prevent their death.

How are we to distinguish devastating conditions that are worse than death from those that are serious, but still preferable to death? The "wrongful life" standard draws no clear line between them. Some may think that being born without two limbs is a devastating condition, while others may say that it is serious, but not so awful as to be devastating. The "wrongful life" standard does not give us a firm notion of the nature of a devastating condition, for some people can reveal extraordinary character and qualities, even though they have severe deficits that make it very difficult for them to function at what others take to be an adequate level. They can render what would otherwise be a devastating condition a less serious one.

Some proponents of the "wrongful life" standard would respond that we can distinguish between a condition that is devastating and one that is serious in specific instances. Yet the difficulty of doing so becomes clear when we consider some of the cases listed as devastating by Feinberg. Many would challenge his view that such conditions as spina bifida or permanent incontinence are so awful that they render the lives of those born with these illnesses worse than death. However, they might well maintain that these conditions amount to serious ones that would make it difficult to justify knowingly bringing children with them into the world. These serious conditions make the lives of children born with them worse than *preconception nonexistence*, rather than death [3].

Many advocates of the "No Harm" view, in applying the "wrongful life" standard, take nonexistence to be a univocal concept. They assume that preconception and posthumous nonexistence are one and the same and that nonexistence is so awful that only a life that is even worse than it could merit not being brought into existence. However, preconception nonexistence and death are distinct notions; they are not conceptually or evaluatively equivalent.

Some would challenge this claim on grounds that we cannot know what it is like not to exist, and therefore cannot compare various forms of nonexistence to each other or to existence. Hare encounters this epistemological difficulty and suggests that the nearest we can come to imagining preconception nonexistence is to compare it with being totally unconscious ([7], p. 73). Others would deny this claim on the basis that it is logically impossible to make such a comparison, for "nonexistence is not a state than can be given a value" ([8], pp. 30). This was the conclusion of several courts in the early "wrongful life" cases in the United States. They declared, in the words of the court in *Gleitman v. Cosgrove*, that it is "logically impossible" to compare "life with impairments against the nonexistence of life itself" [5]. Parfit observes that "Some objectors claim that life cannot be judged to be either better or worse than nonexistence. But life of a certain kind may be judged to be either good or bad—either worth living, or worth not living. If a certain kind of life is good, it is better than nothing. If it is bad, it is worse than nothing" ([12], p. 487). What is the "nothing" to which Parfit refers? It seems to be just that—nothing. And nothing is not something that can be characterized and compared with life.

Yet we can characterize the notions of preconception nonexistence and of death and distinguish them from one another. We can do so without postulating a shadowy world of nonexistence and without consciously experiencing nonexistence. Our concept of death (we must reluctantly set aside the intriguing question of an after-life for current purposes) is derived from what we know about being alive. It is a logical construct, rather than a metaphysical place. Similarly, our concept of preconception nonexistence is a logical construct that we develop from what we know about existence and death. We are able to talk about it and understand it to an extent. We have done so here when we have conceptualized certain things about possible children, compared groups of them with one another, and considered what their lives would be like were we to conceive and bear them. We can talk meaningfully about possible children without falling into gibberish. To do so is to talk about an aspect of preconception nonexistence.

Moreover, we can assess the value of preconception nonexistence and posthumous nonexistence and can compare the value of each form of nonexistence with that of being alive. Contrary to the court in *Gleitman*, it is not logically impossible to compare preconception nonexistence with life. When we do so, we find that we ascribe different degrees of value to preconception nonexistence and to death. We view death as terrible (often even though we believe in an after-life), but consider preconception nonexistence to be neither good nor bad. Why is this?

Death is terrible, in part, because it prevents us from having future goods that we would have had if we had remained alive [11]. The awfulness of death is also grounded in the fact that it robs us of those goods that we already have ([9], p. 40). Preconception nonexistence, on the other hand, does not involve the loss of life's goods, nor does it deprive us of goods that we already possess. There is no loss incurred by possible children who are not brought into the world, for there is no actual "we" who could suffer such a loss at this point. Instead, there "are" theoretical constructs that we can characterize in certain ways that serve partially to identify these possible children as subjects. Further, preconception nonexistence does not prevent those possible children who will be actualized from having the goods that will be theirs.

Other features of death that are not features of preconception nonexistence reinforce our tendency to assess death as extremely bad. In death, the loss of goods of this life is permanent, whereas in preconception nonexistence, the possibility of being conceived, born into this life, and achieving life's goods is still open ([9], p. 42). While possible children who are not actualized cannot realize this possibility, this cannot harm these theoretical constructs in any way. At death, the life of a particular individual in this world ends, whereas in preconception nonexistence, no one's life ends. Once the point at which conception could take place has passed and a possible child is not conceived, no child is injured when the possibility of being conceived has closed permanently. Death involves an event in which nonexistence occurs to someone. Preconception nonexistence, in contrast, includes no such event ([9], pp. 39-42).

Preconception nonexistence, in sum, is not as bad as death. Our comparison of these two kinds of nonexistence reveals that death bears with it a much greater degree of disvalue than does preconception nonexistence. Because we consider death so terrible, we make strenuous efforts to prevent those who are alive from succumbing to it. However, when life is so awful that death is preferable to it, we desist from such efforts. Our attitude toward preconception nonexistence is quite different. It is not so awful that we believe we are obliged to "remove" possible children from it and bring them to life. We are not forced to the conclusion that being alive is always better than never coming into existence at all. Preconception nonexistence, consequently, is a better state than death.

The "wrongful life" standard applies only to already existing children. It requires that we compare their current state to the state of death. When it is applied to possible children in its present form, this standard requires that we compare their death with being alive in order to assess whether these children are harmed by being brought into existence. When we do so, however, we find that this standard justifies allowing us to conceive children with almost any disease or condition, as long as it is not worse than death. This startling conclusion, which is, all sides appear to agree, contrary to common sense morality, indicates that the "wrongful life" standard is too narrow. Its exclusive focus on only one form of nonexistence, death, unjustifiably renders it inapplicable to possible children.

Death does not (figuratively speaking) constitute an option for possible children; the only alternatives open to them (again, figuratively speaking) are not to exist in the first place or life. In assessing whether it would be wrong to conceive and give birth to them, we must compare their preconception nonexistence, not their posthumous nonexistence, with what their lives would be like if they were actualized. The "wrongful life" standard, consequently, needs to be revised and expanded to apply to possible children. *The relevant form of nonexistence that should be used to compare with being alive in an expanded "wrongful life" standard when the question is whether to conceive a child is preconception nonexistence, not death.* [11]

Since preconception nonexistence is not as bad as death, a life that will be worse than preconception nonexistence will not have to be as bad as a life worse than death. A revised "wrongful life" standard that takes preconception nonexistence into account, therefore, will allow conditions that are serious, but not devastating, to count against conceiving possible children. Such conditions can carry considerable disvalue and therefore can be worse than preconception nonexistence. *A "wrongful life" standard, when applied to possible children, will not be restricted to a life of devastating illness, but can also include conditions that are less severe.* Consequently, on an expanded "wrongful life" standard, it would be wrong knowingly to conceive a child with devastating illness, but it also could be wrong to conceive a child with serious disease.

THE INTERESTS OF POSSIBLE CHILDREN

The argument presented here is predicated on the view that possible children have certain kinds of interests. In particular, it holds that possible children who would have serious conditions if they were brought into the world can have an interest in not being conceived. How can this be when they are, as we have argued, only logical constructs and there are, as yet, no living children who could have interests?

The term, "interest," can be used in at least two different senses. In one, we speak of a person being "interested in" something, meaning that he or she has a special affinity, concern, or positive attitude toward something. A person may have an interest in this sense in another person, the opera, or a favorite charity. This sort of interest involves a psychological state, an affinity toward objects or persons. In a second sense of "interest," we speak of something as being "in a person's interests," meaning that something is good for that person, is conducive to his or her well-being. This sort of interest can include having all four limbs or not experiencing great pain and suffering. An interest in this sense is an evaluative one related to a person's good or welfare. A possible child cannot have interests in the first sense, for one has to be alive to entertain psychological states. But can a possible child have the second sort of interests, welfare interests? Can something be good or bad for a possible child?

Initially, it would seem that possible children, as such, cannot have a good; things cannot be conducive to their well-being. After all, they are only theoretical constructs, rather than actual beings, and it seems inappropriate to apply the notion of having a good to them. Yet possible persons can have a good. That is, we can conceive of them not only as having certain grandparents, living in a certain house, and lacking two limbs, but also as living in ways that are or are not conducive to their welfare.

Possible female children, for instance, have a welfare interest in not having their mothers given drugs such as diethyl silbesterol (D.E.S.) that would damage the ability of these children to reproduce. This interest is a feature of all female possible children; it inheres in the very concept of a female possible child. Madison Powers offers a different example:

...imagine a scientist creating a developmental toxin designed to adversely affect newborns who are exposed to the body of the mother who received the toxin prior to conception. What matters morally it seems is the prospect of interests being adversely affected in the future by actions of persons at a time clearly prior to the existence of actual interests of lives in being." [13]

While possible children do not have "actual interests of lives in being" because they are not lives in being, they have the interests of possible children who could become lives in being. In this case, they have a welfare interest in not coming into a uterine environment in which they would be adversely affected by toxins. They need not exist to have this interest, for it is a characteristic of the very concept of what it is to be a possible child. Harm can be done to the welfare interests of those who are not yet conceived.

Thus, when it would be for the good of possible children to live with certain physical and mental conditions, they can be said to have a welfare interest in existing in those conditions. *Pace* Hare, they have no interest in being conceived and born *per se*. Their interest, if actualized, is in living in ways that are conducive to their good. If being conceived and born with certain physical and mental conditions would not be conducive to their good, they can be said to have a welfare interest in not being brought into existence. Thus, possible children can have certain sorts of interests.

If possible children have a welfare interest in not being conceived with a serious or devastating condition, and they are conceived, when does the harm to them occur? Harm occurs when their interest in not being conceived is violated—at the point of conception. At that time, the possible child's interest in not coming into existence is wholly negated and the child is harmed by being conceived. The harm is done when they move from possible to actual children. To ascertain the nature of the harm done to the possible child with a welfare interest in not existing, we must compare preconception nonexistence with being alive and must do so before the point of conception. Living with a serious condition can have a degree of disvalue, depending on the person who is in that condition and his or her actual circumstances. When we compare the value of preconception existence—which is, we have noted above, not as bad as death—with being alive with a serious condition, living with a serious condition can have a balance of negative value. Therefore, knowingly bringing a possible child with a serious condition into the world when this would have an overall negative impact on that child is to cause that child to suffer harm.

Yet harming someone involves making his or her condition worse. Can a child's condition be worsened by being conceived and brought into the world? How can existing be worse than not existing, which, after all is nothing? As noted above, preconception nonexistence is not nothing, for it can be characterized in certain ways. The same is true of death. As the condition of the person who is murdered is made worse when he or she is abruptly brought into posthumous nonexistence, so is the condition of the person made worse who is brought into the world when this is contrary to his or her welfare interests. Hence a possible child can be harmed by being conceived.

Parfit's nonidentity problem does not present a barrier to the view developed here, for the child who is conceived is not a different child from the possible child. You are faced with a decision whether to conceive a child who will only have two limbs. Who that specific possible child is depends on a variety of factors related to when and how IVF would be done, along with many other factors. Should you decide to go ahead and conceive a child by this means, the child you conceive will be the same as the possible child you could have conceived. They are one and the same. Moreover, even though we cannot fully identify who they are at any preconception point in time, this does not affect the interest of the possible child in not being conceived in a condition that is not conducive to his or her good. "The person who will occupy my carrel at the library next may be now unidentified, but it is in his interest that I should leave it tidy," Hare observes ([6], p. 89). Possible children, like the next library carrel patron, can have certain interests, even though we cannot fully characterize who they are or the nature of all of their interests.

OBLIGATIONS TO POSSIBLE CHILDREN

What do we owe possible children who are not conceived, but who could be? Surely, we owe them a life in which they would not suffer devastating illness and live only briefly, if we can avoid this. We owe them a life, for instance, in which they will not suffer from Tay Sachs disease, a condition in which children experience progressive neurological deterioration before they die at an early age. We would harm possible children by knowingly bringing them into the world with this disease if we could avoid doing so. We will have made their life worse than preconception nonexistence. But if we do not bring possible children with the Tay Sachs gene into the world, we do them no wrong; we do not harm them.

What if possible children would suffer a devastating illness much later in life as adults, and would, in all probability, live in good health up to that time? This occurs, for instance, in those who inherit the gene for Huntington's disease, an illness which entails intellectual deterioration, involuntary bodily movements, and eventual death at age 50 or so. Do we owe it to possible children not to bring them into the world to suffer from this illness if we can avoid it? Further, should we apply whatever the standard we develop for conceiving children with Huntington's disease to conceiving of children with polycystic kidney disease? The latter is a condition in which people experience progressive renal failure during their adult years, but it is not necessarily fatal. They can have it corrected by a kidney transplant or dialysis. The questions become even more difficult when we ask whether we should provide our children a life free from what we take to be serious, but not devastating diseases. What if a possible child has a chance of being born deaf or developing bipolar affective disorder? Are these conditions so serious that we should not knowingly conceive a child with them?

We face the specter of a "slippery slope," for we may begin by declining to conceive possible children with devastating illnesses and then rapidly move down the slope to decide against conceiving children with serious illnesses. We may make a final slide toward not conceiving children with any "imperfections" at all. Barbara Katz Rothman cites cases in which parents have decided to have an abortion rather than bring children into the world with mild disorders and goes on to ask whether we will "establish a set of norms of acceptability and then narrow, and narrow, and narrow yet again those norms" ([18], p. 227)?

We tend to assume that those with serious, or even devastating, conditions necessarily undergo a great deal of suffering. Yet some report that what suffering they experience is more a result of societal response—or lack of response—to their condition, rather than a necessary accompaniment of it. Stephen Post observes:

...it is wrong to assume that suffering is the necessary result of every genetic defect, or that lives with degrees of physical suffering cannot be creative and meaningful. Moreover, human beings are finite creatures thrown into suffering, from which there is no ultimate escape. We confront our frailties sooner or later, and much of human enlightenment is to know that even in brokenness there is hope. That suffering and the necessity of meeting its challenge creatively is a universal existential predicament seems perfectly obvious. In this sense, placing all hope in a genetic response to suffering is, finally, misplaced [13].

As we assess what sorts of condition would make it wrong knowingly to conceive possible children, we must avoid assuming that those who are not "normal" will inevitably suffer because of this. Moreover, as Post observes, suffering is an ineradicable part of life, experienced by those with and without debilitating conditions. We cannot hope to spare our children from all suffering, in imitation of the parents of the Buddha.

The standard that we develop for marking off those conditions that are so deleterious for children that it would be wrong knowingly to conceive them cannot rest solely on physical status. This is because the same physical condition could have a strong negative impact on children in one time and culture, but not affect their social function to any significant degree in another. If we aim to provide our children with at least an adequate opportunity for health, this must be relativized to cultural needs, expectations, and practices [3]. The application of the standard will, of necessity, provide different outcomes for possible children with similar serious conditions who are in different circumstances. We should accept this relativization reluctantly, however, for conditions that are remediable in one culture may not be treated in another due to circumstances in which injustice and stigmatization are rampant.

We can take as a general standard to apply across cultures the following: the lower the risk of a serious or devastating condition to the possible child and the more the child's parents and society are able and willing to assume responsibility for the health of children, the more it would be justifiable to conceive him or her. On the other hand, if the probability and gravity of a serious or devastating condition is

great, and the parents and social structure are unwilling or un&
ameliorative measures for the child, there is a greater likelihood
child. In such circumstances, it would be less justifiable to conceiv
assessment of whether serious or devastating conditions would cons
harm to possible children must be made under specific circumstances in specific
cultures.

In choosing whether or not to conceive, knowing that we stand some significant
chance of having a child with a serious condition, what are we saying to those
children whom we do conceive and bear? Our reasons for pursuing parenthood help
to establish our identity and stake out the sorts of choices we will make as parents
should we enter this state. For, as Verhey observes, it is one thing to *become*
parents, but quite another to *be* parents ([19, pp. 176-204). When we deliberately
choose an embryo that, when it matures, will not be born with a serious condition
such as cystic fibrosis over one that would, what are we are saying to the resulting
selected child about ourselves as parents? Are we telling him or her that we do not
want to have to grapple with the problems that would inevitably surface in caring
for a child with a serious condition? Will the resulting child feel used and
manipulated, a means to our ends? Or will that child be grateful that we cared about
his or her welfare?

When we make the difficult choice to forgo biological parenthood rather than
conceive a child who might have a serious condition, there is, paradoxically, no
child to whom we are saying something. There is no youngster to whom we can tell
that we did not bring you into the world for your sake. There is no one who benefits
waiting to greet us at the gates of heaven with thanks. These are circumstances in
which goods and evils collide and in which no matter what choice we make, it will
be a tragic one. Even so, those who have not "produced a man with the help of the
Lord" because to have done so would have been to wrong that child, can live in the
knowledge that they have exercised "their God-given dominion" ([19], p. 202)
responsibly.

BIBLIOGRAPHY

1. Brock, D.: 1995, 'The Non-Identity Problem and Genetic Harms—the Case of Wrongful Handicaps', *Bioethics* 9, 269-275.
2. Chadwick, R. F.: 1982, 'Cloning,' *Philosophy* 57, 201-9.
3. Cohen, C. B.: 1996, '"Give Me Children or I Shall Die!" New Reproductive Technologies and Harm to Children,' *Hastings Center Report* 26 (2), 19-27.
4. Feinberg, J.: 1988, "Wrongful Life and the Counterfactual Element in Harming," *Social Philosophy and Policy* 4, 145-178.
5. *Gleitman v. Cosgrove*, 49 N.J. 22, 227 A. 2d 689 (1967).
6. Hare, R. M.: 1993, 'When Does Potentiality Count?', in *Essays on Bioethics*, Clarendon Press, Oxford, pp. 84-97.
7. Hare, R. M.: 1993, 'Possible People', in *Essays on Bioethics*, Clarendon Press, Oxford, pp. 67-83.
8. Heyd, D.: 1992, *Genethics*, University of California Press, Berkeley, pp. 29-33.
9. Kamm, F. M.: 1993, *Morality, Mortality, Volume I. Death and Whom to Save from It*, Oxford University Press, New York.

10. Macklin, R.: 1994, 'Splitting Embryos on the Slippery Slope', *Kennedy Institute of Ethics Journal* 4, 209-25.
11. Nagel, T.: 1979, 'Death', in *Mortal Questions*, Cambridge University Press, Cambridge, pp. 1-10.
12. Parfit, D.: 1985, *Reasons and Persons*, Oxford University Press, Oxford.
13. Post, S. G.: 1993, 'Designer Babes, Selective Abortion, and Human Perfection', in *Inquiries in Bioethics*, Georgetown University Press, Washington, D.C., pp. 7-21.
14. Powers, M.: 1996, 'The Moral Right to Have Children', in R. Faden and N. Kass (eds.), *HIV, AIDS, and Childbearing: Public Policy, Private Lives*, Oxford University Press, New York, pp. 320-44.
15. Robertson, J. A.: 1983, 'Procreative Liberty and the Control of Conception, Pregnancy, and Childbirth', *University of Virginia Law Review* 69, 434.
16. Robertson, J. A.: 1986, 'Embryos, Families, and Procreative Liberty: The Legal Structure of the New Reproduction', *Southern California Law Review* 59, 958, 988.
17. Robertson, J. A.: 1994, *Children of Choice: Freedom and the New Reproductive Technologies* Princeton University Press, Princeton, N.J.
18. Rothman, B. K.: 1986, *The Tentative Pregnancy: Prenatal Diagnosis and the Future of Motherhood*, Penguin Books, New York.
19. Bouma, H. III, Diekema, D., Langerak, E., Rottman, T., Verhey, A.: 1989, *Christian Faith, Health, and Medical Practice*, William B. Eerdmans, Grand Rapids, Michigan.

INGMAR PERSSON

PERSON-AFFECTING PRINCIPLES AND BEYOND

INTRODUCTION

It has been feared that, if it is allowed that the creation of people can make an outcome better, our intuitive concern for the welfare of already existing persons risks being dissipated. Intuitively, we are inclined to think it better to improve an outcome by making things better for existing persons, especially ones who are worse off, than by adding new persons whose lives represent the same value and, more firmly, we think it better to keep existing people at a higher level of welfare than letting this level drop to have a much larger population at a lower level. To stave off dismal obligations to procreate, it is tempting to impose some person-affecting restriction like:

> (PAN) One outcome is better than another if and only if it is better for non-contingent persons, i.e., persons who either already exist at the time of action or will begin to exist whichever outcome is caused.

Strictly speaking, (PAN) is not a moral principle, but it is intimately linked to such principles. On a purely consequentialist morality, one is morally required to bring about the best outcome one is capable of bringing about. This is not so, however, if there are deontological constraints (to the effect, e.g., that one should not cause an outcome, however good in other respects, if the causing of it involves causing the death of a person in such a way that one has killed her). But the existence of such constraints is nothing I will here discuss.

Despite its apparent attractions, I will argue that (PAN) is false: it does make outcomes better to bring to life persons whose lives will be good for them. Indeed, it is even bad for such persons never to come into existence, and it detracts from the value of outcomes. Furthermore, it will be seen that even a wider person-affecting restriction, to the effect that one outcome is better if and only if it is better for persons, *whether contingent or non-contingent*, is untenable, because one outcome can be better than another, although it is not better for anyone. The reason for this is that there are 'impersonal' values, like, for instance, just equality. As will transpire, this impersonal value however provides resources to salvage our intuitive preoccupation with the welfare of non-contingent persons, in particular existing ones. Additional resources are supplied by a qualitative segmentation of value introduced to block Derek Parfit's repugnant conclusion. By these measures, I hope

41

Nick Fotion and Jan C. Heller (eds.), Contingent Future Persons, 41-56.
© 1997 *Kluwer Academic Publishers. Printed in the Netherlands.*

to show that an intuitively decent emphasis on the welfare of existing persons, especially those worse off, can survive the abandonment of narrow person-affecting principles like (PAN).

Let me however straight-away stress that the notion of a principle for the evaluation of outcomes being 'person-affecting' raises two distinct issues:

> (1) Are all values values for someone, personal values, or are some values impersonal, not values for anyone? (By the way, what does this distinction mean?); and,

> (2) Are the persons or other subjects for whom (personal) values are for only non-contingent ones or may they be contingent as well?

We encounter these two issues in, e.g., David Heyd's defense of a person-affecting morality: his 'volitionism' is a stance as regards the first issue, since it declares 'that value is always *for* human beings; it has to do with what they, in the broad sense, want or need' ([2], p. 84), whereas his 'generocentrism' ([2], p. 96) is a stance as regards the second issue, to the effect that only non-contingent persons count as suppliers of value to outcomes. As opposed to this, I will contend both that there are values that are not for anyone (though perhaps in a narrower sense than Heyd's) and that what is of value for contingent persons, too, is part of what determines the value of an outcome. I start with trying to clarify the notion of personal values, or values for somebody.

THE NOTION OF VALUE FOR PERSONS

Suppose that we embrace, as I (and apparently Heyd) believe we should, a desire relativist theory of value according to which what is of value is defined in terms of what fulfills certain desires. The requisite desires need not be actual desires of any subjects; they may be ones that are rational in the sense of being formed in a situation in which there is possession of optimal factual information. Their objects may also have to meet certain objective (or subject-independent) constraints, for a desire relativist value theory is not necessarily subjectivist. Call these requirements, designed according to your liking, R. A desire relativist theory then declares, roughly, that the fact that p can be of value only if it fulfills a desire that complies with R. Now, since a desire must be a desire of some subject, it seems to follow that values will be relative to subjects, will be values for subjects. If so, the mere truth of desire relativism will make it indisputable that, in some sense, all values are values for persons (or subjects having desires).

However, I think this conception of 'value for' is too broad. Suppose, to take an example relevant in the present context, that I have a desire (satisfying R) that the human species survives at least 10,000 years after my death. If 10,000 years after my death it turns out that there are still humans around, it is absurd to say that something which is good for me then obtains.[1] We had better try to give a narrower sense to the phrase 'value for someone', and I shall now proceed to outline how this can be done.

Let me start by introducing the notion of a self-regarding desire, i.e., a desire that (1) has a self-referential content to the effect that something be true of oneself and that (2) is not, ultimately, derived from another desire whose content is not self-referential.[2] Consider my desire that one of my kidneys be transplanted to a sick relative of mine. This desire has a content to the effect that something be true of me, but imagine that it is derived from a desire of mine that this relative identified independently of me be well and that the latter desire is ultimate or at least not derived from another desire of mine that satisfies (1); then my desire to have my kidney transplanted is not self-regarding, on my proposal, and, intuitively, this seems right. On the other hand, suppose it is derived from a desire that people related to me be well or that I save the life of someone; then my desire is self-regarding. Thus, whether or not a desire is self-regarding is not apparent at face value.

The contents of many of my self-regarding desires are to the effect that I have some experience or other. Typically, these cannot be fulfilled without my realizing that they are fulfilled. For instance, my desire now to see a beautiful sight or to read a book that amuses me can scarcely be fulfilled without my being aware of it. Such desire fulfillment is experiential: when p's becoming the case fulfills a subject's, S's, desire that p in this sense, it causes a change with respect to it, e.g., it causes S to cease desiring p and instead to experience pleasure that p has come to obtain because she is aware of p's having become a fact. For instance, if I desire to spot a pileated woodpecker now, and I immediately spot one, my desire is replaced by a feeling of satisfaction.

There is however also another concept of desire fulfillment that is purely relational: it consists simply in p's becoming the case at a time t such that S desires that p become the case at t. Fulfillment in this sense does not require awareness on S's part of p's being the case, and there need be no causal effect on S's desire; it need not give way to a feeling of satisfaction. My desire that something I have written be read by somebody this very minute is fulfilled in this sense if, unbeknownst to me, somebody is now reading something by me.

On a line of thought akin to, but broader than, psychological hedonism, the ultimate ground of every self-referential desire will be a desire to the effect that one have some experience (among which would be the experience of desire fulfillment involved in experiential fulfillment). But this seems implausible. I may desire that my name be remembered as long as humanity exists, but it is hardly feasible to construe this desire as being derivative from a desire that I have any experiences. Nor is it a desire that I can realistically hope will ever be experientially fulfilled, as opposed, e.g., to my desire that I am now being read. So, we must acknowledge the existence of self-regarding desires, for other things than experiences, that can only be relationally fulfilled. The fulfillment of these will not fulfill the desire most of us probably have to experience desire fulfillment.

We may wonder whether the purely relational fulfillment of a self-regarding desire is any good for the subject having it. I assume that it will be granted that the experiential fulfillment of such a desire (that meets R, i.e., the requirements a desire has to meet if fulfillment of it is to be of value) is so. I think the answer is 'yes': for instance, I think it is good for me if my desire that I not be slandered behind my back, whose fulfillment I cannot consistently hope to ascertain, is (relationally) fulfilled. But if you wish, you may confine the notion of value for somebody to the experiential fulfillment of (e.g.) self-regarding desires.

Sometimes it is not clear from the content of a self-referential desire what must happen for it to be fulfilled. Consider my desire to travel by train tomorrow: will the mere fact that I will travel by train tomorrow fulfill it? Not if the desire is, to borrow Parfit's phrase, implicitly conditional on its own persistence ([3], p. 151), that is, not if it is a necessary condition of my now having this desire that (a) I believe I will still desire to travel by train tomorrow. If, as appears likely, it is conditional in this fashion, it is also necessary for its fulfillment that this desire persists tomorrow.

But even this is probably not enough: suppose that I am sound asleep or unconscious tomorrow when I am dumped on a departing train. This brings out another possible condition for the existence of my desire: (b) my belief that I will be able to experience a possible train journey tomorrow, and so experience the fulfillment of this desire of mine. If my desire is in this way implicitly conditional on its yielding experiential fulfillment, it will not be fulfilled, and a state of value for me will not have materialized, unless this belief is true. My desire to travel by train is then at bottom a desire to have certain experiences that I expect to like at the time. Experiential fulfillment of it is then requisite to constitute a state that is of value for me. On the other hand, supposing my desire is not implicitly conditional on (b), a purely relational fulfillment may do and constitute such a state.

Turn now to desires whose contents are not self-referential. Suppose I desire that a certain sports event be televised tomorrow. In all likelihood, this desire is derived from a self-referential desire of mine that I watch the event on TV tomorrow, a desire that is probably conditional on my belief that tomorrow I will (still) desire that I watch the event on TV and, of course, that I will then be able to do so. If so, it will surely be of no value to fulfill the former desire (that the event be on TV), if my desire to watch the event cannot be fulfilled; it is the (experiential) fulfillment of the latter desire that is of value to me.

Although it may not be realistic in this case, some non-self-referential desires are not to be construed as being derivative from self-referential desires. Suppose, for instance, that I desire that in the future no species of mammals or birds on earth ever be extinct due to human interference. As it is not reasonable to construe this desire as being derivative from any self-referential desire of mine, there is no risk of its fulfillment falling out in favour of the fulfillment of such a desire. Moreover, it is hardly implicitly conditional on its yielding experiential fulfillment, or even on its persistence, since in all probability it concerns what will happen long after my death.

It seems however to be absurd to hold that it is good for me if, thousands of years after my death when humanity comes to an end, my desire is relationally fulfilled by its turning out then that humans have exterminated no species of mammal or bird. The reason for this, on my analysis, is that it is neither the case that the desire is self-regarding nor that the fulfillment of it is experiential. In contrast the experiential fulfillment of a desire that is not self-regarding, e.g., the pleasure I experience when realizing that humans will not in the future rub out any higher animals, so that my desire for this will be fulfilled, is valuable to me. My hypothesis is that this is because I have a self-regarding desire to experience desire fulfillment, a desire that is here satisfied. If this is right, the 'value for' relation will have been explicated in terms of the (experiential or relational) fulfillment of desires of a specific type, namely self-regarding ones.

If a desire relativist, like myself, is nonetheless inclined to say that some state of affairs which merely relationally fulfills a non-self-regarding desire (complying with R) of, say, mine, is of value, this value will of course have to be relative to this desire of mine. But to prevent confusion, we should not make this claim by saying, simply, that this state of affairs is of value for me. I suggest we should rather say that it is of impersonal, as opposed to personal, value for me, and reserve the unqualified locution 'value for me' for the latter case. I find it plausible to hold that many humans have non-self-regarding desires, of ecological, moral, political, artistic, etc., import, whose purely relational fulfillment is of impersonal value (for them). One such impersonal value, which will play an important role later on, is that of just equality.

Instead of being derived from self-referential desires, these desires may generate such desires, to the effect that we contribute to their realization, whose relational fulfillment is also of value, though impersonally so. Thus, the fulfillment of a self-referential desire need not be of value to the subject. This is so only if the desire is self-regarding as well and not, as in this case, derived from a non-self-referential desire.

In something like this way, I propose that desire relativists about value could uphold a distinction between values that are for the subjects of desire, i.e., personal values, and ones that are impersonal (and for them only in the wide desire relativist sense). Consequently, even for those who endorse a desire relativist value theory the claim that all values are (personal) values for subjects is a substantial claim, not one entailed by their value theory. As will be particularly apparent below in the section "Mere Addition and Equality," it is a claim I reject.

NARROW AND WIDE PERSON-AFFECTING PRINCIPLES

I now turn to the other issue of whether the value of an outcome is a function of the value it has not only for non-contingent persons, but also for persons whose existence is contingent upon its realization. It seems to me that a very strong case can be made for the latter alternative, for maintaining that the creation of persons leading lives good for them adds to the goodness of an outcome.

I have set out the view that existence is good for a person to the extent it involves having self-regarding R-complying desires (relationally or experientially) fulfilled. Now, the state of fulfillment is the same regardless of whether the realization of an outcome consists in the fulfillment of a desire existing beforehand or in both the generation of the desire, possibly by the generation of its subject, and its fulfillment. Whichever is the case, the result is therefore a state that is good for the subject; hence, if the value of an outcome is determined by the (personal) value things have for persons existing in it, this state should contribute to its value.

Certainly, in the case of pre-existing or non-contingent desires, an omission to bring about the fulfilling outcome is likely to leave the subjects in a worse state, i.e., the negative state of having frustrated desires rather than in the, presumably neutral, state of having no (fulfilled or unfulfilled) desires, and, possibly, no existence. But this is not to say that the intrinsic goodness of the state of having a pre-existing or non-contingent desire fulfilled is greater, that this state in itself is better for the subject, still less that receiving the whole package of a desire and its fulfillment is not at all intrinsically good for one.[3]

The following considerations confirm this conclusion that it can be good for somebody to be caused to exist. Surely, we think that it can be good for people to be caused to have desires which are promptly satisfied. No doubt, this is at least part of our reason for taking troubles to instill desires in infants and children, through upbringing and education, and not just resting content with passively gratifying whatever desires happen to crop up in them.

So, if a wedge is to be driven in somewhere, it will presumably have to be between implanting satisfiable desires in existing subjects and creating satisfiable desires by creating their subjects as well. The difference here is that, in the former case, we do something to some organism already existing that will actualize its potential to have desires, whereas in the latter case, this is not so. What exists in this situation is, if anything, a pair of gametes. They have the potential of uniting into something else that has the potential to acquire desires, but they do not themselves have the latter conative potential, and they will never be subjects having desires. This may be held to make an evaluative difference: although it is good for an organism to have something done to it that will actualize its potential to develop desires, provided these desires will be satisfied, it is not good for anything when something done to some organism actualizes its potential to make up some other being, not yet existing, which possesses a conative potential that will be actualized in it having satisfied desires.

But the end-product can be the same in both cases, a subject or person with satisfied desires, so how can what was done in the former, but not the latter, case be good for this subject? It may be said that in the latter case, the original action which produces the result cannot be done to the subject, since it does not exist at the time. But, obviously, from the fact that some action is not done to somebody, it does not follow that it cannot have results or consequences that are good or bad for this person (obviously, a nuclear explosion can have bad effects in the future for people not yet conceived). And it is the value of these consequences for all persons existing in an outcome that, on a person-affecting approach, should determine its value.

Hence, I conclude that it can be good for persons to be caused to exist, and that this contributes to the value of an outcome. Therefore, (PAN) that narrows down the value of an outcome to its value for persons, whose existence is not contingent upon its materialization, is false.[4]

Even if this is conceded, it may however be urged that it is not bad for persons whose existence would be good for them, never to be caused to exist (or to be caused never to exist). It may seem that nothing can be bad for somebody who has never existed and never will.[5] If so, an outcome cannot be bad because it fails to bring into existence persons who would lead worthwhile lives. Thus, an outcome in which no-one exists cannot be worse than one in which many persons lead good lives.

Now, it is of course true that nothing can be intrinsically bad for a person in a state of permanent non-existence: since this person will be without desires at every time, none of her desires can ever be frustrated or contravened. Nevertheless, being caused to remain in this state of non-existence can be extrinsically bad because it precludes a state (of existence) which would be intrinsically good for the existent.[6] This only requires that non-existence in itself is not good, and it seems quite plausible to hold that it is intrinsically neither good nor bad for the non-existent, but indifferent. It is intrinsically indifferent because it does not involve any desire that is either fulfilled or contravened.[7]

Thus, my claim is that it can be extrinsically bad for a person not to be caused to exist (when existence would have been good for her). Similarly, in some cases the claim that killing a person would be bad for her may have to be interpreted as the claim that it is extrinsically bad for her, i.e., bad not in itself, but merely because it deprives her of a worthwhile life. Suppose that a person is asleep or unconscious when put to death, so that she has no chance to be upset. Suppose further that she has no plans for the time at which she will otherwise wake up, perhaps she has been unconscious for a long time; or suppose that we are contemplating the killing of an infant who is not yet a person in the established philosophical sense of being self-conscious, i.e., being conscious of itself as a subject being in mental states, and being conscious of itself as such a subject existing at other times than the present. If we regard this contemplated killing as bad for the individual, as we surely would do, it will have to be because it is extrinsically bad in so far as it deprives her of further (valuable) existence.[8] Just as it can be extrinsically bad for an individual to be deprived of further existence, so, I submit, it can be extrinsically bad for her to be deprived of her entire existence.

It may be objected that this parallel breaks down in the following crucial respect: when somebody is killed, it is possible to pick out or identify a particular individual for whom the killing was bad, the victim, but this is not so when we refrain from causing people to exist in the first place: here we cannot pick out or identify any particular individuals and claim that the forbearance was bad for them. This difference is of course due to the fact that in the latter case these individuals are perpetually non-existent.

My reply to this is that it is a mistake to assume that we can pick out or identify particulars only if they are in existence at some time. If our knowledge of the process of fertilization had been greater, we would have been able to predict that exactly one person will result if a certain sperm fertilizes a certain ovum. We could then identify a particular person who has not yet begun to exist and who perhaps never will, as 'the person who were to result if this sperm fertilizes this ovum'. In the light of our extensive (hypothetical) knowledge of genetics, and of the social situation of the parents, we may frame some rough predictions about the quality of life of this possible person. Thus, we could judge whether it will probably be extrinsically good or bad for this particular individual never to be caused to exist.

Resistance to my parallel between causing never to exist and killing may be further eroded by noting that sometimes the latter, too, interferes just with the having of a potential to have desires (e.g., the infant Bob Dole's potential to have a desire to be president) rather than with the having, in a dispositional sense, of desires (e.g., the adult Bob Dole's having had for many years a desire to be president). The latter presupposes that the subject has thought about the matter (e.g., about what it is to be president) and has actually formed a desire in the light of these thoughts. For to have in the dispositional sense a desire is to be, as a result of these mental operations, in a state such that, if an appropriate situation arises, one will have certain 'occurrent' desires (e.g., to give political speeches) that actualize the disposition. In contrast, the former potentiality does not entail that the subject has formed any desires (or has had any thoughts): it merely states that he will form certain occurrent desires (that may 'stiffen' into dispositional desires) if or when certain conditions are fulfilled (e.g., that, when he has grown up and starts thinking about being a president, baby Dole forms a desire to be one).

If a sleeper in the dispositional sense has desires for the future, death is arguably intrinsically bad for her, since it may be held to contravene those desires. But if this subject merely has the potential to form desires in the future, death cannot be intrinsically bad for her, since it does not frustrate any desires that she has (in any sense); it can only be extrinsically bad for her by preventing the conative potential from being actualized in desires that will be fulfilled.

Only the latter is true of a sleeping infant, but it is also normally true of a person who has not (yet) begun to exist that she has the potential to have desires in the sense that she will have certain desires if or when she starts to exist. It is this parallel that makes it possible for never entering into existence to be extrinsically bad for her, just as death is to the infant. To be sure, in the case of merely possible persons, a lot more needs to happen, a lot more value needs to be invested in this cause rather than elsewhere, for the potential to be actualized, but, though relevant to the value overall of a failure to conceive, this is irrelevant to how bad this failure is for the possible person who never becomes actual.

I conclude, then, that not only can it be good for a person to be caused to exist, when existence will turn out to be good for her; under these circumstances, it is also, extrinsically, bad for her never to be caused to exist. This amplifies our reasons for transforming the narrow person-affecting principle, (PAN), into a wider one such as:

> (PAW) One outcome is (intrinsically) better than another if and only if it is (intrinsically) better for all persons, non-contingent ones as well as ones whose existence is contingent upon which of these outcomes is caused.

That an outcome is better for all persons does not mean, of course, that it is better for each person individually, but that it is better for them collectively, i.e., that the sum of the (net) benefits to these persons, or that the average (net) benefit to them, is greater. I shall soon turn to the pros and cons of these alternative specifications.

THE REPUGNANT CONCLUSION

As indicated in the Introduction, many fear that a wide person-affecting principle, like (PAW), will disperse our spontaneous focus on the welfare of non-contingent persons and in particular existing ones. Parfit's 'repugnant conclusion' brings this fear to a head ([3], chap. 17 and [4]). In the present section, I shall however try to indicate how this conclusion can be blocked.

Consider two populations, A and B, the latter of which is twice as big as the former. While the members of A are extremely well off, those of B are just a bit more than half as well off. Which one is the best? As I indicated above, there are two interpretations of (PAW). According to one, the best outcome would be the one with the highest average standard of living. On this interpretation A would be better than B. But, as Parfit argues ([3], § 143), this is not a plausible idea. Consider a world in which everyone is extremely well off, but in which a small minority is slightly better off than a vast majority; then the average principle implies that this world would have been even better if the vast majority had not existed, even though their lives are very good. This is plainly counter-intuitive.

On the other interpretation, what we should go for is the greatest sum of welfare. Now B will be better than A. But consider a third population, C, related to B as B is related to A, that is, C is twice as large as B, and its subjects are a bit more than half as well off as the subjects of B. Of course, C will be better than B just as B is better than A. Consider then a fourth population, D, related to C as C is to B and so on until we reach Z, an enormous population whose lives are barely worth living, but which in virtue of its number will represent the greatest sum of well-being. Given that 'better than' is transitive, we are forced to conclude that Z is better than A, though this conclusion is intuitively 'repugnant'.

It should not be assumed, though, that this repugnant conclusion is invited by taking the step from (PAN) to (PAW) because the former, too, is prey to it. As Parfit points out ([3], p. 498 and [4], pp. 160-1), an analogue of this conclusion can be constructed within the life of a single existing person. Imagine that there is a disease which slows down the intellectual powers of an adult person to those of a toddler. As a compensation, it will prolong the individual's life ten or twenty times. The individual will live as a content toddler for at least a thousand years. Clearly, the sum of fulfillment of such a life could be greater than that of the life of an ordinary human adult. In this sense, a thousand years as toddlers may be better for us. Thus, on the 'greatest sum' interpretation we are considering, (PAN) will imply that that this sort of life is better for us than a normal one, so that, if there were a cure for the illness, it would make the outcome worse to apply it and restore patients to normality. This conclusion is also, I think, repugnant to most of us. Consequently, the widening of the person-affecting principle to (PAW) should not be blamed for paving the way for the repugnant conclusion.

All the same, since (PAW), on the 'greatest sum' interpretation, does allow the repugnant conclusion, some revision of it is called for. As Parfit suggests ([4], p. 161), the single life analogue indicates where the remedy is to be sought: in a distinction between what in the utilitarian literature has become known as 'higher' and 'lower' pleasures. In other words, we must hold that values differ not merely quantitatively, but also qualitatively. To say that a value V_1 is of higher quality than a value V_2 is to imply that a smaller quantity of V_1 is at least as good as some larger quantity of V_2.[9] This statement does not imply the extreme claim that any amount of V_1, however small, is at least as good as any amount of V_2, however big, though the qualitative differentiation idea could take this radical form.

A less radical view, to be developed here, distinguishes between innumerable qualities, ordered hierarchically. It then claims that any quantity of a value at the higher end of the scale is better than any quantity of a value at the lower end, but that, for neighbouring values, a smaller amount of a higher quality can be less good than a greater amount of a lower one. To illustrate, the claim could be that a listening to one of Mozart's best pieces just once is better than any experience of listening to muzak however long, though the quantity of enjoyment is larger in the latter case, but that such a listening to Mozart could be less good than listening to several of Haydn's best works.

How does the introduction of a qualitative differentiation connect with the repugnant conclusion? Parfit remarks that one thing that accounts for the repugnancy of this conclusion is that it involves 'the disappearance from the world of the kinds of experience and activity which do most to make life worth living' ([4], p. 163). Realistically in Z, where people lead lives barely worth living, the best things in life, the activities and experiences instancing values of the highest quality, would be impossible: there would be no enjoyment of the works of Mozart and

Rembrandt, no viewings of sunsets from the top of Mount Everest, etc. There will be just the low quality pleasure derived from barely satisfying the basic needs of life. No doubt, this loss of quality captures a large part of our reason for resisting the conclusion that Z is better than A.

But this resistance can be worked out in two different ways. There are two moves behind the conclusion that Z is better than A: (1) A series of evaluative rankings of intermediate states: B as better than A, C as better than B, etc., and (2) an inference, on the basis of the assumption that 'better than' is transitive, to the conclusion that Z is therefore better than A. Parfit attacks (1), by defending 'the view that what is best has more value…than any amount of what is nearly as good' ([4], p. 164). In terms of an example of his, if Haydn's music is nearly, but not quite as good as Mozart's, no amount of listening to the works of Haydn could be better than hearing one of Mozart's best works just once. That seems to me very hard to swallow. I am inclined to accept the view just indicated that, in the case of neighbouring qualities, a smaller quantity of the higher one can be outweighed a larger quantity of the lower one. So, even if we think of the change from A to B as involving the replacement of a smaller group of listeners to Mozart with twice as many listeners to Haydn, I do not think we can condemn it as a change for the worse.

What remains for me, then, is to try to make credible the rejection of (2), the transitivity of 'better than'. We are generally willing to disregard minute, barely perceptible, qualitative (or indeed any) differences. So, if there is such a minimal qualitative difference between an enjoyable experience E_1 and an enjoyable experience E_2, in favour of the former, but a very noticeable difference in quantity, say, E_2 is twice as long, and therefore brings a larger quantity of enjoyment, we may well be inclined to go by the latter difference and judge E_2 to be better. Similarly, if we compare E_2 to E_3 which is related to E_2 as it is related to E_1. Yet, it could be that when we put E_3 beside E_1, we feel that the qualitative difference is so conspicuous, that the fact that E_3 is four times as long is not enough to make it better than E_1. It would have had to be even longer to make up for such a marked drop in quality. Two qualitative differences that each seems to us easy to ignore because they are hard to notice may add up to a qualitative difference that is glaring and hard not to notice, and disregard of which therefore requires more than twice the quantity needed to outweigh each of the other differences.[10] If the comparison of qualitatively minimally different experiences is continued, we may eventually reach E_n which is so inferior in quality to E_1 that no quantity of it can be as good, let alone better, than a minimal amount of E_1. No amount of listening to muzak can be as good as a single experience of one of Mozart's best works.

It may be objected that, if transitivity is rejected, there will be no alternative that is the best one in the set consisting in E_1, E_2 and E_3. This is not evident, however. I think it can be argued that if the alternatives are E_1, E_2 and E_3, E_2 is the best one, all things considered, since E_3 involves an unacceptable qualitative deterioration (relative to E_1), and of the qualitatively similar E_1 and E_2, the latter is the longer. So far as I can find, this does not contradict the fact that if the alternatives are just E_2

and E_3, the latter is the best one, all things considered, since 'all things considered' does not here cover the same 'things': not the reason that there is a qualitative deterioration.

To conclude, I think there is reason to question the transitivity of 'better than'. We could defensibly maintain that, however large we imagine the population of Z to be, if there is value only of a very low quality, this outcome cannot be as good as A, though B can be as good as, or even better than, A, and so on. A series of qualitative deteriorations, each of which is can be counterbalanced by a gain in quantity, can together make up a qualitative deterioration too gross to be counterbalanced by any such gain.

MERE ADDITION AND EQUALITY

These considerations should be kept in mind when (PAW) is interpreted. If so, it is less apparent that this principle will put in jeopardy our intuitive bias towards existing persons, our predilection for making outcomes better by making life better for them rather than by increasing the number of persons with worthwhile lives. For if a qualitative dimension is introduced, the former measure is given an edge, since it is more likely than the creation of new lives to result in a higher qualitative level. The new lives would add quantitatively to the value of the outcome even if they are barely worth living, but to pump them up to a qualitatively high level would normally require more resources than to raise the welfare of existing people to the same level.

This does not exhaust the means, however, that champions of (PAW) have at their disposal to vindicate our intuitive bias towards existing persons. To bring out these means, we should examine what Parfit calls mere additions of persons who lead worthwhile lives ([3], chap. 19 and [4], pp. 151 ff.). Suppose that we create a state of the world, A+, by adding to the existing population, A, a group of people who, on another planet so distant that there can be no communication between it and the one on which A lives, lead lives well worth living, though less than half as good as the lives of A. Parfit contends that A+ is at least not worse than A ([4], pp. 151-2). It is better in that the sum of worthwhile lives is greater, but, on the assumption that there is nothing to make it just that one population is better off than the other, it also features the bad aspect of a (natural) inequality which detracts from its goodness. However, the former aspect may not unreasonably be judged to outweigh the latter.

Parfit links this thought-experiment to the repugnant conclusion by imagining that an equalization then takes place, ensuing in that the populations become equally well off at a level lower than A's original one.[11] This raises anew the issue of qualitative deteriorations discussed in the foregoing section. So, I will focus on the additive step itself, the addition of new lives that do not affect how well off those already partaking in existence are, to make a rather simple point: if, as seems to me reasonable,[12] we endorse a principle of justice that demands equality in a case of mere addition, like Parfit's, the addition of lives that are worthwhile, though less so than those already existing, will make for an outcome that is worse in one respect, that of justice. Thus, as Parfit admits, there is a disvalue that must be subtracted from the value of the lives added that would be absent had this value instead been injected into existing lives.

It is essential to notice that such a principle of equality will not be person-affecting even in the wide sense. According to it, the transition from A to A+ makes things worse in one respect, but they do not become (personally) worse for anyone: A is not made worse off by the addition of the + population, and this population is made better off through being caused to exist. This is so even if the badness is due to the contravention of a desire for equality these populations have, since this contravention is not (personally) bad for them because the desire is not self-regarding, and its contravention here is merely relational (because they are not aware of it being contravened).

Even though its value is impersonal, however, the badness of an inequality installed must be subtracted from the goodness of the lives added. Of course, this provides a reason to improve matters for existing people rather than to pour the same (personal) value into new persons who are worse off than existing ones. But what if we take as our point of departure a world in which there is already a great deal of inequality, like A+, where inequality will not be created by a mere addition? This is practically a more important question, since our actual world is similar to A+, with its 'have' and 'have not' nations, though there is the significant difference that these know of each other's existence and can affect, and have affected, each other. But, in order to abstract from here irrelevant features (depletion of the earth's resources, compensations for past deeds of injustice, etc.), let us concentrate on the pure case of A+. Intuitively, we presumably want to say that rather than by adding lives to A and, at a much faster rate, to the + population, it would be better to increase the welfare of the latter, even if the value added is somewhat smaller. Considerations of equality will help us to this view only if the first alternative makes inequality worse and the second makes it better.

This has been denied. Suppose that, as the result of the fast increase of the size of the worse-off population, a greater and greater percentage of the total population will be at the same level (namely, the worse-off level), while improvements of the conditions of the worse-off have to proceed by lifting one small group after another, and so will pass through a stage where 50% remains worse off, but the rest belong to the better-off. Then Parfit, for instance, would hold that the first alternative is better in respect of equality, since it is quicker in placing more people on the same level (see [4], p. 156).

But I think that is a mistake, for consider how he himself formulates the principle of equality: 'It is in itself bad if some people are *worse* off than others' ([5], p. 4; my emphasis). The fact that the principle is expressed in this way rather than, say, by the equivalent formulation 'It is in itself bad if some people are *better* off than others', suggests that an inequality is worse if *more* people are *worse* off (assuming that the degree to which they are worse off is constant). Consequently, if we accept this conception of equality, increasing the worse-off population, even at the same rate as the better-off, will make the outcome worse in respect of equality, whereas decreasing it, by aiding the worse-off, will make it better in this respect. Hence, the principle of equality, suitably interpreted, does supply us with a reason to make an outcome better in the latter way. Even the operation of adding new lives as good as those of the better-off has the bad feature of preserving whatever inequality there already is, and may for that reason be worse all things considered than doing less good to existent people who are worse-off (and it will certainly tax our resources to a greater extent). The introduction of a principle of equality may therefore help us salvage the intuitive bias towards existing persons that prima facie seemed destined to go by the board with the shift from (PAN) to (PAW), since it allows us to appeal to an impersonal value alongside the personal value of giving benefits to the (existing) worse-off.

It may be objected: won't we decrease inequality between those who lead worthwhile lives and the non-existent (who 'dwell' in an indifferent state) by dispatching some from the latter to the former category? No, because procreation will augment the number of merely possible persons: the more persons there are, the more they can conceive; procreation does not gradually empty a fixed class of non-existent persons who are worse off than existent ones who lead worthwhile lives.

CONCLUSION

So, perhaps somewhat surprisingly, a principle, of equality, that is not person-affecting even in the wide sense of (PAW) will help prevent an unwanted dissipation of our concern for the welfare of existing persons that people have mistakenly thought to follow from the rejection of (PAN). But to combine (PAW) with such a non-person-affecting principle, we must revise it to state a sufficient condition, ceteris paribus, for the value of outcomes. We can call this a principle of beneficence, since it deals with that part of the value of outcomes that is a function of how they benefit, or are (personally) better for, persons (or other subjects for whom there are values):

> (B) One outcome is (intrinsically) better than another if, other things being equal, it is (intrinsically) better, qualitatively, for all contingent or non-contingent persons, collectively.

This principle can be conjugated with a principle of equality like the following:

> (E) One outcome is (intrinsically) better than another if, other things being equal, those who, through no fault or choice of theirs, are worse off than others in it are fewer and less worse off, i.e., there is a greater degree of just equality in it.

As I have explained, this principle is not person-affecting even in the wide sense, for just equality is an impersonal good.

At the outset I pointed out that two issues have been discussed under the heading of whether our principles for the evaluation of outcomes should be person-affecting: (1) whether all values are for somebody, are personal in contrast to impersonal, and (2) whether the value of an outcome is a function of what has value only for non-contingent persons or for contingent ones as well. To disambiguate the term 'person-affecting', we could confine it to the first issue and contrast it with 'impersonality', whereas we can describe the second issue as dealing with whether our principles should be 'existence-presupposing'[13] in contrast to 'existence-including'. In this terminology, I have sketched in barest outline a set of two principles for the evaluation of outcomes which is existence-including in virtue of incorporating (B), and impersonal in virtue of (E). I have tried to show that this set can be aligned with our intuitive preference for increasing the value of outcomes by improving the lot of non-contingent persons, especially those worse off, instead of adding new worthwhile lives to the world.

NOTES

[1] Cf. Parfit's critique of 'the Unrestricted Desire-Fulfilment Theory' in ([3], p. 494).

[2] I think a desire can be self-regarding without being egoistic or selfish: the latter seems to consist in wanting to fulfil one's self-regarding desires rather than the (conflicting) desires of others, and, thus, presupposes an awareness of the desires of others.

[3] I here assume the falsity of a view that I criticize in [7], namely that fulfilment has no positive value, but is only the absence of the negative value of frustration.

[4] (PAN) also comes up against Parfit's 'Non-identity Problem' ([3], ch. 16). This argument implies that an outcome can be worse though it is better for all non-contingent persons.

[5] Parfit, for one, takes this view ([3], pp. 395, 489-90).

[6] Cf. Feldman's definition: 'Something is extrinsically bad for a person if and only if he or she would have been intrinsically better off it it had not taken place' ([1], p. 138). I would like to add a clause requiring that this 'something' is not intrinsically bad, thereby excluding that something will be extrinsically bad just because it is intrinsically bad.

[7] Here, and below, I repeat some points more fully made in ([6], pp. 27-30).

[8] Therefore, to read 'person' in 'person-affecting' as a person in the sense just indicated is too narrow; we should take it as designating a being with any form of consciousness and desires, however rudimentary.

[9] According to desire relativism, there is no guarantee that the qualitative rankings of different persons will coincide, unless we incorporate some objective normative requirements into R. This means that they may disagree about when the quantitative gains will no longer outweigh the qualitative losses, though they may still agree that this has happened by the time Z is reached.

[10] This argument against transitivity can be made more persuasive on the reasonable assumption that there is a vagueness or indeterminacy in our qualitative comparisons. This would make it possible that, although we cannot detect any qualitative difference between E_1 and E_2, or between E_2 and E_3, we can detect such a difference between E_1 and E_3. If so, then, while the choice between E_1 and E_2 and between E_2 and E_3 will be based only on differences of duration, the choice between E_1 and E_3 will be based on a difference in quality, as well. Certainly, this qualitative difference may be outweighed by the sum of the quantitative differences, but this is not logically necessary, as transitivity requires.

[11] As regards Parfit's so-called Mere Addition Paradox, I would go along with the solution Larry S. Temkin suggests in ([10], pt. II).

[12] Many moral philosophers will disagree with this: utilitarians because this inequality has no bad effects on what is of (personal) value to people; others because an inequality for which no moral agent is responsible cannot be unjust, and therefore not bad. I think these views are mistaken, but I cannot here argue against them. For further discussion of this and some other claims I make about equality, see [8].
[13] Cf. Peter Singer's label 'prior existence view' ([9], pp. 103-4).

BIBLIOGRAPHY

1.   Feldman, F.: 1992, *Confrontations with the Reaper*, Oxford University Press, New York.
2.   Heyd, D.: 1992, *Genethics*, University of California Press, Berkeley.
3.   Parfit, D.: 1984, *Reasons and Persons*, Clarendon Press, Oxford.
4.   Parfit, D.: 1986, 'Overpopulation and the Quality of Life', in Singer, P. (Ed.): 1986, *Applied Ethics*, Oxford University Press, Oxford.
5.   Parfit, D.: 1991, 'Equality or Priority', The Lindley Lecture, The University of Kansas.
6.   Persson, I.: 1995, 'Genethic Therapy, Identity and the Person-Regarding Reasons', *Bioethics*, 9, 16-31.
7.   Persson, I.: 1995, 'Peter Singer on why Persons are Irreplaceable', *Utilitas* 7, 55-66.
8.   Persson, I.: 1996, 'Telic Egalitarianism vs. The Priority View', in Rabinowicz, W. (ed.): 1996, *Preference and Value*, Department of Philosophy, Lund University.
9.   Singer, P.: 1993, *Practical Ethics*, 2nd ed., Cambridge University Press, Cambridge.
10. Temkin, L.: 1987, 'Intransitivity and the Mere Addition Paradox', *Philosophy and Public Affairs*, 16, 138-187.

DAVID HEYD

DIVINE CREATION AND HUMAN PROCREATION:
REFLECTIONS ON GENESIS IN THE LIGHT OF *GENESIS*[1]

So far as I'm concerned, I made up my mind long ago not to
speculate whether man has created God or God has created man.

Ivan Karamazov

CONTINGENT EXISTENCE VS. NON-CONTINGENT VALUE

Human beings are contingent insofar as their existence is not necessary. Logically, there is, of course, nothing self-contradictory in a human-less world, let alone in a world from which any particular individual is absent. From a metaphysical perspective, however, things are less clear. Spinozistic arguments notwithstanding, it is indeed plausible to say that the existence of any individual person is metaphysically speaking a contingent matter; but is the existence of humanity as such similarly contingent? Could the world as we know it be devoid of humans? Some metaphysical and theological systems answer in the negative; naturalistic and positivist approaches answer in the affirmative, treating the evolution of humanity as a contingent, even accidental matter. Without taking sides on this issue, I would like to follow a Leibnizian line by claiming that even if there is a possible world in which there are no human beings, a benevolent God could not have created it since it would not have been the *best* possible world. Indeed, it will be the major argument of this article that a human-less world would lack any value. Or in other words, human beings are non-contingent from the point of view of value: being its source, they are necessary.

There is another sense in which human beings are described as contingent. This sense is neither logical nor metaphysical, but better described as human. It has to do with the kind of control (or the lack thereof) over the process of reproduction leading to the birth of individual persons. This is an agent-related concept of contingency and is accordingly relative. Thus, in a society in which means of birth control are unknown, children are born as a matter of "necessity", whereas typical couples in the developed world, concerned with family planning, give birth to "contingent" persons. Contingency in this sense is derived from the *choice* which gives rise to the existence of a new individual. Contingent future people are thus those potential or possible human beings whose existence depends on a choice made by actual human beings (rather than on natural necessity which lies beyond the control of the biological parents).

57

Nick Fotion and Jan C. Heller (eds.), Contingent Future Persons, 57-70.
© 1997 *Kluwer Academic Publishers. Printed in the Netherlands.*

Now, as has been widely shown in the past twenty years, the moral status of humanly contingent persons is puzzling and raises disturbing paradoxes. As I have illustrated elsewhere, these perplexities can be classified under three headings: existence, number, and identity.[2] Or, in other words, there are three inter-related questions: should we create a new person at all?, how many new persons?, and under what identity? On the practical level these issues relate to the morality of family planning, population policy, and genetic engineering (respectively); they are the focus of "wrongful life cases" in the law, of the restrictions on certain forms of assisted (artificial) reproduction, and even of the justification of moral constraints on education in its more formative aspects. However, on the theoretical level the status of contingent future people raises what might be the deepest question, namely, the very nature of value: is value *impersonal*, that is, attributed to states of affairs in the world independently of acts of evaluation; or is value *person-affecting*, that is, a function of the way evaluators are affected by states of affairs.

The dispute between the two views of value has proven to be the underlying source of disagreement about the moral status of contingent future people. Yet, the discussion of "genethical" problems (that is those relating to the existence, number, and identity of contingent future people) equally plays a role in lending support to either of the alternative views of value. This creates a non-vicious, indeed a philosophically fruitful kind of circularity, in which we are called to formulate a theory of value which would fit our basic intuitions about genethical issues in a kind of a Rawlsian reflective equilibrium. One potentially useful strategy for analyzing the interdependence of our theory of value and our genethical intuitions is to examine what I referred to as the human sense of contingency (the moral status of future possible people in *our* deliberation) in the light of the metaphysical sense (the value of the existence of humanity from a transcendent point of view). My suggestion is that the traditional philosophical discussion of genethical issues, preceding the debates of the last two decades, followed exactly this strategy.

The first and maybe most formative presentation of the subject in the history of western thought is found in the first chapters of the Bible. This article is devoted to a close reading of the verses relating to the creation of humanity, to later interpretations of these verses, and to the attempt to expose the tension between the person-affecting and impersonal approaches to value which underlie them. It will be argued that the overall person-affecting tone of the various readings of the text is associated with a double move: analyzing the divine plan of creation in human terms and understanding human procreation by shifting to the metaphysical depiction of the creation of humanity. By focusing on the first chapters of the Bible, I have a double aim in mind: a better understanding of the philosophical discussions of "genesis problems" for which *Genesis* dictated the agenda and an insight into the particular Jewish perspective and the anthropocentric world-view associated with it.

IN THE IMAGE OF GOD

The specific nature of the image of God in which every human being is created has been extensively discussed by philosophers, theologians, and biblical commentators. Philosophers of a rationalist bent mention reason and intelligence as the divine property in which humans resemble God. Some theologians emphasize spirituality and free will as God's image. However, the juxtaposition of the verses referring to God's image and likeness with the following verse prescribing procreation and dominion has not escaped the notice of biblical commentators, ancient and modern. And indeed the close textual association provides compelling evidence for the plausibility of interpretations of the nature of God's image in terms of these two properties:

And God said, "Let us make man in our image, after our likeness. They shall rule the fish of the sea, the birds of the sky, the cattle, the whole earth, and all the creeping things that creep on earth". And God created man in His image, in the image of God He created him; male and female He created them. God blessed them and God said unto them, "Be fertile and increase, fill the earth and master it; and rule the fish of the sea, the birds of the sky, and all the living things that creep on earth" (*Genesis*, 1:26-28, The JPS edition).

The 10th century commentator and philosopher Sa'adia Gaon, for example, understands "image" as referring neither to form nor to real image, but to "a form of action", which - by the above mentioned juxtaposition - is to be read as the divine delegation of power over nature to man. Man is inferior to God only in having less power: he can only subdue the earth, not create it ([18], pp. 252, 255). The Talmudic sage, R. Akiba, follows the other option of connecting God's image with the immediately following description of man who is created in that image. He explains the prohibition on celibacy:

As though he [the celibate] has diminished the Divine Image; since it is said, "For in the image of God made he man", and this is immediately followed by, "And you, be ye fruitful etc." ([2], p. 63b).

The two interpretations of God's image in terms of the textual proximity refer then to man's ruling of nature on the one hand and to his power of procreation on the other. The literal reading of the verses following the ones quoted above points to the teleological point of the creation of the natural world, namely to serve the needs of man, its master. However, there is a homiletic tradition which interprets the end of creation in terms of the other aspect of God's image, viz. procreation. Since God meant the world to be settled rather than remain waste, this homiletic rendering, as we shall see, understands God as creating the world *in order* that human beings procreate and multiply!

Still, these interpretations, including the last, usually treat procreation as a *means* to achieve a certain divine goal. Thus, in his comprehensive and erudite study of the verse "Be fruitful and increase...", Jeremy Cohen comments that sexuality "enabled [human beings] to work *within* that world toward its transformation according to an otherworldly model" ([3], p. 122).[3] Or, in a similar vein, R. Tifdai says that angels were created in God's image but do not procreate, while animals procreate but are not made in God's image; only man is created with a celestial character but procreates in the terrestrial way ([11], pp. 61-62). But most interpretations stop short of what I would like to suggest is the radical reading of the juxtaposition, namely that being fruitful and increasing *is* God's image, that is, a celestial property. If God's essential image is his creative power, our likeness to him consists in our procreative capacity.

This interpretation, which serves as the guiding principle for my reading of the story of the genesis of humanity, is prima facie suspect. The association of God's nature with sexual reproduction seems an oxymoron. God's absolute and self-sufficient mode of existence seems to be incompatible with replication and proliferation. However, I would like to argue that even if this is true on the logical (and maybe on the abstract metaphysical) level, from an *axiological* point of view God is not self-sufficient and the proliferation of his image in human form is necessary for the constitution of value in the world and even for God's own existence.[4]

A careful reading of the creation of man on the sixth day can help support this suggestion. In the previous stages of creation nothing was created in the image of God. Hence, the world, although it was good *in the eyes of* God, was in itself value-less, that is bare nature. Only a natural creature which has some of God's supernatural properties can make it good in the sense that it is valued and valuable in worldly terms, that is from the point of view of the created, "from within". One such property is being able to serve as the *telos* of the created world, being its master and making use of it, thus investing it with value. The other property is being able to perpetuate the very conditions of valuation, namely the existence of evaluators, by the capacity to create them, to produce more people. The twin power of dominion and propagation is, therefore, what makes humans "the pinnacle of creation", its metaphysical point.[5]

The biblical text testifies to these fundamental differences between the creation of the natural world and that of man. First, after each day of creation it says, "and God saw that this was good"; but after the sixth day it says, "and God saw it was very good" (*Genesis* 1: 31), which can be taken as implyinging that only at that stage does the act of creation reach perfection, or, in other words, only then does the world have value "of its own". This occurs only when the natural world becomes good *for* someone, that is to say, positively affects the needs and interests of human subjects.

Secondly, it should be noted that the act of creation usually takes the "jussive" linguistic form of "let there be" or "let the earth bring forth", or uses the verb "make", while the term "create" is almost exclusively reserved for creation *ex nihilo* (1:1, 1:27):[6] first, at the very beginning, when heaven and earth are created (as the raw material for all the rest which is articulated by fiat later on), and second, at the very end, when man is created. The analogy I wish to draw here is that in the same way as matter is created out of nothing on the first day, value is invested in it, equally *ex nihilo*, on the final day. The metaphysical necessity of there being "something" rather than nothing is complemented by the axiological necessity of a *telos*, a creature for whom the created world is good.

Thirdly, fertility is mentioned in the context of the creation of animals as a *blessing*: "and God blessed them saying, be fruitful and increase" (1:22); but in the case of human beings it is explicitly put as an *injunction*: "and God blessed them and said to them, be fruitful and increase" (1:28) ([15], p. 55). In itself the ability to multiply is a blessing but not a source of value, nor is it an image of God. In its instinctive, purely sexual manifestation, reproduction is just a natural process like any other. What provides it with an ethical nature is the choice involved, the understanding of its meaning, the significance of the intentional perpetuation of the conditions of value in the world. Thus, R. Levi ben Gershom, the 14th century philosopher, says in his commentary to the Pentateuch,

And the point of this injunction is explained in that from it the continued existence of the human species is derived. Since, as man is free in choosing his actions, he could destroy his species by a universal agreement between people to avoid procreation. And at such possibility is the Law's injunction aimed ([9], p. 47).

And for David Hartman, this first commandment to be fertile and increase is the first stage of the covenant between God and man, a relationship of interdependence of man and God. Fertility becomes, through "the capacity for deliberation and reasoned decision making," the obligation of human beings, who by that power acquire the responsibility for the continuity of creation ([4], pp. 22-23).[7] But it no less lays responsibility on God to enable man to increase, as it is reflected in the numerous blessings and promises given later to Noah, Abraham, Isaac, and Jacob. In terms of my person-affecting reading of the nature of value, only the continuity of humanity, based on the *choice* of human beings to procreate, can guarantee the value of the creation of the world.[8]

The obedience to God's commandments (*mitzvoth*) is in the Jewish tradition central to the religiously worthy life. Hence the priority of the commandment to be fertile and increase is of particular significance to later Jewish thinkers. Maimonides, who systematically lists the traditional 613 precepts, notes the double priority of the commandment to multiply: it is the first both in the chronological order of the commandments in the Bible as well as in the logical order: "This is an important *mitzvah*, by virtue of which all the *mitzvoth* in the world are fulfilled" ([16], pp. 82-83). This is not only because the existence of human beings is the condition of commandments being obeyed, but because with no human beings the universe as a whole would lack meaning and value:

As regards the root purpose of this precept, it is in order that the world should be settled, inhabited. For the Eternal Lord, blessed be He, desires its settlement, as it is written (*Isaiah* 45:18) "He did not create it chaos; he formed it to be inhabited" ([16], *Ibid.*, and [12], 1:13).

In other words, the world was not only a chaos on the first day of creation (1:2), but also after the fifth day by which time almost all nature was well-formed and ordered. We find in these later readings of the biblical story a sensitivity to the distinction between metaphysical chaos and "axiological chaos". And while God is the only source of the order of nature, human beings are the necessary source of the order of value. This is a radically person-affecting view.

THE BOOK OF GENERATIONS

This is the record of Adam's line. When God created man, He made him in the likeness of God; male and female He created them. And when they were created, He blessed them and called them Man. When Adam had lived 130 years, he begot a son in his likeness after his image, and he named him Seth (*Genesis*, 5: 1-3).

In this second stage of divine creation the first couple directly created by God takes over the proliferation of God's image by transmitting it to their descendants. At this point the metaphysical account of the first primordial phase paves the way to human history. Thus, the "book of generations" of Adam is both the record of his line (as the above translation puts it) and the story of his evolution. The original Hebrew term for generation(s), "toldot", refers both to begetting and to the history or record of events.

Some commentators hold that Adam begot his first child on the day of his creation, thus directly associating creation and procreation. And R. Abraham ben Ezra notes that "God endowed man with the power of generation in order that he manifest His image so that his act resemble the divine act"([17], p. 81)! And again, the text can be plausibly read as relating the likeness of God to human sexuality or reproductive power ("in the image of God He created him", *namely* "male and female He created them").

From that point on, the task of spreading God's image in the world, namely to invest it with (religious) value, is delegated to human beings (who have been commanded to do so).[9] Adam begets a son in his image and likeness, which is the same divine image in which he himself was created *ex nihilo*.[10] Read in the light of the interpretation suggested here, it is significant that the first account of the beginning of human history consists of a *purely* genealogical record of the birth of one generation after another. The whole of *Genesis* chapter 5 proceeds with a tedious listing of ten generations, mentioning only the names of their first-born representatives and the length of their lives. The primary meaning of human existence is portrayed as lying in its sheer perpetuation, that is, in spreading God's image in the world. The kind of life these people lead is implicitly declared as irrelevant for the understanding of the point of human existence.

The urgency of securing the conditions of religious value in the world is succinctly expressed also in the later Talmudic tradition: permission to sell Torah scrolls is exclusively given for the purpose of either the study of Torah or of *marriage* ([1], p. 27a). This can be understood as saying that Torah scrolls have value only *for* present and future people, who can study it and be subjected to the religious precepts contained in it. Religious study, maybe because of its practical association with the performance of *mitzvoth*, is not completely "self-sufficient" in the Aristotelian sense of the contemplative life.

The story of ben Azai, who hails the priority of the duty to procreate, reveals the tension between that duty and the duty to study the Torah (the two duties which justify the selling of Torah scrolls). The story goes that he was blamed "that he preaches well but does not act well since he remained a bachelor" to which the Rabbi replied, "[b]ut what shall I do, seeing that my soul is in love with the Torah; the world can be carried on by others" ([2], p. 63b). This raises the unresolved conflict between the two basic duties which bestow meaning on life. The pragmatic resolution of the contradiction suggested by ben Azai is based on the elitist assumption that spreading God's image can be achieved by everybody, but the study of the Torah can be undertaken only by the select few.[11]

GOD'S DOUBLE REGRET

The next stage in the story of the creation of humanity and the deliberation about its continuance appears at the end of the first ten generations, that is, in the time of Noah.

The Lord saw how great was man's wickedness on earth, and how every plan devised by his mind was nothing but evil all the time. And the Lord regretted that He had made man on earth, and His heart was saddened. The Lord said, "I will blot out from the earth the men whom I created—men together with beasts, creeping things, and birds of the sky; for I regret that I made them (6:5-7).

Since all we know of the story of man during this long period of ten generations consists in his own reproduction, and the only norm to which humans are subject concerns procreation, it makes sense to interpret the "evil thought" of man as connected to his sexuality. The abuse of the procreative power (by both humans and animals) is tacitly suggested as the source of God's dissatisfaction with the "pinnacle of creation".

And a few verses later, the motive for the divine plan of annihilation is described in terms of "corruption and lawlessness" (6:11-13), which are understood by most commentators as referring to the arrogant disregard of the sanctity and inviolability of human life. As we shall see in the post-diluvian stage of the story, this gravest of offenses is understood as directly related to the idea of God's image and its diminution.

However, this divine regret for creating humanity seems irrational: if the image of God consists, as I am suggesting, of the *free* exercise of (pro)creative power, then once this image is recast in *human* (finite) form, it necessarily yields some measure of evil as well as of goodness. In Kantian terms of "negative freedom", morality consists of the power to choose between good and evil, that is to say, moral value can exist only against the background of the actual possibility of evil. The image of God consists of a radical freedom of choice. Hence, avoiding all possible corruption can be achieved only by the total annihilation of the sources of both good and evil. This would leave the world value-less, as it was before the creation of humanity.

A radical expression of a similar view is expressed by R. Meir, a 2nd century scholar. In a daring reading of the verse "and God saw everything that he had made and, behold, it was very good" (1:31), he notes that the Hebrew words *tov me'od* ("very good"), rather than just "good" (as in the previous days of creation) can be read, in a slight phonetic shift, as *tov mot*, meaning "death is good"! A possible interpretation of this striking exegetical move is that the death of the individual finite human creature is a metaphysical necessity, part of the very force of life, the mirror-image or counterpart of reproductive power. The value of procreation is coupled with the ultimate evil of death as two complementary factors of the same presupposition of (human) life having any value ([11], p. 66).[12]

The necessary coupling of good and evil in the act of creation is also simply presented in R. Berekiah's reflections about God's dilemma:

If I create him, wicked men will spring from him; if I do not create him, how are the righteous to spring from him? ([11], p. 57).[13]

Due to its self-defeating nature, the idea of total annihilation is later replaced by the idea of a second chance for the human race. Noah is chosen as the mainstay of human renewal, but this time on a double basis: Noah's own proven righteousness and God's promise never again to destroy every living being. Unlike the tacit covenant of God with Adam, the covenant with Noah becomes explicit and cosmically guaranteed by the rainbow in the clouds. Any future desire of God to destroy humanity will be checked by the reminder of the rainbow, which connects heaven and earth, divine nature and its human manifestation.

God's second regret is, therefore, his realization that total destruction of human beings would undermine the metaphysical point of the creation of the world. With no human beings there would be no recognition or proliferation of the divine image and the very power of God would be lacking. The dependence of God on human creatures is subtly conveyed in the context of this second regret. When Noah builds an altar and makes his offerings to God,

The Lord smelled the pleasing odor, and the Lord said to Himself: "never again will I doom the earth because of man, since the devisings of man's mind are evil from his youth; nor will I ever again destroy every living being, as I have done (8:21).

Human evil, as God now realizes, is "innate", that is to say essential, or in our terms axiologically necessary. There is no conceptual possibility of goodness without evil. Creating the conditions of value in the world entails making evil possible as well. The 16th century commentator Sforno understands man's "likeness" to God in his being able to act on the basis of knowledge and choice; but then notes that "although God's choice is always for the good, this is not the case with human choice", whose choice is sometimes for the better and sometimes for the worse ([17], p. 30).

God's second regret is typically crowned by the same blessing of the first chapter, "Be fertile and increase, and fill the earth" (9:1), put in the same grammatical form expressing a commandment. Like the blessing to Adam and Eve, this blessing to Noah is coupled with the parallel one of dominion over nature and is repeated in an emphatic formula (9:7). The stronger formulation of the commandment reflects, according to Nachmanides the special urgency of reproduction after the flood due to the paucity of human beings in the world ([15], p. 135).[14] God's dilemma is that on the one hand human beings are the source of the corruption of the whole earth but at the same time are the only natural creatures which can invest value in this world. The total annihilation of humanity necessarily means, therefore, making the whole project of creation null and void.

THE SANCTITY OF LIFE

However, the new covenant includes also a new condition, an explicit commandment which is derived from the identification of human reproductive power with the divine image.

You must not, however, eat flesh with its life-blood in it. But for your own life-blood I will require a reckoning: I will require it of every beast; of man, too, will I require a reckoning for human life, for every man for that of his fellow man! Whoever sheds the blood of man, by man shall his blood be shed; for in His image did God make man (9:4-6).

This verse served later commentators as the source for the interpretation of murder as the diminution of God's image. Thus, the prohibition of murder is portrayed as the "mirror-image" of the injunction to reproduce, both being justified in terms of the expansion of the divine image in the world. Thus, for instance, R. Eliezer, the Talmudic sage, states: "He who does not engage in propagation of the race is as though he sheds blood", supporting his claim on the juxtaposition of the prohibition on murder and the prescription to reproduce in Noah's story ([2], p. 63b, and [15], p. 136). It should be emphasized again that the spilling of human blood is not wrong because human beings are the "carriers" of divine image, but because killing a man is a *direct* impairment of God's image.

This reading has its biblical roots in the story of Cain and Abel, in which the association of blood and life is first suggested. But more significant to our purpose is the later reading of the verse, "Hark, your brother's blood cries out to Me from the ground" (4:10-11). Commentators were quick to note the plural form in the Hebrew term for "blood" (*damim*). The Mishna, in the context of discussing the exhortation of witnesses testifying in capital cases, notes the gravity of an error in such cases since it may lead to the shedding of innocent blood. As in the case of Abel, "his [the innocent victim's] blood and the blood of his offspring...until the end of the world" is at stake ([13], 4:5). That is to say, taking the life of an individual entails the non-life of all his potential descendants, the destruction of life to an almost infinite degree (in Abel's case, exactly half of all potential human beings).

The Mishna continues with the interesting explanation of this idea of the inclusion of the loss of life of "future contingent lives" in the assessment of the loss of the life of an individual:

> Therefore man was created singly, to teach you that whoever destroys a single soul, Scripture accounts it as if he had destroyed a full world. And who saves a single soul, it is as if he had saved a full world ([13], *Ibid.*).

We can see how the ideas of the image of God, human reproduction, and the uniqueness of the value of human life are all tied together conceptually and theologically. The ideal of propagation is just a transgenerational expression of the principle of the sanctity of human life, which is grounded in its being a precondition of any value. Since there is no value with no evaluators, the life of the evaluating subjects, both on the individual and the collective levels, both in the short and in the long run, is a sort of *meta*-value, a second-order value, a basis for all there is, axiologically speaking ([14], p. 519).[15] The above-quoted Mishna concludes that the uniqueness of the individual obliges him to say, "for my sake the world was created", which is a radical person-affecting and anthropocentric formulation.[16]

The crystallization of the principle of the sanctity of life is also reflected in the Noahide prohibition on the eating of "flesh with its blood-life in it" (9:4). In other words, although the scope of human dominion over the natural world is expanded (since in antediluvian times humans were restricted to a vegetarian diet), the respect for life (as such) is extended also to the animal world. No animal organ should be taken for human consumption before the death of the animal. The life-blood of animals should be drained before they are eaten. Blood, exactly like the power of procreation, is directly associated with life and indirectly with God's image, and hence enjoys a special status not only in humans but also in animals. The new covenant and the promise never to destroy life again specifies, accordingly, "all flesh that is on earth" (9:17), rather than just human beings.[17]

From a person-affecting perspective, no particular future life is sanctified. Hence, it seems that the view expressed by the above Mishna is typically "impersonal". However, the association of the sanctity of human life with the divine interest in the expansion of the divine image lends a person-affecting (or rather God-affecting) inflection to the theology of the double injunction to reproduce and to refrain from killing. The whole story of creation is told in the first-person, or from God's individual perspective, always checked by his "personal" assessment of the success of the undertaking. But at any rate, even if no commitment to the impersonal value of the existence of any *particular* future individual is suggested by the Jewish tradition, the value of the existence of future people *in general* is not only highly rated, but made absolute as a necessary condition to any other value.

TRANSCENDENCE AND SELF-TRANSCENDENCE

The deep philosophical divide between person-affecting and impersonal theories of value is sharply, though only implicitly, portrayed in the first chapters of the Bible. The impersonal approach considers the existence of human beings as good "in itself", a value which can be ascribed to the world as such. However, this is a typically dogmatic answer, since it does not specify *why* or *what* is good in the existence of humanity, or why corrupt humanity should be saved from total destruction in the deluge. A person-affecting approach holds that any value must be "anchored" in human desires, interests, ideals - that is to say, in the way human beings are affected by states of affairs. But then, how can one assess the value of the very existence of human beings? One answer is that it simply has no value: it is a value-neutral fact, a presupposition of any ascription of value. From both a theological point of view (trying to account for the various aspects of the created world) and that of human beings (trying to justify the value of the continuation of the human race), this might be an unsatisfactory answer.

This raises another possibility, namely, that the existence of human beings is itself a primary interest or ideal *of* evaluating beings. From the person-affecting perspective, human beings can find value in the future existence of humanity only in their own "self-transcendence", that is their expanded existence in the life of their descendants. Only by begetting children, raising them according to our values and ideals ("image"!), can we hope to infuse value in our own limited life plans and projects. But this leaves open the question whether the existence of human beings in the world "to start with" is a value. The only response to that perplexing enigma is through a move of "transcendence", that is a metaphysical account in which the existence of human beings serves the purposes of some super-natural being, God.

The preceding pages aimed to support the thesis that the biblical story of the creation of humanity reflects this double move of transcendence and self-transcendence as a person-affecting account. The primacy of the value of procreation, the prohibition of murder, the sanctity of life, as expressed in the Jewish tradition from the biblical chapters to the late commentaries, exhibit this idea of self-transcendence as the only source of value of human existence. And the story of the creation of Adam and Eve expresses the "person"-affecting justification of God's finding satisfaction in his creation and in the propagation of his image in the world through man. Beyond that move of transcendence, no questions can be raised (why does God exist? or, what is good in spreading his image?). But once God's point of view is adopted, it looks similar to the person-affecting, self-transcending evaluation of procreation as the ultimate source of value. God expands in the world according to a principle of *plenitude*: both ontologically and axiologically, as the supreme ruler and propagator. But as in the "great chain of being", God can achieve this double role only with the cooperation of created, finite human beings.

This shift of the source of value of human existence to a higher metaphysical level and the interdependence of the two levels (the divine and human bonded in a covenant) is manifest, as has been shown, in various aspects of the biblical story and its interpretations. Thus, R. David Kimhi (Radak) reads the verse "They shall rule the fish of the sea, etc.",

in order to inform all the lowly creatures that they were created only for the sake of man and that he, with his intelligence, will dominate and rule them, since otherwise there would be no one in the lower world who would recognize who created it ([17], p. 31).

Recognition is the condition of the worthiness of creation and a manifestation of the mutual dependence of the divine and the human from a person-affecting point of view. This bi-directional dialectic of human obligation towards God and God's promise to man is the conceptual framework of the whole story of creation.[18]

NOTES

[1] This article was written with the financial support and intellectual encouragement of the Shalom Hartman Institute in Jerusalem. I am particularly grateful to Yair Lorberboim who directed my attention to many of the Jewish sources which he systematically investigated in his Ph.D. dissertation on the subject of the Image of God [10]. I am also grateful to Noam Zohar for his incisive criticism of an earlier draft and his enlightening suggestions.

[2] For a full theory of the moral status of future people and the competing conceptions of value which underlie the alternative approaches to the subject, see [5].

[3] I fully agree with Cohen's reading that mastering the earth does not mean unencumbered exploitation of nature and that there is nothing contrary to ecologically sensitive views in the biblical story. Dominion is to be understood in the sense I am suggesting here, namely, the person-affecting source of the value of nature.

[4] This dependence of God on human beings is formulated also in the mystical tradition of the Kabbalah. Thus, according to Moshe Idel, "for the theosophical kabbalists, intercourse is not an aim in itself. The final goals are procreation and propagation of appropriate *substrata*—human beings—to serve as residences for the Shekhinah" ([7], p. 206). Idel notes that after the destruction of the temple, the divinity dwells on human couples rather than on the two cherubim which were placed at the temple entrance.

[5] Modern feminist sensibilities notwithstanding, it should be noted that the injunction of procreation applies only to men rather than women, since, according to one common interpretation, only man is endowed with the power of dominion.

[6] The only exception are the great sea-monsters (or dragons) which were "created" (1:21) rather than "made" due (according to Nachmanides) to their enormous size. Other exegetes refer to the anti-pagan polemic involved in this depiction of the sea monsters which were objects of Canaanite idolatry as independent deities.

[7] Hartman convincingly points out that by creating human beings endowed with free choice, God is limiting his own power (like a parent who raises a child to be an autonomous self-choosing personality). This, in my understanding, expresses the idea that only the existence of valuing subjects can make the world have value independently of God's own satisfaction with his creation.

[8] R. Jacob ben Asher (Ba'al Haturim), a medieval commentator in Toledo, distinguishes between the blessing of fertility to the animals and the *real* blessing of fertility to humans. Whereas in the first case fertility is merely the power to reproduce, in the second it is an expression of man's dominion over the world. Thus the first two injunctions are connected as the two aspects of God's image ([8], p. 5).

[9] The 13th century biblical commentator R. David Kimhi (Radak) reads the verse "God ceased from all the work of creation that He had done" (2:3) as "God ceased the work of creation [for man] to [continue to] do [thenceforth]": God *created* the world and man; from that point onwards, it is man's *making* through procreation and dominion ([17], p. 38).

[10] Nachmanides emphasizes this "transitivity" of God's image saying that although it is trivially true that offspring resemble the parents, here, "because Adam was elevated in his likeness and image...Scripture explains that his offspring were also in this ennobled likeness" ([15], p. 98).

[11] This association of marriage and the image of God can be found also in the "seven blessings" which constitute the liturgical part of the Jewish wedding ceremony: after a blessing of God for creating the world and a blessing of God as the creator of man, there follows a blessing of God "who made man in His image and in the image of His likeness and pattern, and fashioned out of Himself an eternal line of reproduction". I am grateful to Yair Lorberboim for having drawn my attention to this illustrative source, and to his original interpretation according to which by creating humans God secures eternity for *himself* [10]! This bold reading is fully in agreement with my suggested interpretation of God's image as the power of replication.

[12] R. David Kimhi (Radak) offers a somewhat similar reading, based on the Midrash Rabbah: "good" means "good inclination"; "very good" means "evil inclination". How come? With no evil inclination, man does not marry and beget children! ([17], p. 35).

[13] The same homily proceeds to the other justification of the creation of man: "A tower full of good things and no guests— what pleasure has its owner in having filled it?" ([11], p. 59).

[14] For a similar argument concerning the proportion between the urgency of the duty to beget children and the size of the present human population, see [6]. This is called "the variable value view", and is also illustrated by Noah's particularly strong duty to procreate after the flood.

[15] "Value-seekers", says Nozick, "have a cosmic role: to aid in the realization of value, in the infusion of value into the material and human realm". However, with no shift into the transcendent perspective of God, Nozick can substantiate his statement that "it is valuable that there be values" ([14], p. 429) only from an impersonal point of view.

[16] A traditional distinction between "fertility" and "increase" suggests that the former secures physical continuation, while the latter consists of quantitative and qualitative growth, that is "filling the earth" as well as the augmentation of power.

[17] R. Jacob ben Asher notes that animals have a soul, though of a lower kind than that of humans: animal behavior reflects an effort to avoid pain and death and to choose the best food ([8], p. 6). Compare Nachmanides's view in [15], p. 57.

[18] This covenantal relationship takes the form of three descending levels: first, the metaphysical (the creation of Adam and Eve); secondly, the universally human (the rainbow in the cloud and the promise to Noah); and thirdly, the particularistic, Jewish (circumcision as the covenant with Abraham and the beginning of the history of the people of Israel with its special religious significance for God and for the chosen people). See [4], chap. 1, and [3], pp. 39, 66.

BIBLIOGRAPHY

1. *Babylonian Talmud*, Tractate Megillah: 1936, trans. W. Slotki, Soncino Press, London.
2. *Babylonian Talmud*, Tractate Yebamoth: 1936, trans. W. Slotki, Soncino Press, London.
3. Cohen, J.: 1989, *'Be Fertile and Increase, Fill the Earth and Master It': The Ancient and Medieval Career of a Biblical Text*, Cornell University Press, Ithaca.
4. Hartman, D.: 1985, *A Living Covenant*, The Free Press, New York.
5. Heyd, D.: 1992, *Genethics: Moral Issues in the Creation of People*, University of California Press, Berkeley.
6. Hurka, T.: 1983, 'Value and Population Size', *Ethics* 93, 496-507.
7. Idel, M.: 1989, 'Sexual Metaphors and Praxis in the Kabbalah', in D. Kraemer (ed.), *The Jewish Family*, Oxford University Press, London, pp. 197-224.
8. Jacob ben Asher (Ba'al Haturim): 1961, *Perush Hatur Ha'aroch*, J. Stern, Jerusalem [in Hebrew].
9. Levi ben Gershom (Ralbag): 1992, *Bible Interpretations*, Mossad Harav Kook, Jerusalem [in Hebrew].
10. Lorberboim, Y.: 1996, "Imago Dei in Jewish Thought: Rabbinic Literature, Maimonides, and Nachmanides", Ph. D. dissertation submitted to The Hebrew University of Jerusalem.

11. *Midrash Rabbah* (Genesis): 1951, trans. H. Freedman and M. Simon, Soncino Press, London.
12. *Mishna*, Eduyoth: 1988, trans. E. Lewin, Eliner Library, Jerusalem.
13. *Mishna*, Sanhedrin: 1988, trans. E. Lewin, Eliner Library, Jerusalem.
14. Nozick, R.: 1981, *Philosophical Explanations*, Harvard University Press, Cambridge (Mass.).
15. Ramban (Nachmanides): 1971, *Commentary on the Torah* (Genesis), trans. C. B. Chavel, Shilo, New York.
16. *Sefer haHinnuch* (The Book of Education), ascribed to Aharon halevi of Barcelona: 1978, trans. C. Wengrow, Feldheim, New York.
17. *Torat Chaim Chumash* (Interpretations of the Pentateuch): 1986, Mossad Harav Kook, Jerusalem [in Hebrew].
18. Zucker, M. (ed.): 1984, *R. Sa'adia Gaon's Interpretations of the Book of Genesis*, Jewish Theological Seminary, New York [in Hebrew].

JAN C. HELLER

DECIDING THE TIMING OF CHILDREN:
AN ETHICAL CHALLENGE ONLY INDIRECTLY ADDRESSED BY THE CHRISTIAN TRADITION[1]

Questions concerning the timing of children are common topics of pastoral counseling encounters in the Christian tradition. They may arise as a specific issue for consideration, as when the timing of a birth may adversely affect the health of the child who is born, or as part of a larger constellation of issues, as when the timing of children may adversely affect the overall opportunities afforded a couple and their family. Consider two possible examples.

> Case 1: An older childless couple who is feeling the pressure of the wife's "biological clock" seeks pastoral guidance upon being informed by medical specialists that they will have a better chance of producing healthy children if they delay conception for a period of time. But they were also informed that, should they wait, they will have a greater chance of having no children. They are seeking pastoral counseling because they are not sure morally how to act on this information; they dearly want children of their own, but they wonder if they have any obligation as Christians to bring healthy children into the world when it may be in their power to do so.

> Case 2: A pastor who is counseling a teenage couple in preparation for their wedding points out the well-documented problems encountered by teenagers who marry, among which are the timing of children. The pastor informs them that children born before they as a couple are established financially or before they as individuals are emotionally ready for the responsibility may adversely affect the stability of their marriage and future opportunities for them and their children. However, in a moment of insight, one teen defensively asks the pastor whether the Christian faith gives them any reason to delay their marriage so that their children, who may never be born in any case, will have a greater chance for better opportunities in life.

My intention in posing questions about the timing of children is to focus our inquiry clearly on *future children who do not exist yet but might*, depending on the actions or choices their parents and other agents (e.g., medical specialists) may make.[2] With this focus, I want to ask whether the Christian faith provides moral

Nick Fotion and Jan C. Heller (eds.), Contingent Future Persons, 71-84.
© 1997 *Kluwer Academic Publishers. Printed in the Netherlands.*

reasons that could be used to *constrain* Christian couples in such cases, and whether such reasons can refer *directly* to the children who might be born as a result of this type of action or choice.

To aid my inquiry, I will utilize the work of two moral philosophers—principally, David Heyd, and, to less extent, Derek Parfit—to make three key distinctions: first, between two categories of future persons; second, between two fundamental conceptions of, or approaches to, value; and third, between two perspectives from which, or bases by which, particular value judgments may be made or justified. My reason for using these philosophers should become apparent as the discussion progresses. In short, I believe the categories of analysis they develop with these three key distinctions are relevant for analyzing questions about the timing of children in Christian terms. I conclude that the Christian faith can, in fact, provide reasons that can be used morally to constrain couples in cases concerning the timing of children, but that these reasons can refer only *indirectly* to the children who might be born. As a consequence of the fact that Christians can refer only indirectly to children who might be born, I also argue that those children who are *actually* born as a result of such choices may be overly vulnerable to the interests of the agents who bring them into existence.[3] To the extent that this vulnerability worries Christian pastors and parents, it stands as a possible challenge to the Christian moral tradition (at least as it is typically construed).

THE PROBLEM OF CONTINGENT FUTURE PERSONS

The first distinction concerns two categories of future persons: first, those whose existence, numbers, and identities are *dependent* on the actions or choices of agents in the relevant sense (to be explained momentarily); and, second, those whose existence, numbers, and identities are *not* dependent in the relevant sense. The two couples in the cases above are asking whether they have any obligation as Christians to the future children who fall into the first category of future persons, those who are variously referred to as "possible people" [3], "potential people" [6], or "contingent future persons" [5]. Those future persons whose existence is not dependent in the relevant sense are referred to here as "non-contingent future persons." Heyd uses the term "actual people" for this category of future person and includes in it presently living persons.[4] Moreover, what I typically discuss here as the "problem of contingent future persons" is also addressed under a variety of designations. Parfit discusses it as the "non-identity problem" ([9], pp. 351-355), whereas Heyd follows the economist Partha Dasgupta and treats it as a "genesis problem" ([6], pp. 1-2). By any designation, however, this problem concerns how one ought to evaluate the actions that determine *which* future person or persons will actually exist. Evaluating such actions is perplexing, for those contingent future persons who are actually brought into existence by these actions apparently cannot benefit from or be harmed by the same actions in any conventional sense.

Derek Parfit claims that this counter-intuitive situation arises as a consequence of the fact that the identity of any particular person is *time-dependent* ([9], pp. 351-357). By this he means that the identity of particular humans is dependent on the time of their conception. Naturally, many individuals and prospective parents are indifferent to this fact, but it can become morally relevant for them in cases like the two introduced above, where the timing of children can have significant consequences for the parents and the children themselves.[5] In any case, it is the time-dependency of identity that gives rise to the problem of contingent future persons.

Thus, because identity is time-dependent, if parents deliberately decide to delay the conception of a *particular* (future) child to increase the probability of having a healthy child (Case 1) or to increase the chances of giving their child a better set of opportunities in life (Case 2), a *different* child will in fact be born. And, because a different child is actually born, it makes no sense to say that this child *benefits* from its parents' decision to delay the conception of the other child. For, if its conception had not been delayed, it would never have existed. Conversely, if the decision is made *not* to delay conception, and thus the childless couple in Case 1 gives birth to a handicapped or a genetically affected child or the teenage couple in Case 2 produces a child with a considerably reduced set of opportunities in life, it also makes no sense to claim that either of these children were *harmed* by their parents' actions. Again, any other choice on their parents' part would mean that they would not exist.[6]

This apparent inability to attribute benefit or harm to the effects of actions or choices that hold such dramatic implications for particular future persons is the problem of contingent future persons. And once this problem is explained to Christian pastors and couples, it may leave them wondering if the Christian faith offers any moral guidance in such cases. Said differently, if contingent future children cannot benefit from or be harmed by being brought into existence, it raises the question of whether Christian couples have any moral reason to constrain their own interests relative to these children. To help us address this question, it will be useful to develop the two remaining distinctions mentioned in the introduction.

IMPERSONAL AND PERSON-AFFECTING APPROACHES TO VALUE

David Heyd develops the second key distinction in particularly interesting ways for theologically interested readers as he traces both the practical and theoretical implications of the problem of contingent future persons. This distinction concerns the nature and source of value itself or, as Heyd typically discusses it, the conditions under which value can be attributed to *any* object ([6], pp. 82-83). As mentioned above, he treats the problem of contingent future persons as a "genesis problem," and any choice that involves what he calls the "creation of people" in the relevant sense is discussed as a "genesis choice." Given this terminology, it is perhaps not surprising that Heyd uses the first creation myth in *Genesis* to introduce his discussion. More to the point, he uses the creation myth to establish an analogy between a "pure" or ideal type of genesis choice made by God in the creation of the first humans and an "impure" type of genesis choice made subsequently by humans in the creation of other humans.

Provocatively, Heyd asks:

> ...if the world as a whole does not exist, how can its creation be considered good? Or, alternatively, if no human beings exist (in the inanimate world created in the first five days), how can their creation be considered of any value? God retrospectively judges his creation as "very good," but what kind of good is it ([6], p. 4)?

When Heyd poses this question, he is (here) "not concerned...with either the literary or the theological significance" ([6], p. 1) of the creation story,[7] but instead is using it merely to introduce in an intuitive way a claim that he later develops with an extended argument. This claim has to do with why he believes we are driven by genesis choices to the very limits of ethics and why, when we encounter these limits, we must consider the nature and source of value at its most fundamental level. At this level, the Genesis story illustrates for Heyd's readers how there are only two possible ways to conceptualize value, namely, in impersonal and in person-affecting terms. Thus, Heyd continues:

> There are two possible responses to this question [of what kind of good God's creation is]. The first is to take the impersonal wording of the biblical verse literally, that is to say the state of affairs after Man's creation is better than the one preceding it....The second is to view the value of the newly created state of affairs to God, that is to say to see it as good for him [God being the only "person" who at this point can be affected by the choice] ([6], pp. 4-5).

Heyd argues that this distinction between impersonal and person-affecting approaches to value "consists in the *sort of conditions* that must be satisfied for a value judgment to be applicable: certain absolute characteristics of the world [the impersonal approach] as against certain person-relative states of the world [the person-affecting approach]" ([6], p. 80, emphasis added). Parfit, who is a leading advocate for the impersonal approach to value (and Heyd's principal target), typically defines this approach in negative terms. He claims that an impersonal approach to value "is *not* about what would be good or bad for those people whom our acts affect" ([9], p. 386, emphasis added). But Heyd describes this approach to value more positively. He claims that value conceived impersonally "characterizes states of affairs in the widest global meaning of the term," irrespective of the presence of persons to value these states of affairs. On the other hand, value conceived in person-affecting terms requires or assumes the *prior* presence of a person or "valuer" who can, at least in principle, be affected by some object of value. Thus, Heyd claims, with a person-affecting approach, value originates with and is attached to persons, and states of affairs have value only if persons attribute value to them; if not, these states of affairs remain simply and utterly valueless.

Having defined these two fundamental approaches to value, Heyd argues further that each is "exhaustive and mutually exclusive" of the other. Thus, if we want to treat the problem of contingent future persons consistently, we are forced to choose between them.

> ...I do not argue with the truth or falsity of impersonalism. I only claim that we are confronted with a choice that cannot be avoided: either to adopt an impersonal view of value and pave the way for the inclusion of potential [contingent future] people in the moral community, or adhere to a person-affecting view and treat all genethical [genesis] choices either as a matter related only to actual existing people or consider them as lying beyond the scope of ethics altogether ([6], p. 82).

Now, Heyd does not believe we ought to view such choices as lying beyond the scope of ethics altogether; however, as this quote makes clear, the choice to adopt either an impersonal or a person-affecting approach to value has significant implications for addressing the problem of contingent future persons ethically.

In general terms, an agent using an impersonal approach to value will be concerned with the ways in which the possible existence of contingent future persons (Heyd's "potential" persons) will affect the net quality and quantity of value in the world, rather than with persons as such. It is not that persons are not valued in an impersonal approach, but that they are not valued simply *because* they are persons; again, they are valued for their possible contribution to the net value of the world. Interestingly, then, since an impersonal approach to value makes no reference to the effects of agents' actions on the *particular* future persons who will actually come into existence as a result of the actions, agents using this approach can refer to contingent future persons *directly*. That is, with an impersonal approach, agents can render contingent future persons morally considerable or morally meaningful *as contingent future persons*. This is accomplished by considering their possible existence as a variable in determining the net quality and quantity of value that could result should they be brought into existence.

On the other hand, since contingent future persons are *not yet* and *may never be* persons who can be affected by any choice made about them, Heyd claims that agents using a person-affecting approach to value can treat contingent future persons only *indirectly*. By "indirectly," Heyd means that contingent future persons can be considered morally only by reference to the probable effects their existence or non-existence will have on *other* "actual" persons. And to repeat, for Heyd these "actual" persons include both persons who are presently living and persons who are members of that second set of future persons whom I call non-contingent future persons. Utterly *excluded* from consideration in this approach, however—and this is the point—are contingent or "potential" future persons. In a person-affecting approach to value, Heyd argues, contingent future persons (as such) can have no moral standing.[8] Said differently, coming into existence simply cannot be a harm or a benefit for the person who is born. Existence is viewed merely as a condition of harm or benefit ([6], p. 59).

Now, while one of these two competing approaches to value is presupposed by any treatment of the problem of contingent future persons, neither does all the work that is required ethically. For having rendered contingent future persons morally considerable in two different ways—directly, through an impersonal approach, and indirectly, through a person-affecting approach—we must still decide how we ought to justify particular judgments about them. This question brings us back to more traditional ethical considerations, and to the third key distinction referred to above.

AGENT-NEUTRAL AND AGENT-RELATIVE VALUE JUDGMENTS

This third distinction essentially represents an attempt by contemporary moral philosophers to capture more adequately the most important differences between consequentialism and deontology. For a number of reasons we need not explore here, these differences have recently been reformulated in terms of the perspectives from which, or bases on which, particular value judgments may be justified. An *agent-neutral* perspective requires all agents to use a common perspective. Parfit adopts this perspective ([9], p. 55). It makes no morally significant reference to agents when justifying a particular judgment ([8], pp. 835-836). Heyd adopts an *agent-relative* perspective. It permits agents to adopt *different* perspectives which are "relative" to the *agents'* moral viewpoints. An agent-relative perspective can be further distinguished by agent-relative *constraints* and *permissions*. In contrast to an agent-neutral perspective, an agent-relative constraint may prohibit agents from doing that which would have the best results, and an agent-relative permission may give agents the freedom to do or not to do (at their own discretion) that which would have the best results ([10], pp. 4-5).

My primary concern here is with the perspective Heyd adopts, and with how it influences his treatment of the problem of contingent future persons. Heyd claims that a person-affecting approach to value may substantively be either anthropocentric or theocentric ([9], pp. 1-17). However, these substantive approaches may also be either agent-neutral or agent-relative with respect to the perspective agents ought to adopt when justifying particular judgments. Heyd's own approach is decidedly anthropocentric and radically agent-relative (we consider an agent-relative theocentric approach below).[9] His choice to adopt an anthropocentric approach to value is a humanistic commitment he makes as a contemporary philosopher, but his decision to adopt an agent-relative perspective when making genesis choices may be influenced by the analogy he makes between God's creation of the first humans and our creation of subsequent humans. For just as God is the only reference point or source of value for the creation of the first humans, Heyd argues that human agents are the only reference point or source of value for the creation of other humans: "[I]n the less pure, more contingent, contexts of human procreation, *the actual decision makers are the reference point for the source of value*" ([5], p. 5, emphasis added).

This is a critical move for Heyd, for in cases like the two mentioned above agents have what Heyd calls "god-like" sovereignty over the choice, which is to say they face almost *no* constraints on their choices. For just as God determined which future persons were contingent and which were non-contingent in the creation of the first humans, it is primarily on the basis of the *agent's perspective* that humans determine which future persons are contingent and which are non-contingent in the creation of other humans. Agents are empirically and morally *required* to make this determination in an anthropocentric person-affecting approach to value if they are to know which future persons make a moral claim on them and which do not. Those future persons who, from the agent's perspective, are determined to be non-contingent future persons can make a moral claim on the agent, for they will exist as persons independent of the agent's choice. However, those future persons who are contingent future persons, that is, those who may or may not exist depending on the particular genesis choice made by the agent, can make *no* moral claim on the agent as they cannot benefit from or be harmed by being brought into existence.

On the other hand, agents using Parfit's agent-neutral impersonal approach to value are morally indifferent to the question of *which* future persons are contingent. All these agents are concerned to know is *that* contingent future persons are involved in a given choice and, if so, how their possible existence is likely to affect the net quality and quantity of value in the world.[10] Moreover, these agents are constrained by the agent-neutral qualification from viewing the choice from their own perspective; said differently, it makes no moral difference whether the agent is considering his or her own future children or the future children of strangers. These future children are valued independently of the agent's relation to them, and all agents are morally required to view them in similar terms. In order to get an intuitive sense of the practical implications these two approaches might have, consider again the two cases introduced above.

On the grounds that a healthy child would probably contribute to a greater net quality and quantity of value in the world than a handicapped or genetically affected child would, an agent-neutral impersonal approach might require the childless couple to face the uncertainties of delaying their children in order to secure a better chance of having a healthy child. Similarly, it might require the teenage couple to delay their marriage or, if this is not possible, to delay having children until they are better established as a family and more mature as individuals. Interestingly, an agent-relative anthropocentric approach might counsel the same actions, but on different grounds. For instance, it might suggest that both couples consider the likely negative effects on *them* as individuals, on *their* marriages, and on *their* future opportunities if, in Case 1, an unhealthy child is brought into existence or if, in Case 2, the teenage couple has children before they are adequately prepared. On the basis of an agent-relative anthropocentric approach to value, these couples might even be constrained to consider the wider society and the natural world that sustains it, though due to the cultural and legal protections (i.e., agent-relative permissions) such choices enjoy in western or western-influenced societies, concerns for other persons remotely related to these couples in time and space, and for the natural conditions that sustain them, may be considerably weakened or discounted.

In any case, Heyd believes that parents will usually act in such a way as to protect their own interests and that, in doing so, will indirectly maximize the welfare of their own future children. Nevertheless, he must concede that an agent-relative anthropocentric approach to value does not morally *require* this of parents. Again, Heyd claims,

the fundamental principle…is essentially…that genesis choices can and should be guided exclusively by reference to the interests, welfare, ideals, rights, and duties of those making the choice….” ([6], p. 96, emphasis added).

Thus, in an agent-relative anthropocentric approach to value, *there are few if any constraints* on parents who might wish to bring less than healthy children into the world when it is in their power not to do so, or on parents who may wish to bring children into the world with a considerably reduced set of opportunities in life.

Heyd qualifies this argument in a number of important ways that I will not elaborate here, especially when genesis choices are made by multiple agents on the collective or policy level. On this level, the determination of who is a contingent future person and who is a non-contingent future person can become extremely complex due to the agent-relativism of this approach, for the *same* future person may fall into *either* category depending on which agent's perspective we are considering at a given time.[11] Nevertheless, the basic point stands: the fate of contingent future persons who are brought into existence is empirically *and* morally determined primarily on the basis of the agent's perspective, and the agent faces few constraints when making this kind of choice.

This conclusion worries me morally, for I believe an agent-relative anthropocentric approach to value leaves those persons who are actually born in such cases overly vulnerable to the interests of the agents whose choices or actions bring them into existence. Thus, in cases where parents' self-interest is in potential conflict with concerns for the quality of life of their future children, an agent-relative perspective provides us with weaker constraints at the very time we might want stronger ones. But the agent-relative perspective also worries me on theological grounds, and this is the issue I wish to pursue now. For Heyd claims that the Jewish tradition is largely captured by an agent-relative anthropocentric approach to value [7], and I believe (though, not without qualification) that the Christian tradition can be characterized in very much the same terms and with the same implications for those contingent future persons who are brought into existence.

AGENT-RELATIVE THEOCENTRIC APPROACHES TO VALUE

Admittedly, characterizing a moral tradition as rich and diverse as the Christian tradition with a few distinctions risks misrepresenting this richness and diversity; nevertheless, the second and third distinctions developed above suggest an approach we might take toward making such a characterization, albeit at a high level of abstraction. In any case, I claim that we can fairly characterize the Christian tradition's fundamental approach to value in theocentric terms, and the perspective Christian agents typically adopt in agent-relative terms. However, while I do not try to demonstrate this claim here (this would require an extended review of the tradition), it does need to be qualified in light of the language used by James Gustafson in developing what he calls a "theocentric" critique of the tradition's "anthropocentrism."

Gustafson typically contrasts his own so-called theocentric position with the so-called anthropocentrism of the tradition. He also suggests, however, that we view this contrast as a contrast between two alternative perspectives agents may adopt when justifying particular judgments ([2], vol. 1, pp. 87-113), and *not* as a contrast between two substantive approaches to value. With respect to a fundamental approach to value, I submit that the tradition is theocentric in exactly the same sense that Gustafson's view is theocentric. The discussion above helps to make this point.

The distinction between impersonal and person-affecting approaches to value describes two competing conceptions of the nature of value, or two competing conceptions of the conditions that must obtain for value to be attributed to an object. These are formal conceptions, however, and thus it follows that all substantive approaches to value can be classified as either impersonal or person-affecting. Further, we can perhaps rather quickly conclude that any impersonal approach to value is simply ruled out by the theistic view of God typically adopted by the Christian tradition. I take this theistic view primarily to be an affirmation that it is meaningful to speak of God in agential terms, and thus that God is "personal" in at least this sense. Heyd also suggests—correctly, I think—that an impersonal approach to value denies what a person-affecting approach preserves, namely, that God constitutes value rather than serves it ([6], p. 4). However, if the Christian tradition is committed to a person-affecting approach to value for theological reasons, the question as to what *substantive* approach Christian agents typically adopt is still open. Should it be conceived in theocentric or anthropocentric terms?

The Christian tradition shares with the Jewish tradition a strong commitment to (human) persons and, as mentioned, this commitment has been discussed by Gustafson and others as a form of Christian anthropocentrism. Based in the belief that humans are central to God's purposes for creation, Christian anthropocentrism is reinforced in distinctive ways by the sweeping soteriological orientation of the entire tradition. But in light of the distinctions developed above, we can perhaps specify this commitment somewhat more precisely, since the tradition is not anthropocentric in the same sense that a humanistic person-affecting approach to value is anthropocentric. For instance, Christians would not claim, as Heyd does, that the world is utterly valueless without the presence of *human* valuers ([6], p. 6). Rather, for Christians the world has value simply because God is thought to value it, and this *before* humans were created in the "image of God" (*Genesis* 1:1-2:3). This is an important qualification, for it implies that the existence of value in the Christian tradition depends only on the existence of God. Said differently, God is the fundamental source of value for Christians and the existence of God is the only condition required for the attribution of value. Thus, while the tradition is indeed person-affecting with respect to its approach to value, it is better described substantively in theocentric and *not* in anthropocentric terms.

This said, the question of what perspective Christian agents typically adopt must still be considered (I assume that these agents should not presume to adopt God's perspective when justifying particular value judgments, and that they cannot do so in any case). Here, I think, Gustafson's critique of the tradition may properly be brought to bear. While we cannot deny the sheer diversity of perspectives available to agents within the tradition (compare, for example, a natural law-based perspective to a christologically-based perspective), I believe Gustafson is correct when he argues that these perspectives share a central commitment to (human) persons, and thus that the tradition is anthropocentric *in this sense*. But to avoid confusing Gustafson's analysis of the tradition's perspectives with a fundamental approach to value that is anthropocentric, I suggest that we characterize the tradition's perspectives in agent-relative terms.

The tradition may be regarded as agent-relative both because it permits agents to adopt a wide variety of perspectives and because these perspectives provide agents with moral reasons that refer to these agents in the sense discussed above (which is not to suggest that these reasons refer merely to the agents' interests, though we saw that agents' interests can be given full expression when other "actual" persons are not affected by a given genesis choice). Within these perspectives, then, the tradition's strong commitment to persons can function either as an agent-relative constraint or as an agent-relative permission, depending on circumstances. To take two rather extreme examples, a Christian agent would be constrained from torturing an innocent victim, even if in doing so he would surely save a large number of other innocent victims (an agent-relative constraint); and, if a Christian agent were forced to choose between saving either her own child or four other children who are strangers, the tradition would permit her to save her own child (an agent-relative permission). Interestingly, however, the tradition's agent-relative constraints and permissions may lead to conflicting or ambiguous recommendations when Christian pastors and couples consider questions about the timing of children.

Because questions about the timing of children involve contingent future persons, Christian agents must first determine (as with any possible object of value) whether the tradition gives them any (theocentric) warrants for believing God values contingent future persons. More to the point, Christian agents in such cases must determine whether God values one contingent future person over another,[12] for this is what is finally at stake for Christian parents in choices involving the timing of children. It is not clear to me that Christians have ever addressed this question. Those who may have, like Thomas Aquinas [1], were evidently unaware of the problem of contingent future persons. Nevertheless, we can suggest some possible responses that the tradition might make based on the analysis developed above.

Because of the tradition's strong commitment to persons generally, I take it that there is no question that the tradition provides warrants for believing God values the contingent future children who are finally brought into existence by their parents.[13] When these children are brought into existence they become "actual" persons, and regardless of whether these children are handicapped, genetically affected in some way, or born with a considerably reduced set of opportunities in life, they ought to be acknowledged as persons and treated as such by members of the tradition. Our concern here, however, is focused on the choice that determines *which* contingent future person is actually brought into existence, particularly when there is a potential conflict between parents' interests and the health or opportunities of their future child. In view of the problem of contingent future persons, are there warrants in the Christian tradition to constrain couples in such choices? I believe there are, but (taking our cue from Heyd) I suggest that they are necessarily *indirect* constraints, and this because the strong commitment to persons discussed above is provided only to "actual" persons—those who presently exist and those non-contingent future persons who will exist in the future.

Thus, in addition to the possible effects of the choice on the agents themselves, Christian couples might be morally constrained to consider the possible effects of their choice regarding contingent future persons on other persons presently living and on those future persons deemed to be non-contingent future persons (relative to their choice or action). They may also be constrained by views of Christian stewardship to consider the effects of their choice on the resources of the wider society and of the natural world, insofar as these will be necessary to sustain human persons now and in the future.[14]

However, should such couples be convinced that their own interests ought to override concerns for the health or opportunities of their future child—and the childless couple in Case 1 chooses to bring a less than healthy child into existence and the teenage couple in Case 2 decides to bring a child into existence with a reduced set of opportunities in life—it is not clear that the tradition could offer any other reason to constrain them. For it is unlikely that reference to the additional burdens required to raise such children would be persuasive for a given couple's choice if they are already convinced that it is, in fact, in their interests to bring such children into the world. Said differently, the tradition's strong commitment to ("actual") persons makes it unlikely that the choices of parents (as actual persons) could be constrained by (the largely impersonal) concerns for the health or opportunities of future children who may or may not be born. In such situations, it is quite possible that agent-relative permissions could override any agent-relative constraints these parents might face. Or, at the very least, it is possible that their agent-relative permissions could conflict with their agent-relative constraints, giving agents no clear guidance concerning which contingent future person (if any) to bring into existence.

Thus, just as is the case with Heyd's agent-relative anthropocentric approach to value, the agent-relative theocentric approach of the Christian tradition may leave those children who are actually born overly vulnerable to their parents choices. While it cannot meaningfully be asserted that these children are harmed by being brought into existence in less than optimal conditions, they (and others) may well be forced to bear the adverse consequences of these less than optimal conditions throughout their lives; indeed, they may pass them on to *their* children. If we want to find stronger constraints on such choices, the analysis above suggests that we must discover a way or ways to refer *directly* to the contingent future persons who might be brought into existence. Two options (that I merely mention here) suggest themselves. The first requires Christians to adopt an impersonal approach to value, similar to Parfit's, and second requires Christians to adopt an agent-neutral theocentric perspective when making particular value judgments. The first option (logically) requires Christians to abandon traditional views of God as the ultimate source of value. The second, developed on the basis of Gustafson's work, (logically) requires Christians to adopt a substantive view of God that undermines the agent-relativism or the so-called anthropocentrism (in the qualified sense discussed above) of the tradition [5]. Neither of these two options is likely to be acceptable to most Christians.

CONCLUSION

The three key distinctions outlined above are useful for analyzing cases that involve choices about the timing of children. Such choices involve questions about which contingent future persons to bring into existence, if any. Moreover, as Heyd argues, impersonal approaches to value can treat contingent future persons directly, while person-affecting approaches can treat them only indirectly. Substantively, however, person-affecting approaches to value may be either anthropocentric or theocentric. With respect to the perspective agents ought to adopt when making particular value judgments, they may also be either agent-neutral or agent-relative. I claimed that the Christian moral tradition as a whole may be characterized in agent-relative, theocentric, person-affecting terms. This characterization implies that Christian agents can be constrained in their choices about contingent future persons only indirectly or by reference to the possible effects of their choices on presently living persons and on non-contingent future persons. Thus, while there are some constraints a Christian pastor or couple might face when making choices about contingent future persons, these constraints cannot refer directly to the contingent future persons in question. This may leave those contingent future persons who are actually brought into existence overly vulnerable to the interests of the agents who determine their existence. Moreover, the options that might limit this vulnerability will probably be unacceptable to most Christians. To the extent this analysis is correct, then, to that extent the problem of contingent future persons stands as a possible challenge to the Christian moral tradition.

NOTES

[1] This article is a much re-worked version of a paper presented by the author at the 1996 Annual Meeting of the Society of Christian Ethics, in Albuquerque, NM [4]. The author acknowledges the helpful comments of three anonymous reviewers of that paper and, particularly, those of Harlan Beckley, then Editor of *The Annual*.

[2] With this focus, I hope to avoid confusing questions about how we ought morally to treat future persons whose existence depends on certain choices with other related, but distinct questions concerning: 1) when human persons begin; 2) what morally we may do to those human entities (e.g.,

embryos and fetuses) that may or may not be regarded as persons; and, 3) how we ought morally to treat future persons whose existence is not dependent in the relevant sense.

[3] Some readers might be tempted to think that questions about the timing of children are not morally interesting, possibly because they are typically regarded as "private" choices where couples have the legal "right" to do what they wish (with the implication that they ought not, therefore, be constrained). But this response merely begs the question. For while it is clear that such choices are subject to strong constitutional protections, they have significant implications for the children who are actually born and for the wider society who may be asked to share in their up-bringing and support. Also, these couples are seeking *moral* guidance from the pastoral counselor; that is, they recognize that merely having the "right" (i.e., the legal permission) to do as they wish does not, by itself, answer the question of how they ought to act *morally*.

[4] Heyd uses the term "actual" counter-intuitively, so I tend to avoid it where possible; admittedly, however, my own terminology suffers from some ambiguity too.

[5] It can also be *very* important for public officials, but I will not consider the collective dimensions of the problem here.

[6] Interestingly, this argument holds both for the individual choices illustrated by the cases above and for the collective choices (e.g., choices about tax credits or direct subsidies to parents raising children) made by public officials that might affect individual choices.

[7] However, compare this disclaimer to Heyd's article in this volume [7], where he *is* concerned with the literary and theological significance of the Genesis myth.

[8] I believe Heyd should claim that contingent future persons can have no moral standing in an *anthropocentric* person-affecting approach to value. Some theocentric approaches to value may permit contingent future persons to have moral standing ([5], pp. 130-140).

[9] These distinctions suggest an interesting array of possible positions, each of which could be explored for its potential to address the problem of contingent future persons. Obviously, there is not space to do this here. However, Heyd briefly discusses some of these possibilities in [6], pp. 80-90, and I explore an agent-neutral theocentric position (discussed there as an "impersonal theocentric approach to value") in [5], pp. 130-140.

[10] While this latter question may be difficult to determine empirically, Heyd's approach also does not escape difficult empirical calculations. He must determine how the existence of contingent future persons is likely to affect other people, some of whom will only exist in the distant future.

[11] In fact, I suggest elsewhere that Heyd's agent-relativism renders his approach self-defeating on the collective level, for there is no way to determine which agent's perspective ought to prevail when a given genesis choice is actually made ([5], pp. 100-103).

[12] For the collective choices not considered here, we would need to ask whether God values one *population* of contingent future persons over another.

[13] Again, however, I will avoid discussing when personhood actually begins.

[14] George's discussion [1] is relevant for such arguments. He argues plausibly that at least the natural law tradition can "link" concerns for (what I claim are non-contingent) future persons to their environmental requirements.

BIBLIOGRAPHY

1. George, W.P.: 1992, 'Regarding Future Neighbors: Thomas Aquinas and Concern for Posterity', *The Heythrop Journal* 33, pp. 283-306.
2. Gustafson, J.M.: 1981-1984, *Ethics from a Theocentric Perspective*, 2 vols., University of Chicago Press, Chicago.
3. Hare, R.M.: 1988, 'Possible People', *Bioethics* 2, pp. 279-293.
4. Heller, J.C.: 1996, 'The Challenge of Contingent Future Persons', paper delivered at the 1996 Annual Meeting of the Society of Christian Ethics, Albuquerque, NM, January 5-7.
5. Heller, J.C.: 1996, *Human Genome Research and the Challenge of Contingent Future Persons: Toward an Impersonal Theocentric Approach to Value*, Creighton University Press, Omaha.

6.   Heyd, D.: 1992, *Genethics: Moral Issues in the Creation of People*, University of California Press, Berkeley.
7.   Heyd, D.: 'Divine Creation and Human Procreation: Reflections on Genesis in Light of *Genesis*', this volume.
8.   McNaughton, D., and Rawling, P., 1992, 'Honoring and Promoting Values', *Ethics* 102, 835-843.
9.   Parfit, D.: 1984, *Reasons and Persons*, Clarendon Press, New York.
10.   Scheffler, S.: 1988, 'Introduction', in S. Scheffler (ed.), *Consequentialism and Its Critics*, Oxford University Press, Oxford.

REPUGNANT THOUGHTS ABOUT
THE REPUGNANT CONCLUSION ARGUMENT

I. THE REPUGNANT CONCLUSION ARGUMENT

The Repugnant Conclusion Argument can be construed as follows. Calculating within the framework of utilitarian theory, we can contrast two states of affairs. The first, call it N, represents a state where the world human population has reached beyond five billion and where most people still live (let us suppose) a life worth living. The second state, call it O, has a larger population—let us say beyond six billion. Life in O is also still worth living, but less so when compared to N. Nonetheless, utilitarian calculations might recommend that we seek the life in O over N because the total utility in O is greater. The greater number of people in O compensates for a small loss in quality of life for each person. The Repugnant Conclusion Argument now urges us to consider state P where the population is still larger, quality of life still lower, but where the total utility is still higher. Again, the more people around makes up for the fact that they are less happy. Eventually, we arrive at state Z where the population is horrendously larger than in N and the quality of life disturbingly lower, even though it is still (barely) worth living. The argument now says that, nonetheless, we may be forced to conclude repugnantly that Z is preferred to N since the total utility in Z is greater than N, O, P...or Y.

It should be clear that this argument is not that total (in contrast to average) utilitarianism must arrive at the conclusion that Z is the preferred outcome. Rather, it says that Z *may* be the preferred outcome. But then it should also be clear that state of affairs A could also be the preferred outcome. One way to arrive at A is by moving gradually from N to M and from there to L. With each move, the population of the world (or some nation) becomes smaller; but the life people live becomes more satisfying. Another way is to skip some of the in between states, and still another is to move directly from N to A. In spite of the moral costs of doing so, we could make the latter move by killing off lots of older people and others who do not measure up to some standard of ideal humanhood. However it is done, A represents a state in which the world sustains a minimal human population but, one in which, as the beer commercial says, "life is good."

Thus, in theory at least, what total utilitarianism allows is a series of possibilities all the way from A to Z. It says that under certain conditions any one of these possibilities could represent the preferred choice. The emphasis has to be on "under certain conditions." Until the conditions are specified it will not be clear whether Z, Y or X or, indeed, A, B or C, are repugnant or wonderful. That is part of my argument in this paper. The other part is that once the conditions are specified, it

Nick Fotion and Jan C. Heller (eds.), Contingent Future Persons, 85-97.
© 1997 *Kluwer Academic Publishers. Printed in the Netherlands.*

will be obvious that states Z, Y and X are not realistic options, given the way we humans are constructed, or even likely to be in the distant future. As such, the argument that seems to lead to the conclusions that Z must be chosen, and is repugnant, is flawed. I will develop the argument by first characterizing N. Then the process of moving from N to X, Y and Z will be characterized and, after that, Z itself. Finally, there will be a brief characterization of the process of moving back to N from Z. Once all that is done, a similar trip will be taken, this time from N to A and back again.

II. BACK AND FORTH

N represents now. We are now in state full of variability. Some of us live (or have lived) a very good (i.e., happy) life indeed, others of us live just a good life while still others live a life that has its ups and downs. Still others, many think lots of others, live a life just barely worth living. Whether this variability is due mainly to our numbers is not clear. What is clear, is that there are enough of us on this planet to significantly alter it in a variety of ways. The planet is not what it was with respect to its chemistry because of our massive presence, and because of the technologies that we apply massively. The composition of the air, water and land is significantly different from what it was just two to three hundred years ago. Obviously, it continues to change.

The net emission of carbon to the atmosphere by human action dates back to the origin of agriculture, but half of the total amount released has been released since 1920. Half of the sulfur and half of the lead ever mobilized by humankind have been emitted since 1960; half of the phosphorus and nitrogen, since 1975. The annual human releases of many heavy metals now vastly exceed their natural flows from weathering; those of lead, for example, by more than 20 times. Land used for farming has expanded 400% since 1700, obliterating onetime forests, grasslands, and wetlands, and the area of irrigated cropland has grown by several thousand percent. The annual loss of organic carbon from soil has more than doubled from its average rate over the past three centuries to its rate over the past 50 years ([7], p. 216).

Things living in the air, water and land have also changed [4]. We rightly call some of these changes polluting since many plants and other biological creatures are diminishing in numbers or even disappearing ([9], [3], pp. 167-187).

At the same time, other changes due to our presence are life enhancing. Those of us who live a very good (i.e., happy) life or just a good life seem to be better off because of a wide variety of technologies. Sanitation practices as well as knowledge of medicine give us longer and healthier lives. Transportation allows us to see and enjoy places reserved in the past only for the most enterprising explorers. Hundreds of other technologies help give us a good life in one way or another. N, then, represents a mixed bag. The technologies present in it improve the lives of many; but harm others. It clearly is a state that represents neither the best of all possible worlds, nor the worst.

Perhaps Z is better. If it is, and if we choose to go that way, it will take time to get there. We will have to move from N to O and then to P and so on. It will take many generations, and the transition itself will have costs and benefits that need to be counted in the overall assessment of the claim that we ought to try to get to Z. In part, this is because the people in O, P, R and, finally, Z will have memories. They will not just sit in their more populated states living whatever life is in a store for them, as if they were not aware of what better lives previous generations lived. Hare, in "Possible People," puts it this way:

It will not do to say, as some do, that, by assuming a sufficiently *gradual* transition, the disutility of the transition itself can be made to vanish. For, since people will still be able to compare their state with that of the Golden Age several generations before, they will regret the transition, and that will cause them pain ([6], p. 77).

Actually the following distinctions need to be made to appreciate better the transition costs:

1. The state of affairs reached (e.g., O, P and even Z) without taking memory into account;

2. The memories of N present once O, P or Z is reached;

3. The memories of N present while people are in the process of moving from O to P and eventually to Z.

Numbers 2 and 3 need not be all regretful. As humans move from N to one of the other more populated states, they could be educated to accept these changes, at least to some degree. They could be made proud of the sacrifices they make. But the education process itself would be costly. Time and effort would need to be made to convince people to ignore their regretful and resentful memories of the past. In the end, the educational process would probably only succeed partially. Unless that process incurred more costs by resorting to some form of coercion (e.g., by deceitfully recreating history to make people believe that the goodness of life in N has been overrated and by arresting those who write about the wonderful past), people would still remember or know about the good old days (and nights) and still be resentful that they cannot live like that.

Of course there will be other transition costs. Women would literally bear much of the burden of the population increase. In developed countries many of them would likely have to give up their jobs, move back into their home and get involved big-time in the baby-production business. Both morbidity and mortality rates among women would rise disproportionately to men. They would tend to remember the good old days with a bit of extra envy and resentment. They, and also their husbands (who would have to work harder outside the home) would likely resist making the transition to having a big family. If their resistance were strong, the society would have to resort to still further coercion, which would mean that further costs would have to be borne in moving from N to Z. Even if an artificial womb technology were developed, single parents would be heavily burdened with caring for their children. Couples would not be much better off. One or both members would have to stay home to corral the kids. Either that, or the society would have to bear the massive costs of a massive child-care program.

Given our human nature with its memories, knowledge of the past, emotions, the injustices involved in burdening women to take humans from N to Z and other costs, it begins to look as if Z and perhaps states like X and Y do not represent the happiest of utilitarian options. The costs of getting to these end states are simply larger than they might have appeared at first. It is as if Z and Z-like states would be real options only if human nature itself changed. If, for example, humans evolved or could be genetically altered so that memories and knowledge of the past were erased with "the turn of a switch," so they simply could not be envious, it might begin to make sense to think of Z as having fewer costs than benefits. It might also then make sense to think that Z is a superior state to N. Another possibility is to have human emotions changed directly so that, quite apart from what we knew of the past, we would not become envious, angry or resentful. But now a new problem emerges. With these fundamental changes, it becomes difficult to imagine what Z would be like and therefore whether to assess it as repugnant or not. More on this point in a bit.

Now let us turn to Z itself—with, rather than without, our present human nature. Z, recall, is a state where people abound. Rather than a population of five+ billion, the Z world , let us say, has 50 billion people. The lives in Z, on average, are supposedly still worth living (even if we count their memories, knowledge of the past, what happens to women etc. as part of the overall calculation), although barely so.

Life in Z would not necessarily carry with it all the costs found during the transition period. Women, for instance, might have it better in Z than in O, P, or Q. If the population stabilized around 50 billion, they could, on average, have fewer children once again. In time, memory and even knowledge of N and The Great Transition could even fade so that the level of resentment could diminish. Actually, it is hard to tell what would happen here. As memory of N fades, rumor about what it was like back then could idealize the past. The good old days could be made to seem much better than they ever were, and thus resentment would likely be greater rather than less.

However it turned out, in other respects it is pretty obvious that Z would create problems of its own. To see why, consider what it would be like to have, on average, 50 billion people living just barely above a level where life is no longer worth living. Whatever living just barely above such a level might actually mean to different people, the likelihood is that some of the 50 billion would be living considerably above the average while others would be living considerably below. But, then, what would those below the average likely do? Hare, who considers this possibility, says:

If they are rational and overcome the fear of death, they will all commit suicide. But this will be bad for the proponent of CG [the advocate of Hare's version of Z], because it will reduce the population again, just when he has been at such pains to increase it. In practice, no doubt, the disutility of the suicide process would be considerable, involving as it would overcoming the fear of death. So he would have done better not to produce these people in the first place. But if he resolves not to produce them, then he has the problem of how to raise the population to the optimum, at the cost of decreasing average utility to the minimum level that just makes life worth living, without thereby producing a lot of people who are below this level ([6], p. 79).

Of course many will not be rational and so will not overcome their fear of death. They will exist below a level of life worth living, but will be too afraid to end their life. Or they will have an irrational hope that things will get better. Others living at the same low level will not commit suicide because of their commitment to societal sanctions against such a practice. Once again, the net result will be that Z will contain more misery than it might have seemed at first.

Even if these problems can be overcome by moving to state Y (with, say, 45 billion people) so that the level of life worth living is a little more than slightly over the minimum, there will be problems. One reason is that the goal in achieving Z (or Y) is not to achieve it for one moment but for an indefinite period of time. If we want it at all, we want not a fleeting, but a stable Z. Unfortunately Z (Y, X and possibly W and V) is not likely to be stable. Some people will be so close to the line below which life would be meaningless that they will be tempted to do desperate things to keep from dropping below that line. Many of those already below the line, but who would not commit suicide, will also be desperate. Both groups will likely lie, steal and kill, although surely some will simply give up and "fade away." Beyond the struggles fought between individuals, it will be difficult to prevent more general internal unrest and uprisings as the majority of the population saw that certain privileged minorities such as doctors, political leaders, and business executives were living a very good life indeed. What would exacerbate the situation is the availability of high technology which would not necessarily disappear because of the move from N to Z. This technology would be available to the privileged few, but not to the "dirty masses." The former would profit from medical technology to help keep them alive and well longer, while the "masses" would have no or only minimal access to that technology. Whatever the disparities found in N, they would likely be magnified in Z. So in Z we would have envy and resentment not just about the past, but about what is going on in Z itself.

Apart from factors that would encourage internal conflict and rebellion, there would be wars between nations over the very limited natural resources needed to sustain the 50 billion people of Z. Life might still be worth living in the sense that many people would still do all they can to stay alive, but it would be "poor, nasty, brutish and short," though certainly not solitary.

An attempt could be made to mitigate some of these difficulties by imposing an egalitarian system of government upon the world or, if that were not feasible, upon some of the nations in Z. The egalitarianism need not be strict. It might allow for some variation in incomes and other benefits and still be relatively more just than Z would be if market forces were allowed to dominate the interactions between people and societies. But if this attempt were made, it is not clear that it would help much. The attempt itself would be costly. Even modest egalitarianism would involve the use of strong centralized management of the world or the societies involved in the egalitarian program. With so many people living near and below the edge, it is also not clear just how manageable "the masses" would actually be. Rebellion would still be a reasonable option if these people imagined that there were steps they could take to move away from the edge. They would be especially likely to revolt if they saw, as they inevitably would, the managers living a better life than they were.

Increasingly, then, it appears that Z and other state of affairs like it, are not ones that utilitarians would choose. At least they are not ones to choose given that human nature is as it is. They might be chosen were human nature to change. If humans evolved in such a way that they naturally forgot about the past, or had diminished feelings of envy and insecurity, Z might be a real utilitarian option. But short of such changes, the repugnant solution is no utilitarian solution at all. There just is an incompatibility between Z and human nature as we know it.

We can appreciate this incompatibility still more by imagining what might happen after the world reached Z. Let us suppose that it got there in a fervor of (stupid) utilitarian thinking. If my argument so far is correct, the people of Z would do all they could to get out of the mess they have either put themselves or found themselves in. But this move away from Z would not be easy. Getting out means gradually cutting the world population, nation by nation, significantly down from 50 billion. No doubt many would say that education would help them out of the Z mess. And perhaps advanced, long-lasting birth control technologies would also help. One can only speculate here, but my guess is that even with education and advanced technologies, a good deal of coercion would also be required. The desire for children is strong—both biologically and socially. The latter would be especially strong after the ideal of "(the large) family" had been extolled for several generations. We would expect a good deal of resistance to reproductive policies required to bring the world population down from 50 billion, to 45 and from there to some still lower figure.

In spite of this resistance and the costs of invoking coercive measures, I speculate that if and when people began gradually to move away from the edge, and as a result started enjoying life more, the resentment found in Z would be replaced by more positive feelings. Further, given the impersonal stance I am taking in this article, those who now are not brought into the world because of the population reductions would have to be taken into account. Their lost opportunity for life would count against a policy of moving away from Z, just as the better life of those who are now moving away from X, or U would count for it. But recall that life in Z and Z-like states was not a positive experience for the vast majority. It appeared marginally acceptable before we gave it a good look. But with the resentment, the suicides, and all the rest that would make life in Z unpalatable, the lives of those who never appeared on the scene as the move away from Z took place would not represent a large loss. So moving from Z back toward N sounds like a good move overall. And arriving at Z in the first place not such a good idea.

There are two other reasons for suggesting that moving from N to Z is not a good idea. Both relate to the notion of the irreversible damage done by that move. The first has already been suggested. Moving from Z back in the direction of N may not be possible. Massive attempts to depopulate the world just may not be successful. Resistance to not having children at all, or having only one child, may be so great that once the damage is done it cannot be undone. If traveling back up the road we traveled down earlier is impossible, or highly unlikely, then that too is a good utilitarian reason for not going down that road in the first place. Going down that road thus represents too much of a gamble, just as it would if we thought we could experiment with some strongly addictive drug, and then, later, quit taking it by putting a bit of will power to work.

With the second reason, the damage done is more certainly irreversible. If humans gradually placed 50 billion of their kind on the planet, undoubtedly other species would become extinct at a much more rapid rate than they are now in N. This pattern of extinction would be vicious not simply because of humanity's large numbers, but because so many people would be living just above, on and below the edge. Those on both sides of the edge would scour the planet to gain some survival advantage in the form of space and food, very likely at the expense of non-human animals [1]. So even if humans could return to N in terms of their own numbers, the world would not be the same in so far as these scrubbed-out animals are concerned.

III. FEWER RATHER THAN MORE PEOPLE

So far I have argued that utilitarianism might recommend that humans move to Z, but only if they themselves changed in some fundamental ways. Z is far from the promised land, given the way humans are presently constituted. I have also argued that it is just as likely that utilitarianism would recommend a move to A as to Z. Prior to assessing the facts there can be no utilitarian population recommendations. We can see this by considering what it might be like to move from N to M and then all the way to A.

In some respects such a move represents a continuation of the move from Z back to N. As a population becomes smaller by moving from N to M, and from there to L, the quality of life people will be experiencing would tend to become better; and the joys of expecting that things will improve will continue. To be sure, such a trend is not inevitable. Even with smaller populations, various peoples might still find reasons to go to war, and unusual weather conditions could still cause mass starvation. But other things being equal, life should be better overall as the move is made from N to A.

In one respect, however, such a move is radically different when compared to a move away from Z back in the direction of N. Life in Z, Y and X was so near the edge that the good achieved by creating another human life was minimal, nonexistent or even negative. Such is not the case with movement from N toward A. Now the lives of the contingent future persons who would not be chosen count for something. Had they been created, many of them could have looked forward to a life worth living—one not near the edge. Thus as one moves in the direction of A, the weight of the good lost through non-creation increases.

The state of A itself needs to be described. A is not the Garden of Eden where Adam and Eve satisfy their every desire by themselves. Instead, A is presumably large enough in numbers so that people can profit from varied forms of social interaction; and yet small enough so that conflict between them is minimal and the goods for them to use plentiful. If one had to guess at the numbers in A, seven-hundred million sounds about right. It is a state where humans were about 300 years ago ([7], pp. 27-28). The difference between then and what A would look like in the future is that medical, transportation and other technologies would be in place to make life different from, and possibly better than, what it was back then. Things might also be better given that many nations have, in the meantime, given up some foolish notions such as the divine right of kings.

But, now, would utilitarianism choose A? As one extreme, it certainly sounds more inviting than Z does at the other. For one thing, it likely represents a far more stable state than X, Y or Z. Although rebellion and war could still occur in A, many of the causes for such events would be missing. For another, hunger is not likely to be a problem. Further, there would be plenty of land for most every ethnic and racial group to flourish. A, in principle, could also be far more friendly to the environment. Humans and many other animal (and even plant) species that had somehow already managed to survive human attack before A was reached, could live together happily ever after.

Even so, A would probably not be the preferred option since significantly more good could be brought about (because of the extra future contingents who would be living the good life) if some state between A and N were adopted. So if the world population were to float roughly between seven hundred million and something over one billion, it still might be possible to make the world safe both for humans and most of the other creatures on this planet so as to give meaning to the utilitarian principle of doing the greatest good for the greatest number over the greatest period of time.

IV. A CLOSER LOOK AT THE REPUGNANT CONCLUSION ARGUMENT

This conclusion that some state or other between C and N is the preferred option for utilitarianism will disappoint some. These same people might be even more disappointed if they were told that states just beyond N might also be acceptable. It could be argued, for instance, that humans could learn to harm the environment less even while the human population increased from 5 to seven and perhaps to 10 billion—an increase likely to be reached by the first quarter of the 21st century ([7], p. 24). So utilitarianism could very well accept states starting with E (let us say 1 billion) all the way to Q (10 billion). The disappointment is in the apparent inability of utilitarianism to be more specific. Initially, and perhaps naively, one might suppose that it is utilitarianism's job to pick one optimal state, let us say F, and announce to the world that it satisfies the utility principle more than any other.

Indeed, the disappointment rests on naiveté. It may in the future be possible to do better than exclude the extreme options of Z, Y and X, and possibly even A, B and C as we can now. But for now, because we know so little about population practices, fine choices are not possible. The phenomenon of creating 1 billion, and then 2 and then 5 billion humans and the effect of this creating on humans themselves and the rest of the environment are unique in our history. So is the effect of the technologies these billions of people put to use.

At the time of the agricultural revolution, there were perhaps 5-10 million people. Since then the world population has increased roughly 500 to 1000 fold, and the average impact per person (measured by energy use) has increased about eight times. So one can conclude that the total human impact has increased about 4000 to 8000 fold . . . . Prior to 1850 the human population multiplied over 200-fold while per-capita energy use roughly doubled. But in the last 140 years, the scale of the human enterprise has increased another 20-fold, and it has quadrupled since 1950 ([5], p. 3).

We've never gone through such an experience before. Much of the literature on the environment suggests that one or another form of a catastrophe is imminent not just because of our numbers, but also because of our careless and extensive use of various forms of technology. But there is much disagreement here about catastrophes and how imminent they are. Still, our ignorance about what we are doing to the planet and those living in, on and over it is growing. So in the foreseeable future we can expect that utilitarian thinking about various population options will be in a somewhat better focus than it is now. It is not likely ever be in such complete focus as to pick out state F, or whatever, because of the overwhelming empirical complexities involved in predicting the future, and also because of the complexities having to do with what we as humans place value upon. However, utilitarianism can do two things. It can tell us that certain states can be excluded as realistic options for population policies. And, in so far as utilitarianism encourages empirical research into the effects of population policies, and this research constantly tells us that technologies pertaining to these policies have numerous side effects, it counsels caution. It tells us that we should not go head-down bullishly in any one direction. Rather it counsels that we should perhaps move from N to M slowly and then, after that, "play it by ear." These thoughts further suggest that the extremes, especially Z, Y and Z, are not the preferred options.

Aside from some being disappointed with utilitarianism itself because it is not more focused, others might be disappointed because I have not dealt directly with the force of the Repugnant Conclusion Argument. Rather, I have redescribed it as an alleged practical criticism of utilitarianism, whereas in reality, it represents an *in principle* criticism. Let us see what this means. In his *Reasons and Persons* Derek Parfit says:

The Repugnant Conclusion: For any possible population of at least ten billion [roughly comparable to my figure of 5+ billion for N], all with a very high quality of life, there must be some much larger imaginable population [Z] whose existence, if other things are equal, would be better, even though its members have lives that are barely worth living ([8], p. 388).

He adds that his initial 10 billion people condition and one next to it [comparable to my N and O] could be real alternatives. This is hardly likely since it is difficult to conceive that all 10 billion would have a life of very high quality. But he grants that Z does not represent a real choice. It is in some sense impossible to achieve. So it appears that, for Parfit at least, the Repugnant Conclusion Argument is an *in principle* argument. Both his initial state [roughly my N] and Z hardly represents life as we know it, and thus a choice between them hardly a real choice. Evidently it is conceived in the never-never world of the philosopher's imagination where little attention is paid to details of real life.

Further explaining the Repugnant Conclusion Argument, and Z in particular, Parfit makes a distinction between two kinds of impossibilities. Z might represent either deep or technical impossibility. He says: "An imagined case is deeply impossible if it requires a major change in the laws of nature, including the laws of human nature" ([8], p. 388). So Z would be deeply impossible if we left human nature alone and, as a result, could not achieve that state. I have already suggested as much by saying earlier that Z might be implemented if human memory of the past and/or if human envy were eliminated. I have also already suggested that states of deep impossibility are extremely difficult to imagine so that assessment of them are difficult and perhaps impossible to make.

In contrast to deeply impossible states, those that are merely technically impossible are readily within the reach of our imagination. Z would merely be technically impossible if all that needed changing is "…the nature and availability of resources" ([8], p. 390). Our food resources might increase radically if, for example, those living in Z gave up eating meat. The increase would come about because, by obtaining our food stuffs directly from the soil rather than having much of it mediated inefficiently through domesticated animals, more would be available [11]. Now, presumably, we could envision that there would be enough food to sustain the 50 billion people of Z—just above, on, and below the edge—and to appreciate just how repugnant Z and like states are.

But the main thrust of my argument has equally to do with deep rather than technical impossibility. Even if technical impossibilities were taken care of, the problems with conceiving how Z might be viewed would still be present. Recall that it is human nature and its social structures that contribute heavily to making Z impossible. People in Z will remember and resent the past if they are asked to live below, at, or just above the edge. They will be motivated to move themselves, either as individuals, families or larger groups, to a position well above the edge even if doing so hurts others. Living in Z would be a jungle that just could not, given our physical, psychical and social natures, be more utilitarian than some state considerably different from it.

For Z to make sense, then, one would need to change human nature, that is, to reach a state of deep impossibility. Again, the trouble this sort of change makes for the Repugnant Conclusion Argument is that it would now be difficult to imagine what kind of life these changed people would have, and thus to imagine just how repugnant or unrepugnant such a life would be. In other words, looking at the Argument as if it were a practical rather than a philosopher's argument suggests that it is not so damaging to utilitarianism as it is often taken to be. Utilitarianism, of the total variety, may have its problems, but the Repugnant Conclusion Argument apparently does not identify one of them.

V. SOME REPUGNANT THOUGHTS

But suppose the main argument of this paper is wrong. That is, suppose the Repugnant Conclusion Argument can be presented in such way that Z can be meaningfully recommended by utilitarian thinking as the best population policy for us to follow. As improbable as it may be, suppose that Z represents a state with the following characteristics. Let us call this particular version of this state Z1. There are, as with Z, 50 billion people in Z1. Almost all of them live in a condition just above the level at which life is worth living, and they do so for the greater part of their lives. But Z1 is not only egalitarian in that hardly anyone is far above or below the "level," but egalitarian as well in the kinds of pleasures people have. Food, clothing, housing, means of transportation, work conditions, music, etc. are all the practically the same. Life in Z1 gives slightly more pleasure than pain (even if we take human memory into account), but the pleasures themselves are bland and boring. Beyond that, Z1 is stable. There are few insurrections, rebellions and wars. Finally, Z1 is a state where non-human animals can survive and presumably lead a life, like their human counterparts, just above the level that makes life worth living.

There are other ways Z could be characterized [10]. All are highly improbable. But that is not the point for now. As Cowen expresses it, "The point [of the Repugnant Conclusion Argument] is not whether the highly populated society is possible but rather whether we would prefer it if it were possible" ([2], p. 756). But even so, we need to imagine some version of Z that can be presented where the total utility of Z is greater than N. If we can, based on something like the characterization of Z1, then total utilitarianism would be embarrassed since it would have to recommend Z since it gives us, by definition, more overall utility.

But would it be embarrassed? Under some truly extraordinary set of circumstances it is conceivable that Z yields more total utility than any other state. If so, total utilitarianism would have to concede that this state is the most preferred, by definition. Further, if this state were repugnant, then total utilitarianism would indeed be embarrassed. However, in order to avoid permanent embarrassment, advocates of total utilitarian will likely ask us to take account of three ways of viewing Z.

The first is when Z is very deeply impossible. The problem here for the critic of total utilitarianism is that it is difficult to imagine what Z would be like under these conditions. Nature, including human nature, would be so different that comparisons with N-like states would be difficult and perhaps impossible. If so, it would also be difficult, and perhaps impossible, to say whether Z is repugnant or not.

The second way of viewing Z is when it is still deeply impossible but not extremely so. With this way, we suppose we just might imagine what Z is like. Z could be something like Z1 above. But now Z may not be so obviously repugnant. It may seem obviously repugnant to some who are flourishing in N. However, once Z is described in detail as something like Z1, a case can be made that people's feelings of repugnance with that state may be misplaced. Feelings of repugnance do not necessarily represent genuine repugnance (based on rational and objective thinking about population policies we should adopt). Putting it differently, our intuitions in extraordinary settings cannot always to be trusted. Boring as Z1 may be, it at least allows those who live in it a sense of equality and justice lacking in N, it deals better with animals than we do in N and, by definition, it presents those in the future with more overall good than we possess now. Thus it is not so obvious as some might suppose that Z1 is repugnant.

I have been discussing the third way of viewing throughout most of this article. This way places emphasis on the fact that Z1 *is* improbable. To make it (apparently) vulnerable to the Repugnant Conclusion Argument, conditions have to be postulated for Z1 (and other Z-like states) that make little or no empirical sense. In order to imagine Z1 giving forth with more good than bad, it has to be made stable. But, as we have seen, the notion of a stable Z1 (or any Z) is close to an oxymoron. The same can be said for the notion of a humane Z1. How 50 billion people could live on this planet without making thousands of species of birds, land and sea animals, and fish extinct remains a mystery. So not only is the Repugnant Conclusion Argument not necessarily damaging to total utilitarianism because Z1 may not be so repugnant as those living comfortably in N might suppose, but Z1 itself continues to be an elusive state. It continues to be difficult to imagine what possible set of conditions in Z1 (or Z2, Z3, etc.) could yield more good than a state like N.

The lesson to be learned from all this is that there are dangers when philosophers employ "never-never land" examples in an attempt to make their opponents blush. This is not to say that counter examples should not be given. But when they are, they should be presented in enough detail, and be close enough to the real world, so as to make them relevant to the situations we face. There might be times when nonrealistic examples are useful to help us clear our minds or to help us gain a new perspective. But they should not be the norm when it comes to engaging in criticism of ethical theories. After all, such theories are supposed to help us deal with practical, that is, real life problems. If one of them does this well it should be praised. If this same theory fails to deal with situations that can hardly be imagined, and I am not even granting that total utilitarianism fails in this regard, that failure should hardly count heavily against the theory. In law it is said that hard cases make bad law. So in ethics, "never-never land" counter examples rarely make for serious criticism.

BIBLIOGRAPHY

1. Brown, L. R. (ed.): 1991, *The World Watch Reader on Global Environmental Issues*, W. W. Norton and Company, New York and London.
2. Cowen, T.: 1996, "What Do We Learn from the Repugnant Conclusion?", *Ethics* 106, 754-775.
3. Durning, A.: 1991, "Cradles of Life," in L. Brown, etc. (editors,) *The World Watch Reader on Global Environmental Issues*, W. W. Norton and Company, New York and London.
4. Ehrenfeld, D. (ed.): 1995, *Readings from Conservation Biology: To Preserve Biodiversity—an Overview*, The Society for Conservation Biology and Blackwell Science, Inc., Cambridge, Massachusetts.
5. Ehrlich, P. R.: 1993, "The Scale of the Human Enterprise," in Denis A. Saunders, etc. (eds.), *Nature of Conservation 3: Reconstruction of Fragmented Ecosystems*, Surrey Beatty and Sons Pty Limited, Chipping Norton, NSW.
6. Hare, R. M.: 1993, 'Possible People,' in R. M. Hare *Essays on Bioethics*, Clarendon Press, Oxford. Originally Published in *Bioethics*, 1988, 2, 279-293.
7. Meyer, W. B.: 1996, *Human Impact on the Earth*, Cambridge University Press, Cambridge.
8. Parfit, D.: 1984, *Reasons and Persons*, Clarendon Press, Oxford.
9. Quammen, D.: 1996, *The Song of the Dodo*, Scribners, New York.
10. Ryberg, J.: 1996, "Parfit's Repugnant Conclusion," *The Philosophical Quarterly* 46, 202- 213.
11. Singer, P.: 1975, *Animal Liberation*, Avon Books, New York.

PERSON-AFFECTING UTILITARIANISM AND POPULATION POLICY; OR, SISSY JUPE'S THEORY OF SOCIAL CHOICE

"You don't know," said Sissy, half crying, "what a stupid girl I am. All through school hours I make mistakes. Mr. and Mrs. M'Choakumchild call me up, over and over again, regularly to make mistakes. I can't help them. They seem to come naturally.... [T]oday, for instance, Mr. M'Choakumchild was explaining to us about Natural Prosperity.... And he said, Now, this schoolroom is a Nation. And in this nation there are fifty millions of money. Isn't this a prosperous nation? Girl number twenty, isn't this a prosperous nation, and an't you in a thriving state?"

"What did you say?" asked Louisa.

"Miss Louisa, I said I didn't know. I thought I couldn't know whether it was a prosperous nation or not, and whether I was in a thriving state or not unless I knew who had got the money, and whether any of it was mine. But that had nothing to do with it. It was not in the figures at all," said Sissy, wiping her eyes.

"That was a great mistake of yours," observed Louisa.

"Yes Miss Louisa, I know it was now. Then Mr. M'Choakumchild said he would try me again. And he said, This schoolroom is an immense town, and there are a million of inhabitants, and only five and twenty are starved to death in the streets, in the course of a year. What is your remark on that proportion? And my remark was—for I couldn't think of a better one—that I thought it must be just as hard upon those who were starved, whether the others were a million, or a million million. And that was wrong too."

"Of course it was."

Then Mr. M'Choakumchild said he would try me once more... And I find (Mr. M'Choakumchild said) that in a given time a hundred thousand persons went to sea on long voyages, and only five hundred of them were drowned or burnt to death. What is the percentage? And I said Miss;" here Sissy fairly sobbed as confessing with extreme contrition to her greatest error; "I said it was nothing."

"Nothing, Sissy?"

"Nothing, Miss—to the relations and friends of the people who were killed. I shall never learn!"

Charles Dickens, *Hard Times*

Nick Fotion and Jan C. Heller (eds.), Contingent Future Persons, 99-122.
© 1997 *Kluwer Academic Publishers. Printed in the Netherlands.*

The great insight of utilitarian ethical theories, the feature that makes them seem "so self-evidently correct" to so many of their supporters ([26], p. 84) is surely their insistence that morality is intimately associated with human welfare. As most non-utilitarian theorists would acknowledge, any plausible ethical theory must at least take into account as morally significant the influence of choices and actions on well-being ([23], p. 30). Sissy Jupe, however, cannot accept the classical utilitarian assumption that the misery of the few can be rendered less unfortunate by the prosperity of the many. This paper develops a utilitarian account of choice that explains why she is right. The theory presented also has important implications for population theory, and concerning the moral status of contingent future persons.

I. BRINGING HAPPINESS VS. RELIEVING SUFFERING

Classical utilitarians tell us that "actions are right in proportion as they tend to promote happiness, wrong as they tend to promote the reverse of happiness." Some add that "By happiness is intended pleasure and the absence of pain; by unhappiness, pain and the privation of pleasure" [15]. So far so good: Most utilitarians take this principle to pick out as clear and unambiguous a moral theory as one could want. But as it stands, the utilitarian directive is seriously ambiguous, for it tells us nothing about the relationship between pleasures and pains, or about how we are to reconcile the joint commands to 'promote happiness' and also to 'inhibit the reverse of happiness.' A Benthamic Calculus is no help in this regard, not simply because of its explicit hedonism (which, in any case, is rejected by many contemporary utilitarians), but because Bentham, like Mill and most contemporary utilitarians, fails to distinguish the positive injunction to "promote happiness" from the correlative negative injunction to "prevent unhappiness," and fails to examine the ways in which the two may conflict. Contemporary economic theories of utility are worse than useless in this regard, for they render it impossible to distinguish the two injunctions from one another ([30], pp. 274-5).

There are two important, and seldom noticed differences between these twin utilitarian commands. First, the positive utilitarian imperative to "maximize happiness" is insatiable, while the negative utilitarian command to "minimize misery" is satiable: no matter how much happiness we have, the positive principle tells us that more would always be better. But the negative principle ceases to generate any obligations once a determinate but demanding goal has been reached: if misery could be eliminated, no further obligation would be implied by the negative principle, even if it were possible to provide people (or non-human 'persons') with additional bliss. Second, the injunction to minimize misery is a *person-affecting* injunction: it implies an obligation to respond to the needs of people who already exist, but imposes no obligation to bring people in the world so that their miseries might be relieved. The injunction to maximize happiness, as commonly explained by utilitarians, does not restrict its scope to improving the lives of people who already exist, but goes further to recommend that we should bring more people into existence whenever their existence would facilitate an increase in total or average utility. If happiness is good, and more of it is better, then the positive principle seems to tell us that it would be better to have more well-off people around so that their happiness could contribute to a larger utilitarian aggregate.

Classical utilitarians assume that these twin injunctions are complementary, and that pains and pleasures are commensurable so that they can balance one another out in a grand utilitarian aggregate. But it is far from obvious that pains and pleasures are commensurable in this way, and there is good reason to doubt that the twin utilitarian aims are even compatible—at least not without further explanation. We might well ask how pleasures and pains mix to produce an aggregate, and whether different ways of mixing them might be preferable to one another. Suppose Aristippus and Epicurus are offered a choice between two lives: L1 includes high-highs low-lows, while L2 is as calm and *ataraxic* as an Epicurean could wish. These two lives might well be equal on a utilitarian scale that weighs the aggregate happiness they contain, in one case because the highs are compensated by the lows, and in the other because there are no highs or lows. On the assumption that the pleasures of the former life would precisely outweigh the pains, would it be irrational for Aristippus to prefer L1 on grounds that it is more exciting? Would it be irrational for Epicurus prefer the L2 on grounds that it is less so?

'*Commensurabilism*' is the view that pleasures and pains can cancel one another out in the way that classical utilitarians usually assume. Suppose that Jeremy, a commensurabilist hedonic-state utilitarian, is offered the following proposal by his good friend:

> *Sadist I:* Sam the Sadist offers to stimulate the pleasure centers of Jeremy's brain, if only he will allow Sam to inflict suffering that is no greater than the amount of compensatory pleasure offered in return. Like all sadists, Sam enjoys inflicting suffering. He removes dental fillings and applies drills and sharp dental probes directly to the nerves in his victim's teeth. But Sam is a more reasonable sadist than most: he is willing to "pay" for his enjoyment, by replacing the fillings and providing compensatory hedonic benefits. Thus he claims that he leaves his victims no worse off than they would otherwise have been.

Ignore, for the moment, the interesting question whether Sam's sadistic preferences should be taken into account from the moral point of view, for we have other concerns. The question on which I would like to focus attention is this: Should a commensurabilist hedonist like Jeremy be indifferent between acceptance and rejection of this offer? Most of us, I believe, would reject it, even if trustworthy Sam promised us that the compensatory pleasure would be more than enough to compensate us, so that we would actually be better off as a result.

Let us set aside another potentially confusing issue that might cloud our examination of this example and others: It is worth noting that if we adopt revealed preference theory [RPT] and suppose that happiness is exclusively a function of preferences and their satisfaction, then the example will seem nonsensical. Those who accept RPT would argue that the pleasure Sam offers to Jeremy is equal to the pain he anticipates inflicting *only if* Jeremy is indifferent: Jeremy's indifference determines the quantity of pleasure that Sam will need to provide. This introduces another classical problem in the theory of choice, for it is in Jeremy's interest to overstate the disvalue of the pain Sam proposes to inflict, since he can then bargain for a larger hedonic benefit. There is no easy way to insure that Jeremy will accurately reveal the amount of pleasure that would compensate him, for even if he feels indifferent when offered 100 units of compensatory pleasure, he has good reason to demand 200. Since the defense of RPT is couched in psychological behaviorism, this is a problem. For the assumption that Jeremy has a reservation value beneath which he will not go presupposes that the value Jeremy places on 100 units of compensatory pleasure is sometimes independent of the value he will reveal in his choices.

Behaviorism is no longer a defensible psychological theory, even though its vestigial organs live on in the economic theory of choice. Those who find the implicit behaviorism of RPT implausible must find some other way to determine when pleasures and pains balance out, and this is a problem for any theory that regards preference satisfaction as relevant from the moral point of view (that is to say, for all plausible moral theories). But even if this problem can be solved, we may still be uncertain what to say about whether Jeremy should be indifferent between acceptance or rejection of Sam's offer, or whether Aristippus and Epicurus' decisive but divergent preferences are irrational. For these reasons, RPT cannot be the basis for a *normative* theory of utilitarian choice even if it were the best theory of preference to underlie an economic theory of consumer choice. We might agree that individuals are typically the best judges of their own interests, and that therefore we should not interfere with the choices of others. But this attitude toward others' preferences is consistent with acknowledgment that pleasures and pains may not cancel one another out like equivalencies in the numerator and denominator of a fraction.

In the case of *Sadist I* it seems unlikely that either choice is rationally required or forbidden, and we may acknowledge Jeremy's right to make his own choice. But the problem of comparing pains and pleasures (or, in a non-hedonic case, disappointments and satisfactions) becomes more poignant when Sam's activities involve more than one person:

> *Sadist II:* Before meeting Sam, Alph is already miserable and Beth already is happy. Sam satisfies his sadistic impulses by torturing Miserable Alph. But although he is a sadist, Sam believes that he is obliged to leave the world no worse than he found it, and accepts a commensurabilist utilitarian theory that prescribes when

one situation is better or worse than another. He therefore offsets Alph's pain by providing compensatory benefits for Happy Beth.

As Sam is hauled off by the police, should good utilitarians join him in his indignant protest that he is innocent, since he has left the world no worse than he found it? Derek Parfit argues that they should not. He recommends the following

> *Compensation principle:* One person's burdens cannot be compensated by benefits provided for someone else.[1]

If suffering is bad, and if outcomes that include uncompensated suffering are *ceteris paribus* worse than those that do not, then Sam has failed to leave the world "no worse off than he found it." Parfit claims that the *Compensation principle* is clearly true, but if so, it is notoriously difficult for most utilitarian theories to explain why. Indeed, the objection that 'we cannot rightly pay for the bliss of the fortunate many by inflicting misery and suffering on the unfortunate few' is often given as ground for rejecting utilitarian ideals altogether. According to Norman Daniels, it is utilitarianism's rejection of the *Compensation principle* that founds the common claim that utilitarian theories inappropriately ignore the boundaries between persons ([4], p.95). Kantians might explain the *Compensation principle* with the "dogmatic assertion" that individuals should not be used as mere means in the pursuit of utilitarian maxima.[2] At the least, any theory that would require us to reject the Compensation principle would come in conflict with a widely shared and deep seated (if not ineradicable) moral judgment or "intuition."

Other ground could be given in favor of this principle, but here I will recommend it only for its attractiveness, and will consider the relationship between this principle and Utilitarian theories of choice. I will argue that utilitarians can agree with Parfit's *Compensation principle* if they accept that burdens and benefits, misery and happiness, are not two sides of the same coin, but that they identify two different evaluative currencies altogether. For example, one might maintain one's commitment to utilitarianism while adding that one is never justified in ignoring the injunction to minimize misery even when one has an opportunity to increase the bliss of those who are not miserable. Perhaps it is a view like this one that underlies Sissy Jupe's judgment that it is just as hard on those who starve, whether the others are "a million or a million million:" If what we care about is the minimization of misery and deprivation and if we also accept the *Compensation principle*, then we will not care that the *proportion* of miserable persons to well-off persons is small, we will instead focus our attention on the sum total of suffering. Before developing this into a more substantial utilitarian theory for ordering outcomes, we will consider the relative weight of the twin utilitarian imperatives in another context.

II. POPULATION CHOICES

The ambiguity of the twin utilitarian injunctions is especially confusing when we apply them to decisions about population policy. Some of these confusions generate great paradoxes, as Henry Sidgwick glimmeringly suspected and as Derek Parfit has dazzlingly shown. These paradoxes have in turn driven some theorists toward surprisingly baroque and sometimes brilliantly subtle revisions of the utilitarian view.[3] The examples that follow reproduce the problem utilitarians face in Sadist II in the context of population choices. I consider both total and average utilitarian views: total utilitarians recommend that we should strive to maximize the total amount of utility that everyone enjoys, while average utilitarianism tells us that we should maximize the value we get when we divide the grand total by the number of people who enjoy it.

Maximizing Total Utility: Total utilitarianism [TU] does not take account of the distribution of well being and misery, only its sum total. Under the commensurabilist assumption, TU instructs that we should *ceteris paribus* be indifferent between the following alternatives:

> *Total 1:* The next generation will contain 10 billion blissful people and no miserable people.

> *Total 2:* The next generation will contain 100 billion blissful people and X miserable people, where X is chosen so that the total disutility of X miserable people is equivalent to the additional utility provided by the 90 billion blissful additions. That is, where U(*) is a utility function, choose X such that:
> U(90 Billion Blissful People) + U(X Miserable People) = 0.

Total utilitarians claim that Total 1 and Total 2 are equally choiceworthy, since they both contain the same utilitarian total of well-being. But those who accept Parfit's Compensation principle will join Sissy Jupe in the judgment that it is just as hard on the miserable no matter how numerous are the blissful. Since there are suffering people in Total 2, and since their suffering is uncompensated, the *Compensation principle* would lead one to conclude that Total 1 is better than Total 2. After all, the 90 billion additional blissful people are not worse off in Total 1 than they would have been in Total 2, for they would never exist at all in Total 1.

Maximizing Average Utility: Average utilitarians [AU] tell us to maximize average utility. Again, this injunction implies nothing about the distribution of well-being and misery within the population: if the average utility in two outcomes is equivalent, we should be indifferent between one in which everyone's well-being is the equal, and another in which one person is super-extravagantly blissfully happy, while everyone else is miserable. In population choices, AU recommends indifference between the following alternatives:

Average 1: The next generation contains 9 Billion Blissful People each of whom enjoys a happy life at a Utility Level of B.

Average 2: The next generation contains 9 Billion Blissful people, X BlissPlus People, and 9 Billion Miserable People, where BlissPlus people are even better off (much better off) than blissful people, and where X is chosen so that:

$$\frac{U(X \text{ BlissPlus People}) + U(9 \text{ Billion Miserable People})}{(9 \text{ Billion} + X)} = B$$

The average utility level is the same in *Average 1* and *Average 2*. But those who accept Parfit's Compensation Principle will again note that *Average 2* contains uncompensated suffering and a lot of miserable people, while *Average 1* does not. Acceptance of the compensation principle would lead one to conclude that *Average 1* is better than *Average 2*.

Some utilitarians will bite the bullet, and will reject the Compensation principle [13]. Those who are more firmly committed to the Compensation principle than to utilitarianism may be led to conclude that utilitarianism is an unacceptable theory [4]. I will urge that the problem is not with utilitarianism but with the commensurabilist assumption that well-being and misery can balance one another out like the two sides of a see-saw. In section III I develop a non-commensurabilist utilitarian theory for comparing outcomes. This theory maintains the tight utilitarian association between morality and welfare, but without violating the Compensation principle. Section VI will incorporate this theory into a broader account of obligation.

III. EVALUATING OUTCOMES: A NON-COMMENSURABILIST THEORY OF UTILITARIAN 'BETTERNESS'

Theories are *utilitarian* if they rank outcomes in terms of their relative 'betterness' and if they further hold that the 'betterness' relation takes account only of the well- or ill-being of the persons who will exist if one outcome comes about rather than another. Theories are *non-commensurabilist* if they reject the claim that misery and well-being are commensurable qualities that balance one another out in a grand utilitarian aggregate. Only non-commensurabilist theories are consistent with the Compensation principle. Is it possible to develop a utilitarian theory for ordering outcomes that does not violate the Compensation principle? I will show that it is. But the Compensation principle limits the structure of such a theory. The requirement that one person's burdens cannot be compensated by benefits to another person implies that the obligation to minimize misery is lexically prior to the correlative obligation to maximize well-being.

It is worthwhile to re-emphasize that terms like 'happiness,' 'well-being,' 'misery,' and 'ill-being' should be understood to refer to whatever makes life go well or ill, and should be interpreted as evaluative criteria that apply to complete lives, and not necessarily to momentary mental states like pleasure, satisfaction, pain, or frustration. Momentary hedonic states like pleasure and satisfaction may indeed contribute to making lives go well, just as pain and frustration may contribute to making some lives go badly. But for the purposes of this theory, we need not take a stand on whether hedonic states are the only determinants of well-being and misery. For now I will simply describe a system for ordering outcomes. A full defense of this system, including comparison with plausible alternatives, must wait for another time.

Utilitarians can accept the compensation principle if they formulate the negative utilitarian imperative as a first principle for the ordering of prospective outcomes:

> *Negative Ordering Principle* [NOP]: Outcomes are worse if they contain more misery, less bad if they contain less.

Fred Feldman plausibly holds that misery and unhappiness have a different moral status when they are freely chosen, compensated within a life, or deserved as punishment [8]. On this view, NOP should take account only of ill-being that is undeserved, uncompensated, and unchosen. I raise this issue only to set it aside, for acceptance or rejection of Feldman's view will not affect the argument made here. In ordering outcomes according to their relative betterness, the first step is to use NOP to divide outcomes into indifference classes—classes of outcomes that contain the same amount of misery or ill-being. NOP orders these indifference classes according to the aggregate misery they contain. For those indifference classes that contain more than one member, positive ordering principles may be used to further order outcomes within these sets. As a first approximation, we might adopt the following:

> *Positive Ordering Principle* [POP]: Outcomes are better if they contain more happiness, less good if they contain less.

To avoid conflict with the Compensation principle, POP may appropriately be applied only for further refinement of the ordering given by NOP. On this view, NOP is thus lexically prior to POP. We must distinguish different interpretations of POP that apply to its application in different contexts. In particular, different interpretations of POP are associated with its implications for the ordering of outcomes that contain different numbers of persons. Many different number choices will be settled by NOP, but some will remain, since NOP gives no ground for ordering outcomes that contain the same amount of misery, regardless of the number of well-off persons they contain. Before considering the difficult issues raised by those different number choices that remain after application of NOP, we can see that POP has the following implication for the ordering of outcomes that contain the same number of persons:

Positive Ordering Principle for Same Number Choices [POP-SN]:
If the same number of people would exist in either of two
outcomes, O1 and O2, O1 is better than O2 if those who would
exist in O1 are better off than those who would exist in O2.

POP-SN tells us that we should make those who exist as well off as possible. As
stated here, POP-SN is more or less identical to Derek Parfit's "Same Number
Quality Claim," which he calls Principle Q ([21], p.360). Like Parfit's *Principle Q*,
POP-SN is subject to a variety of interpretations. A weak paretian interpretation of
POP-SN requires that at least one person is better off in O1 than in O2 while no one
is worse off in O1 than in O2. A strong paretian interpretation requires that everyone
must be better off in O1 and O2. Non-paretian interpretations might require that
there be less aggregate misery, or more aggregate happiness, or some combination
of these requirements. While I cannot sort these interpretations out here, any of them
is consistent with the view I develop in later sections of this paper.

How should comparisons be made when outcomes contain different numbers of
persons? Four alternative views have been defended concerning the purported value
of adding additional well-off people to the world: Richard Hare argues that it is
better if more well-off people exist [10]. Christoph Fehige argues that it not better if
more people exist, regardless of how well-off they would be [7]. In a similar vein,
Jan Narveson claims that the existence of additional well-off people is a matter of
moral indifference ([17], [18]). And Thomas Hurka argues that additional people
make outcomes better when total population is low, but that the value of additional
people diminishes as population levels rise [12]. These views correspond to four
different refinements on the POP that might be used to order outcomes in different
number choices:

Positive Ordering Principles for Different Number Choices
[POP-DN]:

POP-DN1: Outcomes are better when they contain more well-off
persons [Hare].

POP-DN2: Outcomes that contain more people are ceteris paribus
no better than those that contain fewer, no matter how well-off the
additional people would be [Fehige].

POP-DN3: The value of additional persons is a decreasing
function of population size [Hurka].

POP-DN4: The existence of additional well-off persons makes
outcomes neither better nor worse [Narveson].

All of these, with the possible exception of POP-DN3, accept that it is worse when more miserable people exist. While they are not all inconsistent with one another, they clearly have quite different implications concerning the moral status of future persons, and there is little agreement about which we should accept. Arguments that have been provided in favor of one of these principles over others usually appeal to our intuitions, but intuitions provide a less reliable when they are applied to novel domains, and population theory is surely a novel decision domain.

But even if agreement cannot be reached on the choice among these alternatives, it is important to note that different number choices that involve more or less ill-being have already been settled by the application of NOP, and the set of possible outcomes already has a high degree of order, given by NOP and POP-SN, before we even come to these divisive issues. In most practical circumstances, our ability to describe or predict likely outcomes is limited, and our descriptions will be coarse grained enough that most different number choices will be definitively settled by NOP. The negative principle is far less controversial than the positive principle in its implications for most different number choices,[4] since its application does not raise metaphysical questions about the relative value of persons and the well-or-ill-being that they enjoy. Although the theory of obligation developed later in section VI is consistent with any of the positive ordering principles for different number choices identified above, it is worthwhile to take a moment briefly to sort out some of the arguments that motivate the different views, and my own reasons for preferring POP-DN4 over the alternative views. Section IV will discuss some of the issues that divide advocates of the different positive principles listed above.

IV. THE VALUE OF WELL-BEING
AND THE VALUE OF WELL-OFF PERSONS

The different principles deserve, and have received, more extensive consideration than they can be given here, and the issues that separate their advocates are among the most divisive issues in normative population theory. If one accepts the *Compensation principle*, however, the set of cases over which these divisions range is rather small and the set of prospective outcomes already has a high degree of order before we even come to these issues.

Richard Hare's argument for the view that the existence of additional well-off people makes outcomes better is based on his view that to be moral is to have analogous preferences for analogous situations. Since some real life people want to have been born, Hare's view implies that morality requires us to prefer the existence of any other people who would, if they existed, want to have been born.[5]

Some people are persuaded by this argument. But one wonders what it is that people think they are preferring when they view themselves as having a preference for having been born. Such a preference might have its source in vague fears about the emptiness of nonexistence, or nebulous worries about *what it would have been like for them* had they never been born. Since there is *nothing* that it would have been like *for them* if they had never been born, such sources would render this purported preference poorly formed or poorly articulated. In order to have a preference among options, one must have at least some idea what those options would involve, and when alternatives are vaguely or nebulously understood, people may be mistaken in their beliefs about what they prefer. Partha Dasgupta writes "The impossibility of imagining our own nonexistence gives spurious credence to the view that nonexistence must be a long dismal night from which we must try to rescue people"([6], p.114). If one suspects that people's purported 'preference for having been born' might derive from such a spurious source, one may reasonably reject Hare's argument. The Epicureans believed that the fear of death would be extinguished once people had a proper understanding of the state of nonexistence. Since nonexistence before birth is usually far less frightening to people than post-natal nonexistence (death), it is perhaps even more plausible to think that a proper understanding of nonexistence would extinguish or render superfluous Hare's purported preference for having been born.[6]

Christoph Fehige's argument for the claim that existence is never preferable to nonexistence is presented in one of the most interesting papers to have appeared on this subject since the publication of Parfit's path-breaking book. The claim is founded on an antecedent theory of preference, *Anti-Frustrationism*, for which Fehige offers a detailed independent argument. According to an anti-frustrationist, "we don't do any good by creating satisfied extra preferences. What counts about preferences is not that they have a satisfied existence, but that they don't have a frustrated existence" ([7], p. 497). On this view, satisfaction of a preference at best brings us to the level of well-being we would have enjoyed if we had not had the preference at all. Since non-existent people have no preferences to be frustrated, this view implies that they enjoy the same level of well-being that they would have enjoyed if they had existed and had all of their desires fully satisfied. Thus Fehige concludes that people who might have existed but who never do exist are always at least as well off as actual persons who exist and who are sure to enjoy less than complete preference satisfaction. It follows from this theory of preference that nonexistence is always at least as good as existence. This theory of preference has ancient roots in the works of Epicurus and his followers, but also perhaps in Sophocles, who writes "Not to be born is, past all prizing, best; but when a man hath seen the light, this is next best by far, that with all speed he should go thither, whence he hath come."[7] Unlike Sophocles, Fehige does not claim that people are better off if they die sooner; for many of us this would frustrate our desires to go on living. But like Sophocles, he claims that those possible people who are never born are better off than we less fortunate actual persons, since the terminally unborn will never suffer frustration of their desires. Those who find this view absurd on its face should surely examine Fehige's brilliant contemporary defense of it. While Fehige begins by defending this theory of preference directly, he later demonstrates that his view implies plausible solutions for many of the most perplexing paradoxes of population theory. Even without the direct argument Fehige offers, the tidiness of his solution to Parfit's *Mere-Addition Paradox* should lead population theorists to give his argument the most respectful consideration.

Although I cannot discuss all of the features of Fehige's detailed and careful defense of this theory of preference, I believe that his view may reasonably be rejected. In particular, anti-frustrationism may pass too quickly over the very plausible possibility that some preferences might be enjoyable and desirable in themselves, and that some pleasures may constitute positive benefits rather than simply the removal of painful longings. Sometimes people are better off if they have preferences to be satisfied than they would have been had they not had those preferences. Perhaps some desires are like afflictions which we seek to free ourselves, either by extinguishing or satisfying them. But surely there are other desires and preferences possession of which makes our lives better. Why else would people take pains to develop expensive and refined tastes if their possession didn't make life richer by virtue of the rare but profound satisfaction enjoyed when these tastes are satisfied? Fehige is perhaps too quick to conclude that there is no independent value for sweet longings and cultivated preferences, and that no desires are desirable for their own sake.[8]

It may help to compare *anti-frustrationism* with an ancient precursor: the Epicureans recommended that we should endeavor to extinguish sexual desire altogether so that its frustration would not trouble our happiness. But they also allowed that those who find such desires difficult to extinguish might permissibly satisfy them so to be rid of them. Later Epicureans (Lucretius) added that in such circumstances these desires should be satisfied without any passionate feeling or attachment, since turbulent passions would undermine the calm and unperturbed happiness of the Epicurean ideal. Most find this argument unconvincing, and for good reason: sometimes turbulent passions, loves, and attachments make our lives richer, even when they disturb the placidity of our happiness and even though they render us susceptible to loss and pain. If some satisfactions provide positive benefits that are worth pursuing for their own sake, these benefits cannot be explained by an account of happiness as absence of pain and painful desires. But Fehige's anti-frustrationism is not quite the same as the Epicurean view: in particular, Fehige does not characterize unsatisfied desires as *painful*, and can explain the benefit of acquiring new preferences in terms of the preference that a persons may have to do just that. Anti-frustrationism allows that it may be reasonable to acquire preferences as a way of avoiding the frustration of meta-preferences. But like Epicureanism, anti-frustrationism offers a negative account of well-being as the absence of frustrated or unsatisfied preferences or desires, and we may have reason to want an account of desire that better captures the positive role that desires, satisfactions, and passions play in our lives. While this brief argument cannot do justice to the subtlety of Fehige's position, we may still have good reason to want an account of preference that recognizes this positive role.

Thomas Hurka famously argues that additional persons have positive value, but that the value of additional persons diminishes as total population size increases [12]. Hurka brilliantly shows that this hypothesis about the value of persons collects many widely shared considered judgments about extinction and the value of individuals. But like Hare, Hurka completely separates the value of additional persons from the value that their lives have for them. For Hurka, the value of a person is decisively dependent on population size, and when population size is low, Hurka implies that it might even be appropriate to bring miserable persons into existence for the purpose of perpetuating the species, and that sometimes it would be better to increase population than to increase the welfare of existing people ([12], p.504; [11] p.142). This would violate the *Compensation principle*, since these people would suffer personal misery in the service of an impersonal population total. For these reasons, and once again acknowledging that my brief discussion here can not do justice to Hurka's subtle argument, I believe that one may reasonably reject this account of the value of persons in the context of population choices.

These questions raise issues at the foundation of ethics, concerning the value of well-being and the value of persons: Is well-being is valuable because it is *good for people*, or are people valuable because their lives contain well-being? The problem does not arise in the case of ill-being or misery, because the negative utilitarian injunction places no independent value on the existence of any evaluative unit, independently of the persons who might possess it. No one would suggest that the injunction to minimize misery might impose an obligation to bring people into existence that their misery might be relieved. Because I find it implausible that the value of well-being could be independent of its value to those persons who enjoy it, and because acts that fail to bring well-off persons into existence are worse for no one, I am inclined to accept Narveson's view that it is neither better nor worse to bring additional well-off persons into existence.

Those who are antecedently convinced by the argument for one of the alternative views discussed in this section may well be unconvinced by the brief responses given to those arguments in the discussion above. But as I have argued, the set of options over which this disagreement ranges is small, and agreement on these issues may not be necessary for agreement about what we should do. As noted earlier, I believe that the theory of obligation I develop in what follows could be accepted by advocates of any of these views. But one important reason theorists have given for opting for an impersonal theories like those recommended by Hare and Hurka is that they believe that only impersonal theories can give an acceptable account of population choice. If successful, the theory developed in section V and VI undermines that reason.

V. TWO DEONTIC ASYMMETRIES

The examples considered in sections I and II motivate the suggestion that misery and well-being may not balance one another out in the way that classical utilitarians typically assume. Sections III and IV take steps toward development of a non-commensurabilist theory of utilitarian betterness. In this section I move from the evaluation of outcomes to the evaluation of actions in terms of their permissibility, impermissibility, and obligatoriness. In particular, I consider a set of asymmetries in our commonsense understanding of our obligations concerning the value of promoting well-being versus inhibiting misery. In section VI, I show how the theory of betterness developed in III and IV can be incorporated into a plausible theory of obligation.

It is sometimes thought that there is an asymmetric relation between the normative status of acts that prevent harm, and those that provide extra benefits for persons who are already well off and who are not experiencing harms. This gives us the

> *First Asymmetry Thesis:* We have an obligation to prevent harms, at least when we can do so without excessive risk or cost, but no obligation to provide additional benefits for persons who are well off and who are not miserable or deprived or experiencing harms. It may be a good thing to benefit those who are adequately well-off, but it is not morally obligatory.

Suppose we have the opportunity to provide an additional benefit to Keith, who is already quite well off and who is living a happy and fulfilling life. But we could instead use our resources to improve the lives of others who would be doomed to lives squalor and misery in the absence of our aid. Those who accept the *First Asymmetry Thesis* might acknowledge that it would be nice to provide Keith with an additional benefit, but would not claim that failure to do so would be morally reprehensible. Failure to provide a benefit to someone who is well off might show that one lacks certain virtues of beneficence or generosity, but would not be a serious moral wrong. But failure to prevent harm and misery, when one could have done so without risk or excessive effort on ones own part may sometimes be a serious moral wrong.

In a slightly more fanciful context, suppose that Well-off Keith is exceptionally efficient at turning resources into well-being: if we used our resources to feed the hungry or house the homeless, we would decrease their misery by a given amount, but if we instead gave them to Keith, his welfare level, already quite high, would go through the roof.[9] Almost everyone would agree that our obligation to aid the miserable should take precedence, even if Keith's prospective utility gain would be larger than theirs. It would be nice to send Keith's welfare level through the roof, but it is not morally obligatory, and it would be wrong to do so at the expense of the hungry or the homeless.

A second deontic asymmetry arises in the case of "genesis choices,"—choices that will result in the existence of persons who would not exist otherwise:

> *Second Asymmetry Thesis:* We have an obligation not to cause people to exist if those who would exist will be miserable and deprived, but we have no obligation to cause people to exist who

would be happy ([7], section 7; [14], p.100; [17]; [18]; [21], p. 391).

Those who accept the *second asymmetry thesis* believe that people are not doing something wrong when they choose not to have a child who would be happy. But if one knows that any child one has will be miserable, then it would be wrong to have children. In general, those who accept the *second asymmetry thesis* hold that when our choices might cause the existence of well-off persons who would not have existed otherwise, the happiness those people would enjoy does not by itself constitute a reason for bringing them into existence. But when our choices might cause the existence of miserable people, the misery they would suffer does constitute a reason for not bringing them into existence.

It is plausible to think that this asymmetry has its source in the difference between misery and well-being, and in the differences between the positive and negative utilitarian commands: when one fails to bring into existence a person who would be well-off, the person who would have existed is not well-off or badly-off as a result, since nonexistent persons cannot be well-off or badly off. But if one brings into existence a miserable person, that person's misery is a consequence of one's choice. It seems likely that the folk theory of obligation that underlies these asymmetries has roots that stretch to the same source that makes the *Compensation principle* so plausible. The unhappiness of the miserable cannot be compensated by benefits to the happy, no matter how efficient the happy may be at converting benefits into welfare.

VI. AN IMPURE CONSEQUENTIALIST THEORY OF OBLIGATION

Pure consequentialists hold that there is no sharp distinction between the theory of betterness and a theory of obligation. They believe that our obligation is always to do what would be best, and actions are better or worse depending only on the betterness or worseness of the outcomes at which they aim. Pure consequentialist theories have come under criticism on ground that they conflict with commonsense moral judgments: such theories accord no weight to promises, integrity, or moral desert. Some have argued that such theories demand too much of us, and that they eliminate entirely some commonsense normative categories like supererogation— actions that are good, but which exceed the requirements of obligation. I hope that the *impure* theory I develop here will avoid such objections.

Some terminological issues must be settled before we will have an adequate interpretation of the theory I will propose: To say that an agent A has an obligation to do X is to say that A's failure to do X would reveal that A is a *schmuck*. For the moment, I rely on the reader's intuitive understanding of what it means to be a *schmuck*. Unless a contravening obligation or prerogative justifies an agent in overriding or rebutting a *prima facie* obligation, A has a duty to do what obligation assigning principles prescribe. On this understanding, the function of a theory of obligation is to distinguish the *schmucks* from people who are minimally morally decent. Most people are imperfect, and sometimes fail to do what they have obligations to do: that is, most of behave like *schmucks* in at least some of our actions and choices. But there are some people whose general propensity to do what they are morally obliged not to do justifies the judgment that they are *schmucks tout court*. I believe that this account of obligation captures well both our common usage, and the usage of obligation-talk in most discussions of moral theory. In effect, this account makes the theory of obligation depend on the theory of what it is to be a *schmuck*—a theory of vice.

To say that it would be good for A to do X even though X is not obligatory is to say that A has a moral reason to do X. But while A is no saint if she fails to do what would be good but is not obligatory, she is not thereby a *schmuck* either. Thus one function of a theory of beneficence is to separate those who are only minimally decent from those who are saints and heroes. Again, I believe that this captures commonsense and philosophical notions of supererogation.(See [28]) On this account, the theory of moral goodness and supererogation depends on a theory of virtue.

I would like to suggest a theory of obligation and supererogation that is consistent with the Compensation principle and with the non-commensurabilist theory of utilitarian betterness developed in sections III and IV. If it is acceptable, this theory would also explain the two deontic asymmetries described in the previous section. As in previous sections, it should be understood that the unit of comparison is complete life expectations and not momentary hedonic states. The theory is not a pure consequentialist theory, since it allows that people do not always have an obligation to do what will result in the best outcome, and since it leaves room for actions that are supererogatory. I will call this theory the

Impure Consequentialist Theory of Obligation [ICTO]:

> 1. *Negative Principle of Obligation* [NPO]: Actions that reduce (or minimize) misery are prima facie obligatory.

> 2. *Positive Principle of Beneficence* [PPB]: Actions are good if they increase well-being. Actions are better or less-good depending on their propensity to promote well-being: better when they do so more effectively, less good when they do so less effectively.

In the non-commensurabilist theory for the ordering of outcomes, the negative utilitarian principle was given priority over the positive principle. This was necessary to render the theory consistent with the *Compensation principle*. In ICTO, the negative principle is understood as obligation-generating, while the positive principle is not. In this case, the difference in treatment of positive and negative consequences gains support from four different sources: First, the ordering of our obligations described by ICTO is consistent with the non-commensurabilist theory of betterness developed in section III. Second, it is consistent with and supportive of the commonsense judgments of those who accept the first deontic asymmetry discussed in section V. In general, most of the actions we classify as obligatory or supererogatory fit ICTO fairly well. Third, this account of the separation between obligation and supererogation reflects the difference in urgency between acts that are necessary to prevent the perpetuation of harmful circumstances, on the one hand, and acts that would provide additional benefits for persons who are already adequately well-off on the other hand [24]. Failure to respond to others' urgent needs, when one could easily do so, is a grave moral wrong. There is no similar moral urgency concerning actions that provide extra benefits to those who are already well enough off.

Finally, this account of the ordering of our obligations and supererogations explains the intuitions of those who believe that there is an obligation not to have children who would suffer and who would be badly off, but who do not believe that there is an obligation to have children who would be well off. ICTO is *consistent with* the view of those who believe that there is a good moral reason to bring more well-off persons into existence, but it is also consistent with the view of those like Narveson and myself, who hold that such actions are, from the moral point of view, a matter of indifference.[10]

Disagreement about what would be better need not yield disagreement about what we have obligations to do. But there is good reason to want one's theory of obligation to capture the moral difference between outcomes that involve the existence of additional well-off people, and outcomes that involve the existence of additional people who are badly off, for in the context of genesis choices, the value of well-being is formally different from the disvalue of misery. When we choose not to bring into existence a person who would be happy, there is no one who is worse off. But when we fail to meet the obligation assigned by NPO by bringing a miserable person into existence, there exists a badly-off person who would not have been badly off but for our moral mistake. It is a virtue of ICTO that it captures this difference and its moral significance.

Different substantive moral theories will allow different circumstances to defeat or override the obligation assigned by NPO. Some hold that such obligations can only be overridden by contravening *prima facie* obligations of equal or greater moral 'weight.' Others hold that there are *agent centered prerogatives* that justify an agent in giving more weight to her own interests than to the interests of others. Since ICTO is offered not as a complete moral theory, but as an account of the way in which consequences and well-being should be taken into account in the context of moral choice, we need not try to stipulate here all of the circumstances that might justify or excuse an agent in failing to fulfill the *prima facie* obligations assigned by NPO. Utilitarian theories are often criticized on grounds that they demand too much. While ICTO is less demanding than other utilitarian theories, it is still quite demanding, and probably implies that most of us fail to fulfill our obligations much of the time. The degree to which ICTO is demanding is partly a function of our circumstances (what misery are we positioned to respond to?) and partly a function of the circumstances under which our obligations may be defeated.

VII. IS ICTO A PERSON-AFFECTING THEORY? AND DOES IT MATTER?

It is sometimes claimed that our theories should be *person-affecting* in their treatment of well-and-ill-being, but it is not always clear what this requirement is supposed to mean. Sometimes this claim is associated with the dictum that it is good to make people happy, but that we should be indifferent about making happy people [18]. Sometimes it is associated with the claim that the part of morality that is concerned with human well-being should be explained entirely in terms of what would be good or bad for those people who will be better or worse off ([21], p. 39; [9], p. 66), and at other times with the claim that all and only those people who are or will be actual fall within the scope of morality ([1], p. 70; [11]). It is clear not only that these proposals are different from one another, but that some are not consistent with others. This ambiguity makes it difficult to say what philosophers mean when they claim that moral theories should be (or should not be) person affecting.

On some accounts, ICTO is not a person-affecting theory, since it incorporates obligations to some persons who will never be actual: it implies a prima facie obligation not to bring people into existence if they would be miserable. There is no person to whom this obligation is owed unless it is violated. On the other hand, ICTO captures what many have wanted in a person-affecting theory: The value of well-being is a function of its value for persons, not vice versa, and the disvalue of misery is also a function of its value for those who suffer it [1]. ICTO is also consistent with Narveson's insistence that it is good to make people happy, but that we may be indifferent about making happy people [18]. I believe that this justifies regarding ICTO as a person-affecting theory. But surely its plausibility as a theory of choice does not depend on the aptness of this ambiguous label.

VIII. SOME COMMON OBJECTIONS

Because ICTO is closely related to negative utilitarianism [NU], it is subject to several of the obvious objections that have been levelled against NU. Most theorists seem to have regarded these objections as decisive, and to my knowledge, no one has seriously considered or defended negative utilitarianism since Karl Popper briefly proposed that it would "add clarity to ethics" if we would "formulate our demands negatively, i.e. if we demand the elimination of suffering rather than the promotion of happiness."[11] Indeed, some theorists have not made the distinction between negative utilitarianism as articulated in NPO and a quite different view that has been defended by Narveson and others: Narveson claims that we have obligations not to harm, but no obligation to give aid.[12] Obviously Narveson's theory of obligation is different from ICTO, which assigns a positive obligation to aid others whenever doing so would minimize misery. In this respect, ICTO is similar to commonsense reflective morality, since most people would agree that there is a duty to aid others in at least some circumstances—that is, there are circumstances in which failure to aid others would clearly reveal to the world that one is a *schmuck*. Here I consider three common objections to views like ICTO that incorporate the more plausible negative utilitarianism represented by NPO and its role in ICTO.

(i) *The Marginalist Objection*: Some economists and philosophers regard lexical orderings as intrinsically irrational. They would conclude that the non-commensurabilist theory of 'betterness' developed in section III is unacceptable, since the value of relieving suffering is taken to be prior to the value of providing additional happiness to the well-off. This first objection can be dismissed as a marginalist prejudice. In order to make the theory of consumer choice work properly, economists need to assume that people's indifference curves are smooth and twice-differentiable, but the fact that commensurable values are easier to manipulate mathematically is no reason to think that *value* is structured in this way. A theory that forbids lexical ordering would also force us to accept that Seneca's unwillingness to sell his honor for no-matter-how-much monetary profit is also an irrational (since lexical) ordering.

(ii) *The Anti-Natalist Objection*: Several theorists have argued that negative utilitarian views imply that we have an obligation never to have children. Hermann Vetter argues that this is an implication of any view that accepts Narveson's claim that we (i) have a duty not to conceive a child if we could reliably foresee that it will be miserable, but (ii) we have no duty to conceive a child even if we could be sure that it will be very happy. But because we don't know the future, having children always involves imposing on them some risk that they will not be happy. Vetter writes: "It will be seen immediately that the act "do not produce the child" dominates the act "produce the child" because it has equally good consequences as the other act in one case [if the child is or would have been happy], and better consequences in the other [if the child is or would have been unhappy]. So it is to be preferred to the other act as long as we cannot exclude with certainty the possibility that the child will be more or less unhappy; and we never can."[13]

If ICTO implied that people always have an obligation not to conceive children (and by implication, that people who have children are all *schmucks*!), it might indeed be an unacceptable theory. Fortunately, the Vetter dominance argument fails, because it fails to take into account all of the morally relevant considerations at stake in the decision to bring a child into existence. Our prospective children may contribute to making our lives better, and to making the lives of others better as well. Thus *failure* to conceive a child will put at risk the welfare of all those who might have been better off (or less badly off) if one's child had existed. However, ICTO may imply that parents have certain obligations with respect to their children: since the choice to have a child is justified only if our decision to conceive them leaves the world less badly off than it would otherwise have been, we have good reason to teach our children not only that they should flourish and find happy lives for themselves, but also that they have obligations to those who are badly off. If we have good reason to believe that our children will have happy lives, and that they will make the world a better place in some respects, then it is permissible to have them.

Far from implying that it is always wrong to conceive a child, ICTO implies that people sometimes have a *prima facie* obligation to do so if the existence of their child would make the world a less miserable place overall. The happiness that the children might enjoy is not, on this view, an independent reason for conceiving them. But their ability to contribute to the lives of others is an independent reason of this sort. But even in this case, the obligation to have a child would still be a *prima facie* obligation, and a full moral theory would need to include an account of the circumstances under which this obligation might be defeated.[14] Acceptance of ICTO will not turn us into organic baby-production machines.

(iii) *The Apocalypse Objection*: But what if one could painlessly stop the entire human endeavor all at once? Some have argued that the best way to minimize misery would be painlessly to kill off all sentient beings, perhaps by blowing the planet to smithereens with bombs. Since NU and ICTO imply that we have an obligation to minimize misery, it has been argued that they must also imply that we have an obligation to destroy the planet and all conscious beings on it. No theory with this implication can be acceptable ([27], pp. 542-3; [11], p.60).

Those who take ICTO or something like it to be a complete moral theory could respond by emphasizing the extent to which the case for the continuation of our species can rest on the utilities of people who are or will be actual even if humankind dies out.[15] One might then focus on the frustrated hopes and plans, and disappointed expectations that would result. Some have argued fairly persuasively that it is far from clear that the continuation of our species would be justified if not for these contingencies ([1], p.71). But there is another way around this objection. While ICTO does provide an excellent account of the way in which welfarist considerations should be taken into account in moral decision making, one might also urge that welfarist considerations are not the only morally relevant considerations. Other considerations might come into play in two ways: First, we might have a contravening *prima facie* obligation not to kill other people. Such an obligation might then defeat the *prima facie* obligation to alleviate suffering and would provide the basis for a plausible argument against the annihilation of our world. Since most people accept that we *do* have a *prima facie* obligation not to kill other people, this might be sufficient.

But second, we might accept that ICTO describes one species of moral value among others, and that the continuation of the species has only person-affecting value of a sort that is not incorporated in ICTO, but which is not ruled out either. I have offered no argument for the claim that only person-affecting values are significant from the moral point of view, and cannot imagine what such an argument would look like. Few would deny that person-affecting welfarist considerations represent one important kind of moral value and have a special moral status, but some people hold that there are other types of value as well. If the continued existence of persons has value in itself, this value must be explained and justified in non-person affecting terms. For example, environmental ethicists have sometimes argued that the value of animal species and ecosystems is a non-person-affecting value. Some readers may agree that there are other species of value, and that their pursuit can sometimes override or rebut our *prima facie* obligation to relieve suffering and to aid those who are badly off. If the perpetuation of the species has value in itself, as Hurka, for example, claims that it does, then this value would need to be taken into account before we could have a complete understanding of our obligations. ICTO is offered as a theory of the way in which person-affecting welfarist values are relevant to moral decision making, but there may be no reason to believe that all relevant values can be summed up in a simple utilitarian rule.[16]

X. CONCLUSION

If accepted, ICTO would explain why Jeremy would not be irrational to reject Sam's offer in *Sadist 1*, and why Sam makes the outcome worse by torturing Alph and compensating Beth in *Sadist 2*. ICTO would explain why *Total 1* and *Average 1* are respectively better than *Total 2* and *Average 2* and would account for the two deontic asymmetries described in section V. It would explain why Sissy Jupe is right to think that the suffering of some cannot be compensated, in the grand utilitarian equation, by the well-being of others. ICTO would have practical implications for social choice theory and for theories of poverty and development: it implies that we should regard poverty as getting worse when there are *more miserable impoverished people*, and should regard development efforts as successful when they reduce total destitution, not when they increase GNP or decrease the proportion of population that lives in destitution. It would thus sanction a shift from relative or proportionate measures of progress toward absolute measures.

The theory developed here provides a way to order prospective outcomes without running into many of the paradoxes and confusions that plague alternative theories. ICTO has generally plausible implications for population choices—at least, its implications seem much less *implausible* than those of alternative views. It captures the most compelling considered convictions that lie behind the claim that welfare-theory should be person-affecting. It implies that well-being is valuable because it is good for people, denies that people are good because they can serve as loci on which well-being may be heaped, and incorporates the claim that it is good to make people happy, but not necessarily good to make happy people. Finally, ICTO forbids the purchase of bliss for some at the price of misery for others. As far as I know, it is the only utilitarian theory that possesses these virtues. Who could ask for anything more?[17]

NOTES

[1] See Parfit ([21, p. 337), and Daniels ([40], p. 170). Parfit adds one qualification to the *Compensation Principle*: Our burdens can sometimes be compensated by benefits to those we love, but they cannot be compensated by benefits to total strangers.

[2] Some utilitarians never mention Kant without using the word 'dogmatic.' But it is clear that one may be a nondogmatic Kantian (see the work of Barbara Herman, Christine Korsgaard, or Thomas Hill) as that one may dogmatically propound the utilitarian view. Bentham and James Mill are safe, dead examples of dogmatic utilitarians. Indeed, J.S. Mill passed the same judgment on Bentham. Of living utilitarians, we need say nothing if it is not good -- perhaps the dogmatic variety became extinct in the mid-Nineteenth century.

[3] See especially [6], [8], [12], [17], [19], [26] and [30].

[4] There is a set of different number choices concerning which the Negative principle is highly controversial. These will be discussed in section VIII.

[5] See Fehige ([7], p. 439) for a brief examination of Hare's view. The concise pesentation of Hare's view given here is adapted from Fehige, and from Hare ([10], pp. 70-73).

[6] In act III Scene ii, Hamlet whines "Who would fardels bear, To grunt and sweat under a weary life, But that the dread of something after death, The undiscovered country from whose bourn No traveler returns, puzzles the will And makes us rather bear those ills we have Than to fly to others that we know not of?" If we intperpret Hamlet's fear as fear of nonexistence rather than fear of unknown prospects for life after death (admittedly a textual stretch), then Hamlet's fear of death might be mistaken for a preference for life (or for existence). Such misconceptions about the evil of nonexistence are still widely shared. Is it implausible to suppose that these misconceptions might be the source of Hare's speculation that people can rationally prefer existence to nonexistence? Hare considers and rejects the possibility that our preference for having been born might be inextricably associated with fear of death ([10], p. 70-71). It seems unlikely that Hare's argument or this one can settle the question once and for all.

[7] Sophocles, *Oedipus at Colonus*, at 1225 in the text. Cited in Dasgupta ([5], p. 116). For similar sentiments see Job 3:3 and Ecclesiastes 4:2-3.

[8] Actually Fehige discusses this possible objection. He writes: "All this is to say that nobody wants new and satisfied preferences, or that it would be irrational, or morally irrelevant to want them. Mary's *wish* to have additional wishes conveys instrumental value on their existence--the value of avoiding to frustrate another (*viz.,* the highest order) wish. (. . .) The argument here is not a crusade against wanting more. All it denies is that even if people *don't* want to want more, wanting more (and getting it) would benefit them." ([7], p. 434). Once again, my discussion here cannot settle the question. I can only point toward the sources of disagreement. Those who find Fehige's independent argument for *anti-frustrationism* convincing may be unimpressed by my objections here.

[9] Perhaps Keith is a "utility monster" like those described by Nozick ([20, p. 41]. The example here was inspired by Allen Buchanan, who suggested during my oral prelim exam that Keith Lehrer just gets more enjoyment out of things than most other people do. Anyone unconvinced by the *First Asymmetry Thesis* might consider sending contributions to Keith Lehrer at the University of Arizona. I would suggest that such contributions should go to OXFAM instead.

[10] Not that parents should be or will be indifferent about bringing more well-off children into the world, but their decision to do so, on Narveson's view, is not better because of the happiness that these children will enjoy.

[11] Popper, [22], vol. I, chap. 5, n. 6(2). Also vol. i, chap. 9, n. 2. Quoted in Smart ([27], p. 542).

[12] Narveson, [16]. See Glover ([9], pp. 66-69) for criticism of this view.

[13] Vetter ([29], p. 301). Heyd ([11], p. 60). Interestingly, Vetter does not regard this as an ojbection. He argues that we really do have an obligation not to have children, and that it would be a good thing if the human race could quietly go extinct.

[14] There is much more to be said in response to Vetter's objection. Having children changes parents too, sometimes making tham more responsible, kinder, and more understanding people than they would have been if they had not had children. If one has reason to think that parenthood would change one in these ways, then the additional good one might do as a result might constitute an additional reason for coneiving a child, not decisive in itself perhaps, but not irrelevant either. The general point is that

Vetter's game theoretic analysis of the problem leaves out consideration of the interests of persons other than the child herself.

[15] Bennett [1] emphasizes these costs on pp. 70-71. My presentation of the case owes much to his earlier presentation of it.

[16] It has also been suggested that this kind of negative utilitarian view implies Parfit's Repugnant Conclusion. In Wolf [30] I argue that some negative utilitarian views do not imply a repugnant version of the repugnant conclusion.

[17] I received helpful comments on this project from Christoph Fehige, Frederick Ferre, Nick Fotion, Claudia Mills, Michael Tooley, and colloquium participants at the University of Colorado. I would like to thank them, and to absolve them from responsibility for any faults—or at least from any of the *paper's* faults!

BIBLIOGRAPHY

1.   Bennett, J.: 1978, "On Maximizing Happiness." In R. I. Sikora and B. Barry (eds.), *Obligations to Future Generations*, 61-73. Philadelphia: Temple University Press.
2.   Broome, J.: 1992, *Counting the Cost of Global Warming*, Cambridge: White Horse Press.
3.   Broome, J.: 1994, "The Value of a Person", *The Proceedings of the Aristotelian Society*, supp. vol. LXVIII.
4.   Daniels, N.: 1988, *Am I My Parents' Keeper? An Essay on Justice Between the Young and the Old*, New York: Oxford University Press.
5.   Dasgupta, P.: 1974, "On Optimum Population Size." In *Economic Theory and Planning*, Ashok Mitra, ed. Calcutta: Oxford University Press.
6.   Dasgupta, P.: 1994, "Savings and Fertility: Ethical Issues", *Philosophy and Public Affairs*, 23:99-127.
7.   Fehige, C.: 1997, "A Pareto Principle for Possible People." In Christoph Fehige and Ulla Wessels (eds.), *Preferences*, de Gruyter: Berlin/New York.
8.   Feldman, F.: 1996. "Justice, Desert, and the Repugnant Conclusion." Forthcoming.
9.   Glover, J.: 1977, *Causing Death and Saving Lives*, NY: Penguin Books.
10.   Hare, R.: 1993, *Essays on Bioethics*, New York: Oxford University Press.
11.   Heyd, D.: 1992, *Genethics: Moral Issues in the Creation of People*, Berkeley: University of California Press.
12.   Hurka, T.: 1983, "Value and Population Size," *Ethics*, 93:496-507.
13.   Leslie, J.: 1989, "The Need to Generate Happy People," *Philosophia* 19:29-33
14.   McMahan, J.: 1981, "Problems of Population Theory", *Ethics* 92:96-127.
15.   Mill, J. S.: 1979/1861, *Utilitarianism*, Indianapolis: Hackett Puishing Co.
16.   Narveson, J.: 1967, *Morality and Utility*, Baltimore MD: Johns Hopkins Press.
17.   Narveson, J.: 1967b, "Utilitarianism and New Generations," *Mind* 76:62-72.
18.   Narveson, J.: 1973, "Moral Problems of Population," *The Monist* 57:62-86.
19.   Ng, Y-K.: 1989, "What Should We Do About Future Generations? The Impossibility of Parfit's Theory X," *Economics and Philosophy*, 5:235-253.
20.   Nozick, R.: 1974, *Anarchy, State and Utopia*, New York: Basic Books.
21.   Parfit, D.: 1982, *Reasons and Persons*, Oxford: Clarendon Press.
22.   Popper, K.: 1962, *The Open Society and its Enemies*, Princeton N.J.: Princeton University Press.
23.   Rawls, J.: 1971, *A Theory of Justice*, Boston: Harvard University Press.
24.   Scanlon, T.: 1975, "Preference and Urgency," *The Journal of Philosophy*, 72(19):655-669.
25.   Sidgwick, H.: 1981/1907, *The Methods of Ethics*, Indianapolis: Hackett Publishing Co.
26.   Singer, P.: 1976, "A Utilitarian Population Principle", in Michael Bayles, ed. *Ethics and Population*, Cambridge: Schenkman Publishing Co.
27.   Smart, R. N.: 1958, "Negative Utilitarianism," *Mind*, 67:542-3.
28.   Urmson, J. O.: 1958, "Saints and Heroes." In A. I. Melden, ed., *Essays in Moral Philosophy*, Seattle: University of Washington Press, 198-216.
29.   Vetter, H.: 1971, "Utilitarianism and New Generations," *Mind* 80:301-2.

30. Wolf, C.: 1996, "Social Choice and Normative Population Theory: A Person-Affecting Solution to Parfit's Mere Addition Paradox," *Philosophical Studies*.81(2-3):263-282.

AVNER de-SHALIT

DOWN TO EARTH ENVIRONMENTALISM:
SUSTAINABILITY AND FUTURE PERSONS[1]

> And she promises the Earth to me
> And I believe her
> After all these times
> I don't know why
> Paul McCartney (from *Girl*)

INTRODUCTION

In the environmental philosophy literature one is likely to find two very distinct models of 'environmentalism'. According to one, the 'dark' green, or 'deep' ecology, in order to save the environment we need a total motivation change, a new psyche. The question is how to save our souls rather than simply the 'environment'. As for international political and economical arrangements, all international trade should be boycotted, production should be limited, and Consumerism should be regarded as an evil. Trade is the key factor leading to environmental degradation and to the speciesist outlook human beings have adopted since the age of enlightenment. Finally, people should change their lifestyle completely, and adopt 'voluntary simplicity'. These 'deep' ecologists claim that only Deep Ecology is a genuine environmental philosophy.

According to the other model, 'shallow' ecology, in order to save the environment, structural and political reforms should be made. One necessary step is the democratization of all our political institutions. Trade and economic activities should not be stopped, but rather be guided according to ecological sustainability rather than only considerations of cost and benefit. In addition, those whom the North call poor, but in fact are not poor, should be encouraged to protect their rights against the interests of huge multinational firms. Finally, saving the environment does not necessarily involve a theory of agency or changing one's lifestyle. For the Shallow Ecology model, Deep Ecology is nothing but a theory of lifestyle.

It goes without saying that these two portraits are caricatures rather than real portrayals. But they are portrayed this way in order to demonstrate the starting point, which is that Dark Greens or Deep Ecologists and pale Greens or Shallow Ecologists refuse to see the complexity of the other's position. Rather they see each other in a stereotyped way.[2] In this paper I defend one version of Shallow Environmentalism which is anthropocentric. I show that it is not so shallow in its policy implications and that it is morally sound.[3] I do so by referring to a book I

123

Nick Fotion and Jan C. Heller (eds.), Contingent Future Persons, 123-135.
© 1997 *Kluwer Academic Publishers. Printed in the Netherlands.*

wrote about justice between generations [6], and to the criticism I received [1; 4; 8; 9; 12]. In that respect I shall return to the scene of the crime—or at least so it was seen by most of the critics—anthropocentrism.

My argument is that sustainability is related to justice in a very simple way: sustainability is about activities of human beings and the future ecological impact of these activities. It is about living within the carrying capacity of supporting ecosystems, and respecting the latter. The term sustainability implies that we have in mind more or less similar activities done in the future as well.[4] Justice is also related to these activities: it is about how these activities affect the distribution of a variety of goods (including money, free time, status, etc.). But since sustainability implies that what happens in the future counts as well, justice now relates to a trans-generational distribution of goods. In other words, intergenerational justice already encompasses the relationships between justice and sustainability. Notice, however, that I am not making a more radical claim, namely that justice and sustainability are somehow the same. Such a claim would have to rest on metaphysical assumptions with which I am uneasy, e.g. radical holism.

However, the package of sustainability and justice, namely intergenerational justice, is also an effective idea in the service of the Green case. This is not to deny the importance of non-anthropocentrism. There is no doubt that the latter is one of the most interesting and exciting innovations of moral philosophy in the post-war era. Indeed, there are times when one cannot do without it, for instance when one wants to explain one's standpoint against vivisection. But there are different sorts of moral principles that suit best different actions—and the Green case represents political action, rather than simply an armchair exercise in philosophy. Environmental philosophy is there to be used when convincing politicians, policy makers and the public in general of the need for drastic political, structural, and economic reforms. One way of doing so is to stick to non-anthropocentric arguments. But I am afraid that just like Paul McCartney's 'Girl', radical Greens and environmental philosophers who have done so have been promising the Earth to us while achieving very little. Perhaps, then, it is wise to allow shallow environmentalism to have its say as well.[5]

One further introductory note: environmental anthropocentrists have been accused of being indifferent to nature. But my interpretation of this position is that they tend to be less harsh on people. They therefore are likely to have the ear of their audience. Indeed, morality should not make demands beyond what is reasonable (although it should not simply approve people's current attitudes and behavior). If it is suggested that we all move to part-time jobs and reduce our economic activities to the very basic ones (i.e. what guarantees the fulfillment of basic needs only), people will say 'to hell with morality' and will continue to deplete resources and pollute in the way they have been doing. There is also no point in denying the achievements of science and development. As Jonathon Porritt rightly argues, 'it serves little purpose to deny that enormous progress has been made over the last two hundred years, and there is certainly no question of the politics of ecology harking back to some pre-industrial Golden Age. It wasn't golden; it was often mean, miserable and moronic' ([18], p. 19). Whereas if morality demands gradual changes in modes of behavior, this could be accepted as 'reasonable', and within several years produce the results we have all been longing for almost twenty years now.

But how are people convinced? Philosophers are convinced when the theory is consistent and intuitive; the general public is convinced when the theory is reasonable and appealing. So environmental philosophers have a more difficult task than it seemed at first: they must construct a theory which is both consistent and intuitive on the one hand, and reasonable and appealing on the other. Because if one takes seriously what Deep Ecologists have been arguing about the state of the environment (viz., that it is extremely vulnerable now and that something must be done), then one still has to consider what can convince the general public to change its attitudes and behavior—which, we all know, is very difficult to do anyhow.

INTERGENERATIONAL JUSTICE:
THE THEORY IN VERY ROUGH TERMS

I want to outline the theory I have suggested in broad outline. In fact, for the sake of my argument here, the details of my theory do not matter because the position I want to defend is this: 'Suppose we have a theory of intergenerational justice which is consistent and coherent. It is then not wrong to claim that this theory is the right way to make the connection between sustainability and justice. In addition, this theory is also reasonable and appeals to a wide audience.' The theory's summary in the rest of this section is mainly for the curious reader. Other readers may simply skip this and move to the next section.

Philosophers and political and economic theorists have come to discuss obligations to future generations—and, in particular, the moral grounds for these obligations—for three main reasons: (1) because of the implications of different population policies; (2) because of the problem of fair savings and the multi-generational accumulation of capital; and (3) because of the environmental damage that contemporaries (and previous generations) have inflicted on future generations, and the risks to which they have exposed them while pursuing economic growth and the improvement of the material welfare of contemporaries. These are also the three main aspects of sustainability. Thus, philosophers who have discussed intergenerational justice have argued that the treatment of such problems as the depletion of non-renewable natural resources, the pollution of the soil, the contamination of water, the production of toxic and radioactive waste, the destruction of rare species, conservation, and preservation represents the neglect of our duties not only to other contemporaries and, perhaps, to the environment itself, but also duties to the people of the future. Failure on our side to fulfill these duties incurs much economic cost and considerable difficulties in terms of health and quality of life for future people.

In my book I argue that the question of the moral grounds for our obligations to future generations raises many theoretical difficulties. The most obvious one is that this kind of relationship is different from the regular intra-generational relationship. For example, relevant information is absent. And so, although environmental policies may be seen in terms of intergenerational distribution of access to goods, such as clean air, beautiful landscape, etc., and although we may assume that a certain act or policy will affect future generations, we do not know precisely how bad the consequences of our actions will be. We also don't know what future generations will want or need, what will bring them happiness, and how many people will be affected (indeed, the very existence and identity of future generations depends on our actions today, and, at least theoretically, we can decide not to reproduce). These are the difficulties faced by consequentialist theorists (e.g. utilitarians), when constructing a theory of intergenerational justice.

But contractarian theories find other sorts of difficulties. For example, the basic idea of contractarianism is that a policy is approved if all concerned people would have approved it had they been asked about it. Therefore, the first question which arises is, who will be 'invited' to decide upon the principles of justice between generations: one's contemporaries, all possible people, or all actual people? Once again the difficulty is that our decisions and policies will also affect the identity and number of future people. Hence, we find ourselves in a vicious circle: do we first decide upon the policies (that will determine the identity of future people), or upon the identity of the parties to the contract (who will decide upon the policies)?[6] It is then suggested that if neither of the preceding theories provide satisfactory answers, perhaps our obligations to future generations derive from the sense of a community that stretches and extends over generations and into the future. However, unlike the Burkeian notion of trans-generational community that looks backwards and sees an obligation to continue the heritage of previous generations, this notion of community is based on the argument that we regard the future as part of our 'selves'. These, then, would be the relationships that form the trans-generational community, which constitute the source of our obligations to future generations.

Often, the concept of community is related to face to face interaction. It goes without saying that such interaction does not exist in relations between distant generations. But community is arguably a level of relationships, which stands beyond contractual or legal relations. As such, the trans-generational community is not necessarily defined geographically but rather as a moral entity which does not have to rely on face to face interactions. Instead, it describes a framework from which people derive their cultural and moral identities and from which they draw their values. (In that sense my theory is also based on the idea of trans-generational identity.) It is within this framework that the discourse on the moral and political ideas which constitute social life and identity takes place. This discourse is carried on through critical discussion, mass media, art, literature, academic research, and so on. But is there—and should there be—an interaction of this kind between distant—and not necessarily overlapping—generations?

The answer seems to be affirmative: the moral discourse extends and should extend beyond one's lifetime. There is no reason why, if I want to do something because I think it is good, I should be indifferent to its value if it turns out that it could only be accomplished after my death.[7] And thus, when we conceive ideas or create something, we reflect on their relevance, not only to the political and moral environment in which we live, but also to the political and moral environment of the future. This is illustrated in many spheres of human activity. For example, what is pure mathematics today may become applied mathematics within a few generations. Also several technological inventions that are utilized now will still be useful in a generation or more. The same applies to the humanities and arts, and also to political theory and reflections on the values a society holds. Thus, philosophers consider how the future will view their ideas, and politicians do certain things because they wish to be remembered in the future in a certain way. Indeed, it seems completely arbitrary and groundless to assume that what my contemporary thinks of my values is important, whereas what future persons think is not. Just as contemporaries study and reflect on the ideas of Plato, Kant or Hume, so will future people discuss ideas which were conceived by our contemporaries. Distant generations reflect on each other's cultural and moral ideas, and these reflections are always directed towards the future. In that sense, even our notion of the present is future-oriented. This notion constructs the multi-generational community which extends into the future, and is the source of our obligations to other members of this community, i.e. future generations.

SIX ARGUMENTS OF CRITICISM

The following are the arguments that have been raised against my theory, which—except for one—are all against *any* theory of intergenerational justice:

1. The theory is anthropocentric and too rational and thus only sustains human domination over nature;

2. The theory guarantees the satisfaction of future persons' needs/rights/etc., at the expense of the present poor. Thus it is not justice we are talking about at all.

3. The theory cannot and does not take into account population policies, and thus neglects the most urgent environmental issue.

4. The theory considers only those future generations who are not very remote in time. It therefore neglects serious environmental issues and Green intuitions.

5. This theory is communitarian. But the idea of community is either conservative, hence not radical enough to serve as the moral grounds for radical policies, or simply does not elude the non-identity problem.

6. This theory may at first appearance look different from anti-environmental theories, but it must rest on the notion of nature as capital or as resources; hence it is no better.

These are heavy charges. Let me try and answer them one by one.

1. This argument is that only non-anthropocentric theories are 'valid' environmental philosophy. The question, of course, is what is meant by 'valid'. One way of understanding such a critique is that only non-anthropocentric theory is 'authentic' environmental philosophy. In that case the question of whether the theory of intergenerational justice should be regarded as an 'environmental philosophy' or as 'mainstream philosophy with regard to the environment' is important for the typology of ideologies, but bears no normative implications. The second meaning could be that anthropocentrism is not the *right* way to do environmental philosophy. In that case, sustainable development is an anthropocentric notion, but environmental sustainability is not. So it has been argued that *environmental* philosophers should really care for the state of the environment. Sustainability refers to ecological systems; justice (in environmental philosophy) may then refer to relationships between human beings and other objects in nature.

To answer this, imagine a world in which there is a growing gap between the very rich and the very poor. The very rich form about 1% of the population, whereas the rest 99% are extremely poor, consuming very little, not using aeroplanes or cars, etc. The result will be much less industry, transportation, pollution, toxic waste, and so forth. Those who want 'environmental sustainability', or 'strong sustainability' should favor this. Or shouldn't they?

It seems to me that they should not and will not. This is why we should use the term 'sustainable *development*'. It indicates that we are not indifferent to the needs of the least advantaged populations, and that sustainability—even environmental sustainability—involves social and moral sustainability as well. I would therefore urge non-anthropocentric philosophers to be non-monists as well[8], and to allow anthropocentric thought side by side to biocentric or ecocentric theory. While it is important to argue in support of non-anthropocentrism, it should not imply the abolition of any anthropocentric considerations. Of course, there is a case for non-anthropocentrism; but we shouldn't forget that we also have obligations to other human beings.

At this point, a more spiritualistic critique has been raised. Nicholas Albery, for example, suggested that basing an argument in favor of obligations to future generations can be basically accepted, but it cannot rest on rational argumentation. Rather, he argued, the difficulty 'stems from philosophers trying to construct reasons for concern about posterity without dependence on spirituality, love, compassion or intuition' ([1], p. 64).

But it seems to me that not only is sustainability a very rational notion, dependent on activities such as measurement and scientific calculations, but so also are obligations—especially political ones, of justice—since they are far from being based on love or passion. On the contrary, if justice were so based, love would lose its meaning as an exclusive emotion, whereas these obligations must have to do with inclusive ideas. But more importantly, since the love advocates cannot argue that they simply 'love' all future people—because they do not even know who these people are and how they will behave, etc., then they must be arguing for a certain chain of love: I love my children, they love their children, they will love their children, and since I love my children, I love whom they love, and so forth. But this, again, contradicts the very idea of love; it's not contagious. If Diana loves Charles, but he loves Camellia, Diana is fully justified not to love Camellia. The argument for a chain of love fails; spiritualism is fine, but sustainability and justice are a very rational matter.

A rather more moderate but somehow related critique has been put forward by John Barry [4]. He would rather see the trans-generational self extended to include the 'ecological self.'[9] But this is precisely what I want to avoid. Although I have a lot of sympathy for a variety of arguments of that sort, I do not think they have an appeal beyond the community of already convinced environmental philosophers. The aim in constructing an anthropocentric theory of intergenerational justice is to justify sustainability in terms which are taken from outside the jargon of main stream Green theory. It is all about justifying environmental policies without relating to nature fantasies or to controversial metaphysical assumptions.

2. This argument is put forward by radicals, socialists, and so forth. They claim that talking about future generations is misleading both in terms of justice and of sustainability. By talking about the needs of future people, they claim, the needs of contemporaries are neglected. Thus no justice is done to them. Moreover, this way these people remain ignorant and poor, and ignorance and poverty are the main reasons—so it is claimed—for environmental degradation.[10]

My first answer is that it is time we stop patronizing the least advantaged of contemporaries. Contrary to what many people assume, they do not think only in terms of more food and more basic consumption. The interests of the economically least advantaged surprisingly enough include sustainable development and the interests of future people, because, apparently, just as the rich care about the future, so do the poor. This was proved two years ago when Gallup conducted a survey in the Third World: in all but two countries the state of the environment was either the most or the second most urgent political issue, according to people's views.

It is, however, true that ignorance and poverty contribute to the degradation of the environment (for example, because the poor lack the means of overcoming temporary crises, as well as access to information such as advice on risk-reducing agricultural practices, and because often they have little choice but to overexploit a certain natural resource). It can be further argued that favoring the rights and needs of future people while at the same time ignoring the misery and ignorance of the contemporary poor is unacceptable because it is unjust. But the very idea of sustainability implies not going to one extreme, but rather striking a balance. This is another good reason for not going all the way and adopting the radical green standpoint. If you care more for the non-human environment than for human beings, you eternalize the situation that the least advantaged are ignorant. This is not only unjust and unfair, but also helps the interests of capital to control our common and public lives, thereby sustaining pollution and environmental degradation rather than sustainability. We need a balance between caring for people, their well-being, and caring for the environment. The theory of intergenerational justice provides us with this because it treats the environmental issue as an important part of people's well-being.

3. This argument is that sustainability is a function of basically three parameters. One is the rate of economic, industrial, agricultural, and social activities; the second is the question of the distribution of goods. But, the argument goes on, while the intergenerational theory is sensitive to these two, the most important parameter is population policies. Simple arithmetic shows that the growing number of people is the most serious component of environmental impact assessment. Thus, the challenge goes on, an intergenerational theory that leaves aside population policies has nothing to do with sustainability. The size of the human population is 'an environmental fact like any other'.[11]

But, as argued earlier, sustainability is related not only to the environment, but also to social and moral sustainability. Thus although pessimist theorists like Garret Hardin and William Ophuls and recently Laura Westra are advocates of authoritarian and less democratic regimes, it seems that environmental policies must be taken within the framework of democracy if we want them to be just and sustainable in the full sense of the term.[12] Imposing environmental policies on people who do not understand why they are asked to do this or that misses the idea of sustainability, which is to insure that certain contemporary institutions will also function in the future, that certain goods that are available now will still be available, and that species that exist now and ecosystems that function now will still be there. With regard to institutions, it seems that people do value democracy and liberty. I therefore do not see how one can argue in favor of sustainability and at the same time for imposing population policies against people's wills. These policies have to do with the most intimate and private aspects of our lives. It may well be that we need a lower growth of population (although see the discussion below), but this must be achieved voluntarily. So either people realize this by themselves, in which case there is no need for population policies, or they do not, in which case any population policy will be totalitarian and will alienate people from an environmental consciousness, thereby inflicting more harm then good.

There is, however, a paradox which I only wish to raise as food for thought at this point. According to scientific research, men's fertility has suffered a severe decline in recent years. According to data published in the UK in February 1996, there is a 25% decline in the mobility and number of sperm cells. The reason is claimed to be pollution. So if the state of the environment continues to deteriorate due to the lack of population policies, male fertility will continue to decline, hence there will not be so many people. Then, if indeed there are fewer people there will be less pollution, which means that male fertility will again increase, thereby increasing the number of people. This seems to be a circle. There is no way out of it, and it may indicate that population policies are not relevant here at all.[13]

4. This argument is put forward by people who think that it is not enough, morally speaking, to care for and fulfill our obligations to people who will live ten generations from now. Justice between generations assumes a certain reciprocity or community with the not-yet-born, hence is limited in the scope of time. But, it is

argued, we do have obligations to people who will live in the year 2996 and 3996 as well.

Yes, indeed we do. But one wonders just what they are. In the final analysis, one cannot imagine, or even perceive the world in the year 3996, just as if we bring a person who lived in the first century back to life, s/he wouldn't even know how to name strange things like computers, rockets, or Michael Jackson. There are some things we can and should do for the sake of such remote future people, like, perhaps, conserve aesthetic landscape, although it is not quite clear that they will appreciate what we think is good or beautiful. But even the very assumption that these people will need clean air should not be taken for granted, as many scientists have argued. It seems better to stick to *reasonable* theories, rather than to discuss what we actually (indeed unfortunately) cannot do or even perceive.

5. This set of arguments is against the particular, communitarian theory, presented in my book. First, it is argued that a theory of intergenerational justice is acceptable and feasible, as long as it is not a communitarian one. Second, it is argued that *even* a communitarian theory of intergenerational justice cannot escape the ontological question of potential vs. actual persons.

Let me start with the critique of communitarianism in general, and by implication, to intergenerational relationships and sustainability. There are two sub-arguments here. The first is that counting on the goodwill of the community is too risky. What if there is a certain selfish community, or a very urban one, whose members decide that the best life is one of rapid depletion of resources, and that this is their moral message to future generations?

My answer is that there are two ways to conceive of the trans-generational community. One is put forward by Bryan Norton and Bruce Hannon [16]. It is the community of place. Its advantage is that it connects the notion of one's identity to a sense of place and belonging, thereby inserting a strong motivation to conserve one's environment. The drawback, as I see it, is that this kind of community is vulnerable to the above critique. What if people's sense of place is indeed related to rapid development rather than to sustainability? Moreover, this theory of community is vulnerable to another critique. At the end of the day, in order to have sustainability—strong or weak—we need some kind of global orientation or awareness. So rather than having a consciousness of the local (place), we need a consciousness of the local and the global. I have therefore suggested that the trans-generational community is based on the moral, political and social debate. One may then be a member of various communities simultaneously. For example, one is a member of the English nation, the working class, the community of Kent, the Labor party, the community of academics, a feminist group, the Royal Society for the Protection of Birds, and so on. It is more reasonable to assume that at least a few of these communities will be in favor of conservation, or sustainability, and therefore this model of community is not vulnerable to the critique mentioned above. Also this model is global-oriented, and so is not vulnerable to the other critique.

The second sub-argument against the communitarian theory is that 'positive ethical theories are partly a reaction against ethics based on custom and tradition;

and whatever the attractions of communitarianism, it may be doubted whether it can gain the leverage to achieve radical reform'. 'Since social changes have erased many of the traditional communal and familial ties' the argument continues, 'the change in outlook we now need before we shall pay due respect to the future is likely to be more radical then anything a communitarian ethic can produce' ([12], p. 92).

But is community necessarily a conservative and traditional idea? It may very well be so, if we have in mind the primordial community, based on ethnic or blood relations. But obviously the trans-generational community that extends into the future cannot be such a community, because the identity of the not-yet-born is obscure, to say the least. Nor can the trans-generational community be based on everyday interaction. Rather it is based on the political and moral deliberation which is oriented towards the future and is taking place within the framework of the trans-generational community. Therefore this community is far from being conservative: the main characteristic of this deliberation is critical scrutiny of values and ideas, and thus it is very unlikely that it will lead to any objection to reforms simply in the name of conservatism.

Now there is a second sort of argument, admitting the force of communitarianism, but still claiming that environmental policies have nothing to do with considerations of future generations' rights or intergenerational justice, and that any attempt to base obligations to future people on their rights etc. will crash against the walls of the non-identity problem.[9] The argument starts by suggesting that since the trans-generational community is based on moral similarity (to be distinguished from unanimous agreement on moral questions), and since it is plausible that 'our values are a function of our state of economic and technological development', and since 'it is easy to imagine that increased resource scarcity in the future will erode commitment to liberal democratic norms', then it may well be that 'those people inhabiting that future will not be members of our own intergenerational community'. Indeed, the argument goes on, according to this theory nothing prevents us from depleting resources, since if we deplete, those who will live in the future will live in such scarcity that they will adopt different values, thereby forming a different community, and hence we have no obligation to them.

My first response is that the moral community is based not only on values, but on the debate about them as well; so long as there is a debate going on this may very well be a community. But more importantly, this argument only looks at half of the communitarian theory of intergenerational justice. Those who accept the communitarian argument will see that we start from the point where we do believe that the future (and therefore future people) is part of what constitutes us, hence we acknowledge obligations at least for the not-very-remote future. We therefore start from obligations to conserve. Consequently we are unlikely to deplete resources in a manner which will leave future people in such scarcity that they will adopt different values. Although we have an interest in welfare, we should not look for endless prosperity, precisely because we also have an interest in future people, and in future people thinking highly of us. So if one's motivation is sheer materialistic selfishness, then Elliot is right [9]. But if one has an interest in the future, which is an interest related to one's identity, the latter overrides many materialistic interests. In other words, it may be true that according to the communitarian theory of intergenerational justice if we choose a depletion policy, then 'provided it left people in the further future with lives worth living, then we would have committed no injustice, since those members would not be members of our intergenerational community'[14]. And yet, we would not do this, because we would be miserable had we done so: we would lack this future which is so significant to one's personality.[15]

6. The last critique I want to consider is that, in the final analysis, the intergenerational justice theory tries, but cannot depart from, mainstream anti-environmental premises. Since we are talking about a transfer of goods from contemporaries to future generations, nature must be regarded as capital or as resources. So nature, albeit being distributed fairly among generations, is regarded instrumentally. Indeed, I have argued that aesthetic landscape can be regarded as a resource, and if we have as large as possible definition of resources we will be able to construct a sensible theory of intergenerational justice. But according to this critique the intergenerational justice theory is not a departure from the rationale of those who attach to nature economic value only, which is the source of evil and of environmental degradation.

In reply I would like to distinguish between relating to nature as capital as part of one's ideological standpoint, and relating to nature as resources as an argumentative standpoint for the sake of persuasion, and as, in the final analysis, a metaphor. One, then, would acknowledge intrinsic value in nature, but will adopt this language as a means of persuasion. The former leads to the actual destruction of nature because only instrumental value is considered and because ecological sustainability is pushed aside for the sake of cost-benefit analysis and, indeed, greed. But relating to nature as resource as an argumentative standpoint is different. It is claiming that environmental policies and sustainable development need not (although they can!) be couched in terms of the rights of rocks and mountains, an idea which alienates huge parts of the general public from the Green case. Governments and the public at large will find it more easy to grasp the rationale for sustainable development: it is easier for them to understand that any conception of social justice cannot neglect the effects of the present distribution of resources on the distribution in the future or on the distribution of resources between the present and future generations, than to understand that bees or bears have intrinsic value.[16] Thus, relating to nature as resources as an argumentative standpoint is nothing less than Green Realism or, if you want, down-to-Earth environmentalism.

To conclude, intergenerational justice is justice with sustainability—environmentally, socially and morally. It is also a fertile tool for the Green movement.

NOTES

[1] While writing this paper I benefitted from the hospitality of Oxford Centre for the Environment, Ethics and Society and Mansfield College. An earlier version of the paper was presented at the Keele University Seminar on Sustainability and Justice. I am thankful to Andrew Dobson and the participants for their comments.

[2] By 'shallow' and 'deep' I refer to the distinction made by Naess [15].

[3] For a much broader consideration of the distinction between 'shallow' and 'deep', see Barry, John [3]. Barry argues that this distinction is philosophical rather than political, and that deep ecology has had disproportionate influence among environmental philosophers, which restricted the chances of constructing a working realistic theory. In that sense my argument here sustains his thesis.

[4] For more precise definitions see Jacobs [11] and Kirkby [13].

[5] I elaborate on the difficulties with the radical Green standpoint elsewhere [8].

[6] This is sometimes called the non-identity problem, or the problem of potential vs.actual future persons.

[7] Compare Rolston [19] and Barry, Brian [2].

[8] See Norton [17].

[9] For a comprehensive theory of the ecological self, see Fox [10] and most importantly, Mathews [14].

[10] Bob Brecher, for instance, writes that 'if posterity matters, it matters less than living people do' ([5], p. 77).

[11] Brecher [5]. It should be noted that the German Green party is rather ambivalent about this issue.

[12] I elaborate on this in 'Is liberalism environment friendly?', Social Theory and Practice Vol. 21, 1996.

[13] I have no intention to discuss this in details, because we still have to wait for more scientific evidence. I should, however, admit that at the moment this is speculative on the basis of the recent scientific information.

[14] Although I think that my discussion of human rights prevents such an option.

[15] Elliot admits this, but argues that 'this is all well and good, but it does not seem to have much to do with justice'. I wonder. It seems to me that every theory of justice has to discuss both the principles and the motivation. In other words it answers two questions: how to be just, and why be just. This transgenerational identity is the motivation to be just. The framework of justice and the political reflection of these psychological assumptions is the transgenerational community.

[16] This is true in particular in societies that haven't become accustomed to the idea that other human beings have rights.

BIBLIOGRAPHY

1.   Albery, N.: 1995, 'Planetary Caretakers' *Resurgence*, 173, 63-64.
2.   Barry, B.: 1977, 'Justice Between Generations', in P. Hacker and J. Raz (eds.), *Law, Morality and Society*, Clarendon, Oxford.
3.   Barry J.: 1994, 'The Limits of the Shallow and the Deep: Green Politics Philosophy and Praxis', *Environmental Politics*, 3, 369-394.
4.   Barry, J.: 1996, Review of 'Why Posterity Matters', *Environmental Politics*, 4, 299-300.
5.   Brecher, B.: 1996, 'Eat Your Greens', *Radical Philosophy*, 78, 77-78.
6.   de-Shalit, A.: 1995, *Why Posterity Matters*, Routledge, London.
7.   de-Shalit, A.: 1996, 'Is Liberalism Environmentally Friendly?', *Social Theory and Practice*, 21, 287-315.
8.   de-Shalit, A.: (forthcoming), 'Environmentalism for Europe: One Model?', *Journal of Applied Philosophy*.
9.   Elliot, R.: 1996, 'Contingency, Community and Intergenerational Justice', this volume.
10. Fox, W.: 1995, *Toward a Transpersonal Ecology*, Green Books, Devon.
11. Jacobs, M.: 1996, 'Reflections on the Discourse and Politics of Sustainable Development', (unpublished paper).
12. Johnson, A.: 1995, Review of "Why Posterity Matters", *Environmental Values*, 4, 91-92
13. Kirkby, J.: 1995, *The Earthscan Reader in Sustainable Development*, Earthscan, London.

14. Mathews, F.: 1990, *The Ecological Self*, Routledge, London
15. Naess, A.: 1973, 'The Shallow and the Deep, Long-Range Ecology Movement', *Inquiry*, 16, 95-100.
16. Norton, B. and Hannon B.: 1996, 'Democracy and Sense of Place Values in Environmental Policy', unpublished paper.
17. Norton, B.: 1996, 'Why I am Not a Non-Anthropocentrist', *Environmental Ethics*, 17, 341-359.
18. Porritt, J.: 1984, *Seeing Green*, Basil Blackwell, Oxford.
19. Rolston, H.: 1981, 'The River of Life', in E. Partridge (ed.), *Responsibilities to Future Generations*, Prometheus Books, Buffalo.

MORE THAN THEY HAVE A RIGHT TO:
FUTURE PEOPLE AND OUR FUTURE-ORIENTED PROJECTS[1]

INTRODUCTION

Can our concerns for future people and their well-being be fully accounted for by rights-based considerations? Here I will assume without argument that future people can be said to have rights vis-à-vis us[2] and that they have rights vis-à-vis us. More particularly, I will assume that neither the futurity of future people nor the dependence of their number and identity upon our decisions speak against their having rights vis-à-vis us. Thus rights-based considerations may not just bear upon "Same People Choices" but also upon both types of "Different People Choices" that Derek Parfit distinguishes, including what he calls "Different Number Choices" ([31], pp. 355-56). Also, let us assume that future people actually have general (human) rights vis-à-vis us ([14], pp. 116-119). Thus, our correlative duties are very strong and set a normative framework for most of our decisions concerning future people. Granted, these are huge assumptions to make. But even if we assume that much, there are concerns for future people, that many of us share which cannot be accounted for by rights-based considerations—or so I hope to show in section 1 of this paper.

What I will argue is that rights-based considerations cannot account for important concerns that most of us have for future people. Future people cannot coherently be said to have a right to existence (sections 1.1 and 1.2, below). Further, they cannot be said to have a right to a life that is well above a minimal level of well-being or to a particular way of life (section 1.3, below). Then, considerations based on the rights of future people cannot fully guide us in a good number of decision-making situations concerning the future. Nonetheless, we might believe that it is important that there be future people and that they have lives that are well worth living. In section 2 of this paper, I will suggest that we can account for some of our concerns for future people in terms of duties towards them to which no rights of future people correspond. While rights-considerations may be important in accounting for our relations to future generations they do not amount to the whole story.

1. LIMITS OF A RIGHTS-BASED ACCOUNT
1.1 WE HAVE NO OBLIGATION TO PROCREATE

Quite plausibly we may want to attribute some qualified right to survival to future people. For example, we might want to say the following: As with our

Nick Fotion and Jan C. Heller (eds.), Contingent Future Persons, 137-156.
© 1997 *Kluwer Academic Publishers. Printed in the Netherlands.*

contemporaries, future people have an interest in remaining alive or an interest in being able to participate in future events and actions and in achieving valued goals. Based on that interest both our contemporaries and future people have a *prima facie* right not to be killed when innocent and against their will; future people have such a right to survival against all, including us; we can violate future people's rights now. Saying that does not imply that future people have rights now. Rather, we may rely on an account that says ([20], 98-102): Not only can we now, at a time t_1, harm an interest that exists only at some later time t_2, that is, the interest of future people in their survival, but the bearer of the interest also has to exist only at time t_2.

Could one not argue that a person who is said to have a right to survival based on her interest in survival also has a right to the necessary presuppositions for her existence? I do not think so. It is one thing to harm someone's present or prospective interest in survival. It is a very different thing to hinder such an interest from coming into existence. In explaining this difference I rely on David Heyd's account of the distinction between "actual" future people and "possible" future people. This distinction is based on a difference between decision-making contexts wherein we may relate ourselves to future people in different ways: If we make a decision about an action or a policy and the likelihood of the existence of future people is (relatively) *independent* of our performing the action or carrying out the policy, then these future people are *actual* future people for us with respect to their existence and in this decision-making context. If, on the other hand, we make a decision about an action or a policy and the likelihood of the existence of future people is (highly) *dependent* on our performing the action or carrying out the policy, then these future people are *possible* future people for us with respect to their existence and in this decision-making context.[3]

We can harm the prospective interest of someone in her survival only if the interest exists independently of the action under consideration. In other words, we can harm the interests of actual future people in their survival. On the other hand, when we make a decision on whether to reproduce or not, the existence of the possible child and its corresponding interests in survival may vary considerably depending upon what our decision is. Hindering the coming into existence of a bearer of an interest in survival does not harm such an interest. We know with certainty that hindering the coming into existence of a bearer of an interest precludes the possibility of the existence of such an interest. Thus, the person's existence and corresponding interests cannot properly be used as a factor for the decision on whether or not to bring the person into existence. We cannot harm possible future people. Then, claiming that actual future people have rights vis-à-vis us now does not commit us to claiming that possible future people have a right to existence against us. Not to bring about the existence of future people does not harm any interest of 'these' people. Possible people have no right to be brought into existence. We do not have an obligation to procreate.[4]

1.2 CAUSING THE CESSATION OF HUMAN LIFE ON EARTH

Can considerations based on rights of future people bear upon our choices of population policies? Let us first imagine that we could make a decision on the very existence of future people, that is, the continuation of human life on earth. In this decision-situation all future people are possible future people for us. Can rights of future people speak against our taking a decision to cause the cessation of human life on earth? No, they cannot. Possible future people cannot be said to have a right to existence.

Admittedly, it is hard to imagine that we could ever be in a position in which we relate to future life on earth simply as a matter of our procreational choice without there being any interests of actual future people to be taken into account. In many, if not most cases procreation is not the consequence of choice and, if people do choose to procreate, this tends to reflect the values and interests either of the prospective parents alone or, in any case, of not many others besides them. Prospective parents' freedom of making a procreational choice is backed by the idea that being able to choose freely whether to procreate or not is somehow constitutive of leading an autonomous life. For all practical purposes it is pointless to speculate about the possible circumstances of our making a decision concerning the continuation of human life on earth.[5] It might be worth noting, however, that if we were to face collectively a procreational choice concerning the continuation of human life on earth, there are no considerations based on the interests and rights of future people that would speak against our coming up with the decision to cause the cessation of human life on earth.[6] Thus, were we to face a choice between a future of people who all have lives worth living and a future of no people, considerations based on future people's rights could not guide us. However we chose, our choice would reflect solely our preferences and interests. At the same time, at least some of us strongly believe that, even under the highly speculative circumstances of this choice, we *should* prefer a future of people who all have lives worth living to a future of no people. For those holding this belief, preferring the continuation of human life on earth is not simply a matter of our interests or preferences. Rights-based considerations cannot account for this belief.

1.3 CHOOSING AMONG POLICIES WITH
QUALITATIVELY DIFFERENT OUTCOMES

The notion of collectively deciding on the very existence of future people is highly unrealistic, mainly because most cases of procreation are not the consequence of reflexive choice. Thus, when we are choosing a population policy, we may at best hope to be able to influence the reproductive choices of a segment of the population ([19], pp. 154, 198). This, predictably, will have some effect on the total number of future people and on the quality of life of those who will live in the future. Some future people will live in consequence of reproductive choices that were influenced by the population policy adopted, but the procreation of most future people is going to be beyond control. In choosing the population policy these people are actual future people for us. Now, it can be the case that we may choose between a population policy P_1 that will predictably lead to violations of rights of actual future people and a population policy P_2 that will not violate future people's rights. Other things equal, P_2 is to be preferred to P_1. But things are not likely to be equal. P_1 and P_2 are likely to have different implications for the limitations to be imposed on the freedom to procreate. Only some contemporaries' procreational behaviour can be influenced. It is likely that P_2 will imply the more burdensome limitations on these people's procreational freedoms.

Choosing, then, among population policies raises the question of whether it would be just to limit the procreational freedom of those whose freedom can be limited when many other people's freedom to procreate is beyond control. Even if we think that restricting a minority's freedom to procreate can be just under these circumstances, we will also have to ask how much we may restrict a minority's freedom of procreation for the sake of, *inter alia*, the offspring of those whose freedom cannot be restricted. Furthermore, we will have to think about how to distribute the burdens of implementing a population policy over generations. Here I do not even want to begin answering these questions. It is important to note, however, that when we choose among population policies, we will often have to balance rights claims of contemporaries against rights claims of actual future people.[7]

Balancing rights claims of actual future people against those of contemporaries, however, may not account for all of our concerns for future people. Let us say that we face a situation in which we may choose between population policies $P_1{}^*$ and $P_2{}^*$. Choosing population policy $P_1{}^*$ will predictably lead to a future $F_1{}^*$ in which no future people's rights are violated. They live decent lives. Choosing $P_2{}^*$ will predictably lead to a future $F_2{}^*$ in which people live lives above the level of a merely decent life. In $F_2{}^*$ there will be sufficient resources available to provide tertiary education for all those who demand it. These resources are not available in $F_1{}^*$. Will people's right to education be violated in $F_1{}^*$? Hardly so. The duties that are grounded in a right to education depend on the circumstances under which people have a right to education. People might plausibly be said to possess a right to tertiary education only if there are sufficient resources available for the satisfaction of all demands based on the right.[8] The lack of these resources in $F_1{}^*$ might reflect the fact that many more people are living in $F_1{}^*$ than in $F_2{}^*$. Thus, considerations based on the rights of future people do not allow us to prefer one future over the other. At the same time, we might believe that we *should* prefer $F_2{}^*$ over $F_1{}^*$.

This insufficiency of rights considerations in guiding our choices concerning future people is not restricted to our choices of population policies. Rather, it will show whenever we are choosing between securing decent conditions of life for actual future people and securing conditions under which actual future people will be able to live lives above the level of mere decency. For example, assuming that future people have general (human) rights against us, there are considerations based on the rights of future people that prohibit us from choosing a policy of depletion. However, such considerations might well be insufficient in guiding us in choosing among alternative conservation policies that have different consequences with respect to the quality of life future people can be expected to enjoy.

Clearly, considerations based on the rights of future people cannot or cannot fully account for all the concerns we might have for future people. Considerations based on rights of future people do not speak against our taking a decision to cause the cessation of human life on earth. On the basis of such considerations we could not prefer a future with people who all have lives worth living instead of a future with no people. Considerations based on the rights of future people, furthermore, cannot guide us in choosing among policies that have different consequences with respect to the quality of life of future people when we do not violate future people's rights by choosing any of the alternative policies. Thus, considerations based on the rights of future people do not allow us to prefer a future with people who have lives far above the level of decency to a future with people with lives just above the level of decency.

What considerations besides rights-based considerations can guide us in our relations to future people? In the following section I will discuss one alternative type of consideration. I explore the idea that we might have duties towards future people that have no correlatives to their rights vis-à-vis us, and that these duties can partly address those widely shared concerns about future people which cannot be accounted for by rights-based considerations.

2. DUTIES TOWARDS FUTURE PEOPLE BASED ON RESPECT FOR PAST PEOPLE'S AND CONTEMPORARIES' FUTURE-ORIENTED PROJECTS

I shall argue that the respect that we owe to past people's activities that were meant to benefit us as well as more remote future people can amount to a duty. Governments and individuals can be under a duty not wilfully to destroy the conditions that allow future people to choose to continue those projects that past people or presently living people take to be valuable and that allow future people to make good use of the results of the projects that past people and presently living people have been pursuing.

2.1 STRONGLY FUTURE-ORIENTED PROJECTS

People's self-understanding transcends the boundaries of their life-time in both directions: the past and the future. They pursue projects that stand in a tradition of past people's earlier endeavour.[9] The projects are situated in practices that are historically formed and that themselves are defined against the background of past practices and the possibility of other practices being realized. The value of people's projects partly depends on the value of the practices on which they are based.

People's self-understanding in pursuing their projects can transcend their life-time into the future. It is not simply that people can care about what future people might think of them, how future people will evaluate their endeavour and their success in them. Rather, many if not most people pursue projects that may be valuable for future people if there should be future people with certain dispositions, tastes and so on. Pursuing such projects is typically worthwhile whether future people are going to benefit from them or not. These projects are valuable to the people who pursue them and, possibly, to some of their contemporaries.

However, there are also projects that are future-oriented in a strong sense. From the perspective of those who individually or collectively are pursuing such projects, it is constitutive for their meaning that mainly future people are to benefit from them or that future people are likely to continue to pursue them. The planting of trees that will not bear fruit for many years to come is the classical example of the former type of project.[10] But there are, too, the large investments in the construction of, for example, (public) buildings and land reclamation projects and the investments in the conservation of knowledge and cultural achievements, as carried out by many societies establishing and maintaining libraries and museums as well as by the preserving of historical monuments. These large investments are likely to be justifiable only under the assumption that in the main it is future persons who are going to benefit from them.[11] More exclusively concerned with the well-being of future people are investigations into the questions, for example, of how the oceans can be more effectively used as a resource base for food by, say, the farming of algae, or research into the question of how deserts might be turned into fertile soil. Investments in projects like these are justifiable only under the assumption that large numbers of future people (often of generations we cannot possibly know) are likely to benefit from them. Without our making this assumption, these investments would lose their point—or at least partly so.[12]

People also pursue projects from which not only mainly future people are meant to benefit, but projects that would lose their point if future people were not likely to continue to pursue them. People pursue scientific projects whose success depends on intergenerational cooperation. The project of compiling, writing, editing and re-editing ambitious encyclopedias[13] involves not only many people but, indeed, people of many generations. Also, while we obviously want to create benefits for future people by investigating alternative forms of energy, these investigations often depend on the cooperation of researchers of several generations for their success, as can be illustrated by the research undertaken into nuclear fusion. The existence of nuclear fusion energy and its vast potential was identified in the 1920s. Exploratory research on the possibility of releasing the energy began in the decade 1946-1955. By about 1970 the research had reached such a stage that it appeared worthwhile to build a large experimental infrastructure with sufficient capacity directly to explore conditions approaching those needed for self-sustained thermonuclear reactions. The fusion research programmes of the countries of Western Europe were combined in such an experiment, called the Joint European Torus (JET) and commissioned by the European Council of Ministers in 1983. The International Thermonuclear

Experimental Reactor (ITER), initiated in 1987, represents the first step to world-wide collaboration between the EC, USA, the Russian Federation and Japan, under the auspices of the International Atomic Energy Agency. Optimistically judged, these efforts may demonstrate the technological feasibility of gaining surplus energy out of fusion in 50 years time ([35], [11]). Investigations into other alternative forms of energy have a similar history.

It is true that such scientific projects are often expected to show preliminary results in the near future and are thus partly justifiable in terms of the benefits that accrue from them to contemporaries or the next generations of future people. Indeed, while those who invest their work-time at an early stage in the execution of the project cannot know for certain whether the project will show significant results in the end, future people working on the same project will be able to reach their results only on the basis of the preliminary results handed down to them by their predecessors. Nevertheless, the results and the corresponding benefits that could justify today's investments are not expected to be gained in the near future.

It is not only scientific projects that depend for their success on intergenerational cooperation. The goals of certain policies depend on such cooperation for their success. Some policies, such as the use of atomic energy with the side-effect of producing atomic waste, have negative consequences for remote future people while possibly at the same time being beneficial to present generations and their successor generations. Other policies, such as a policy of conserving biological resources, will mainly benefit remote future people but impose burdens on present generations and their successor generations. Without their successor generations adopting a policy of the same kind and imposing certain burdens on themselves, present generations cannot achieve their goal of preserving these resources for remote future people. The goal of our policy, then, can be realized only if future generations of people are equally willing to bear the costs of the policy for the sake of remote future people. Only if there is intergenerational cooperation in achieving the goal of the policy, can the goal of the policy be realized.

2.2 LIVING IN A SOCIETY THAT IS OPEN TO THE FUTURE

Being successful in the pursuit of valuable projects is of the utmost importance to the well-being of people. Thus, for those many contemporaries who pursue projects of the two types as characterized in the preceding paragraphs, it is important for their well-being that they can place the pursuit of their projects in an ongoing and unfolding story. In particular, it is important to them that they can expect the continuance of human life on earth under such conditions that future people will be able to understand the point and value of the projects they have been pursuing, that they can make good use of them or may choose to continue pursuing them. Being able meaningfully to choose a project whose success partly depends on intergenerational cooperation presupposes living in a society of a certain quality. It presupposes living in a society that is sufficiently open to the future to allow that there be future people who, in turn, are able to choose to continue valuable projects that their predecessors pursued before them.

For future people to be able to make good use of our efforts in conserving knowledge or of the scientific results handed down to them and for them to be in a position to choose to continue long-term projects that depend on intergenerational cooperation for their success, a number of conditions must be fulfilled. First, future people will be able to pursue valuable activities and projects only if certain material conditions obtain. Depending on the project, at the very minimum these conditions will have to be held at a level above that of people who are primarily occupied with survival; people should not have to be concerned, every day anew, solely with the satisfaction of their basic physical needs. For the pursuit of many of those projects that we take to be particularly valuable, for example, the pursuit of a professional career such as becoming a violinist, it is essential that people, for the most part, do not have to concern themselves with having their basic needs fulfilled, for their success in pursuing such projects turns in large part on their being able fully to concentrate on their pursuit.

But, equally important and second, they must be able to choose to pursue these valuable activities, and for that these activities must be known to them so that they can aim at them in a way which is consistent with their continuation and prosperity, when that is desirable ([40], p. 20). We cannot invent the valuable activities we want to pursue out of nothing. On the contrary, valuable activities are typically replete with details that make it impossible for future people to engage in them except by means of internalising, within a process of socialisation, the forms of conduct that constitute them, that make for the successful pursuit of such activities. Hence, for future people to be able to continue valuable activities and practices, they will have to engage in social practices with us that will make the acquisition of the required implicit knowledge possible for them. Future people sharing in social practices is also a necessary condition for their being able to choose between continuing projects and activities and rejecting or deviating from them. In other words, they must be in a position to know what counts as the continuation of a project. This is possible only against the background of social practices that not only allow for the continuation of projects and activities but also establish the standards for judging what constitutes continuation of and deviation from long-established practices and activities.

Having an adequate range of options to choose from is constitutive of an autonomous life. For us today, the range of valuable options to choose from importantly includes pursuing what I have called (strongly) future-oriented options. Saying that implies neither that people could not live an autonomous life without pursuing projects of this kind nor that living a good life depends on being able to choose among a range of options that includes such options. It does imply, however, that for those of us who are pursuing projects that have this orientation, success in them is important for our well-being and that our being able to choose among valuable options that include such options that have a strong orientation towards the future is constitutive of a good life. In other words, being able to choose meaningfully to pursue future-oriented projects is a contingent condition of the good life, a condition that can prevail in a society and seems to prevail in our society.

As I pointed out above, the existence of options with that orientation consists in part of the existence of a society that is open to the future. Thus, for the great number of our contemporaries who are actually pursuing projects whose point cannot fully be understood without taking into account their strong orientation towards the future, living in a society of this quality is important to their well-being. Living in such a society is not only relevant to the well-being of those who are actually pursuing such projects. Rather the value of living in such a society consists in people being meaningfully able to choose among valuable options that include those options that imply pursuing projects that are partly constituted by their strong orientation towards the future. For these options to be available to us, we must have good reasons to believe that future people are likely to be in a position to choose to make good use of our having chosen so or even to continue to pursue the projects of their predecessors. In other words, we must have good reasons to believe that future people's range of options is itself partly constituted by their being able to choose to continue the projects of their predecessors or to make good use of the results of their having pursued certain projects. Thus, living in a society that is open to the future in the specified sense is of value to both presently living people and future people. Living in such a society is valuable for presently living people only if they have good reasons to believe that it will benefit future people as well.

Living in a society open to the future in the sense specified is best understood as a public good ([39], pp. 198-203). The benefits that accrue from living in such a society are not subject to voluntary control by anyone other than each potential beneficiary controlling her share of the benefits. Different people will benefit from living in such a society to different degrees, but no member of the society can be involuntarily excluded from the enjoyment of living in such a society.[14] All members of such a society benefit from living in such a society in that they may choose a project that is partly constituted by a strong orientation towards the future. Assuming that pursuing such projects is a valuable option and that, for us, an adequate range of options to choose from importantly includes the option to pursue projects with that orientation, living in such a society is generally beneficial to its members. At the same time, not all members are likely to end up choosing such a project. Thus, different members will benefit differently from living in such a society. The degree to which they benefit depends, however, on their character, interests, and dispositions, and cannot be directly controlled by others. Nor, of course, do people themselves have perfect control over these factors. A second feature of public goods is that their enjoyment is shared by all in a non-competitive way. That is, the enjoyment of one person does not detract from that of others ([40], p. 9). When a society provides the public good of being future-oriented, my choice of pursuing a future-oriented project normally does not undermine your chance of mastering a future-oriented project.[15] Thus, the social conditions on which the existence of the options to pursue strongly future-oriented projects depends are plausibly analyzed as the public good of living in a society that is open to the future in the sense I specified above. By being constitutive of the existence of highly valuable options the public good is itself highly valuable.

Individuals may want to realize an autonomous life in the pursuance of projects for whose existence the existence of a specific public good is constitutive. Typically, an individual cannot be said to have a right to live in a society in which the public good on whose existence the possibility of pursuing such projects depends is realized. Individuals are thought not to have a right to live in a society of a certain character, though an individual's interest in living in a society of a certain character is clearly a reason to develop it in that direction. Why so? Because an individual has a right only if an aspect of her well-being is a sufficient reason for holding some other person or persons to be under a duty.[16] Providing the public good in question depends on the contribution of many, if not most, members of the society. An individual's interest in living in a society that is open to the future in the sense specified and that allows the individual to realize her autonomy in the pursuance of projects of a specific kind is not likely to be strong enough to impose a duty on people to make her society and environment so ([39], pp. 201-2, [41], [1]).

This is not to underestimate the importance to an individual person of the public good of living in a future-oriented society. Indeed, living in a society of that character is likely to be more important to an individual than many things she has a right to, say, her right vis-à-vis a friend to keep his promise to meet her next Tuesday afternoon. However, as I noted above, neither living a good life nor living an autonomous life depends on living in a society that is open to the future. Thus, the legitimate interests of many people can be thought to conflict with an individual's interest in pursuing future-oriented projects. Nor, because it is possible only in a society of a certain character, is it likely that an individual's interest in continuing to pursue a certain type of project is strong enough to hold anyone under a duty to maintain that society and environment as it is. Of course, there are costs involved in being disrupted in pursuing one's projects and in having to adopt another one, but these costs to an individual are not likely to be so weighty as to legitimate holding many people, if not most members of the society under a duty to preserve the environment or the character of the society by keeping up their cooperative schemes. Though being forced to give up one's future-oriented projects is costly, it is highly likely that after a person was disrupted in the pursuit of one such project she will afterwards succeed in adopting a project that lacks this specific quality. Often people can successfully change their projects.[17]

Future people are meant to benefit from these projects by being able either to choose to make use of the results reached by their predecessors or by continuing the pursuit of these projects. It is highly unlikely, however, that a future individual can be said to have a right vis-à-vis us that we pursue such projects. At least, we cannot be said to have an obligation to future people to undertake most of the future-oriented projects that we are actually undertaking. First, future people cannot coherently be said to have a right to existence (see above, section 1.1 and 1.2). Second, what rights those who will live are going to be entitled to enjoy will partly depend on the environmental and societal conditions under which they will live (see above, section 1.3). Third, we are in a position to influence these conditions. Thus, it is highly unlikely that our undertaking most of the projects that we undertake and that are future-oriented in the sense specified above is a necessary condition for not violating future people's rights.

As has been often observed, the current 'Western' style of life is, morally speaking, highly short-sighted and likely to result in violations of the rights of future people by degrading the general conditions of their lives.[18] Some of the future-oriented projects that we are pursuing, such as research into the question of how we can make more effective use of the ocean as a nutritional resource, are likely to have positive consequences for the general conditions of the lives of future people, with the result that they can be expected to counteract the negative consequences of our way of life. If that is so, then a change in this way of life rather than the adoption of projects that can somewhat compensate for its negative consequences is likely to be required to protect future people against violations of their rights.[19] Other future-oriented projects of ours are meant to preserve highly valuable aspects of our particular way of life for future people. For example, Derek Parfit has suggested that we should preserve for future people the possibility of enjoying the most valuable experiences of our own culture, such as, for example, the experience of listening to a first class performance of Mozart's music ([31], pp. 161-63, [22], pp. 81-82). Clearly, future people cannot be said to have a right to that.[20]

2.3 INHERITED PUBLIC GOODS

The fact that presently living people are not the first people to pursue future-oriented projects tends, however, to complicate our moral relations to future people to some degree. Or so, at any rate, I should like to suggest. Presently living people have inherited goods from past people either by mere luck or because past people wanted to benefit them by bequeathing these goods. Here I am interested only in the latter case. Some goods bequeathed to presently living people are individual goods. As lawful heirs of specific past persons, some of us may have a right to what those persons intended us to possess, should there be sufficient moral reason to recognize the disputed right to pass on private property and to inherit it. Other goods were handed on to all of us, that is, to all members of a specific society or all presently living people. We all inherit a social order, a cultural tradition, uncontaminated water, techniques of land cultivation and so on, not as heirs of private will-makers but as members of an ongoing society or simply by being descendants of past people.

What can be a quality of individual goods bequeathed by specific past persons to presently living individuals is typical of inherited public goods such as constitutions, civil liberties, universities, parks, water, techniques of extracting resources and so on: We inherit them not as sole beneficiaries but as persons able to share and pass on these goods to our descendants. As Annette Baier puts it: "It was, presumably, not for this generation in particular that public spirited persons in past generations saved or sacrificed" ([3], p. 173). The public goods we inherit from our predecessors are often extremely valuable to us and they might also be important for the well-being of future people. I will suggest that the respect owed to our predecessors' sacrifices and savings, which were intended to benefit not only us but more remote future people as well, amounts to a general obligation not to dispose of or use up those goods for their own private interests. For example, it would be wrong for us to destroy a highly advanced system of tertiary education that we inherited from our predecessors for the sake of gaining a more luxurious life.

Future people certainly do not have a right to tertiary education. Like ourselves they have no right to their predecessors' achievement of having founded and passed on to them universities including the institutions supporting and financing them. But we owe respect to the sacrifices and the good intentions of past people in passing on public goods to their descendants, including us as well as more remote future people. Future people can blame us for not having respected our predecessors' sacrifices and good intentions in bequeathing public goods to both us and them. Had we, as the intervening generation between them and their public-spirited predecessors, destroyed the public good of higher education for our greater luxury, future people could certainly blame us for not having passed on a public good to them that was intended to benefit them as much as us and that we would have passed on to them had we not acted in an irresponsible and ill-willed manner.[21]

The respect that we owe to certain efforts, sacrifices, and good intentions of past people is simply an instance of the respect that we generally owe to people's highly valuable activities and the conditions that are constitutive of them, that is, the social practices in which these activities are embedded and on whose existence the possibility of people pursuing these activities depends.[22] We also owe this respect to the highly valuable activities of our contemporaries. Though the possibility of our choosing future-oriented projects is merely a contingent condition for our realization of an autonomous life, for those people for whom an adequate range of choice implies having the possibility of choosing future-oriented options, this range of choice is most important; further, under such conditions, pursuing future-oriented projects is highly valuable for those of us who actually do so. No one will want to deny, I assume, that we owe respect to highly valuable activities of past and present people. Also, our owing respect to highly valuable activities and their constitutive conditions is completely independent of whether we happen to have the talent, character, or interests to pursue these projects ourselves or to benefit from past people's activities. Thus, the respect owed to past and present people's highly valuable activities and their constitutive conditions minimally amounts to a general duty (of individuals and governments) not to dispose of and use up these goods for our private interests, say, for the sake of gaining a more luxurious life. Carrying out the duty serves a good, the protection of which is thought to be of such importance that people are thought to have categorical reasons for doing so, that is, reasons whose validity does not derive from the contingent desires of the people to whom they apply.[23]

To whom do we owe this general duty? I analyzed, above, the constitutive conditions for strongly future-oriented activities in terms of a public good. The supposed duty not to dispose of them is then not owed to individuals. An individual typically does not have a right to a public good. Rather, these duties are owed to the society as a whole. The duties are based on the interest of members of the community generally in the existence of these goods. More particularly, they are based on the interest of past, present, and future people in living in an ongoing society that is open to the future. It can be said to be in the interest of past people since the success of some of their projects critically depends on the possibility of prospective inter-generational cooperation in pursuing the projects or on the possibility of more remote future people being among the beneficiaries of their efforts and sacrifices. Also, it is in the interest of particularly those present members of the community who are pursuing projects whose possibility depends on the public good in question. Finally, it is in the interest of those who will benefit from their predecessors having pursued these projects. Governments certainly have a duty not irresponsibly to dispose of public goods in whose existence the citizens have a strong interest. It is one of the main functions of a government to serve the members of its society by securing the conditions under which the public goods of the society can be preserved and by improving society by creating new public goods where this is feasible. Members of a society enjoying public goods may well have a duty to do their share in providing and protecting public goods. For example, they may well have a duty to contribute financially to the preservation of public parks. In any case, they have a duty not to, say, misuse a public park as their private rubbish dump.[24]

How is this duty to be understood in the wider context of how we individually and collectively may relate to what was bequeathed to us? Importantly, the duty is compatible with the idea that the heirs of individual goods as well as the heirs of public goods can legitimately refuse to accept what is bequeathed to them, even if these goods could have been highly valuable to them. People can have morally valid reasons for doing so. What is a good to one person is not necessarily a good to another. For example, some people pursue projects of such character that the acceptance of material individual goods is detrimental to their well-being. Such people might have good reasons for not wanting to be put in a position in which they had to make a decision on how best to dispose of material goods they inherited. Certainly, an individual's right to choose her own way of life can override her duty to respect past people's actions which are intended to benefit her by bequeathing individual goods to her. At the same time, it is true that the individual could have chosen a way of life in which the same bequeathal would have been constitutive for her living a good life.

Much the same is true for public goods. What is a public good in one society at one time may not be a good for people at some future time. We do not have to deny the value of a public good to our predecessors in order to argue that we should get rid of it or replace it with some other good that suits us better. First, human affairs often can be collectively organized in a number of alternative ways, none of which can be said to be better than the other. When we change our predecessors' way of collectively organizing, say, the raising of children, the change might be valuable not because our way of raising children is better, but because the change reflects our autonomous choice of how we want to organize our common life. We might well have chosen to stick to our predecessors' way of raising children, and the corresponding practices and institutions that they bequeathed to us would then have been highly valuable to us. Second, such a change will often reflect not only our legitimate interest in collectively choosing our way of life, but also the changed social, economic and environmental conditions in which we find ourselves. Indeed, in contemporary societies with their generally fast rate of social and economic change people will often be induced to change and replace public goods they inherited. Given that our predecessors could not possibly have fully conceived how society would develop, it is highly likely that at the same time as we show respect for what they bequeathed to us, we also use the inheritance in ways that they could not possibly have been intended or predicted. Much the same will be true for our descendants even though we have comparatively greater power to affect the well-being of future people as well as a comparatively more extensive knowledge of the long-term effects of our policies.[25]

I have stated two reasons for people to change and replace the (public) goods that they inherited even though those goods were highly valuable to their predecessors and could have been highly valuable for them. Obviously, there is a third reason for changing and replacing (public) goods: Our predecessors might have been badly mistaken in matters of the organization of society or of certain aspects of their social life. Then they were mistaken, too, in believing that they could have benefited us by passing on their social order to us. We hardly owe much respect to the mistaken intentions of past people and none to anyone's malicious intentions. There is nothing wrong with disposing of a public evil.[26]

Thus, we owe respect to highly valuable goods that our predecessors bequeathed to us as well as more remote future people and also owe respect to the highly valuable future-oriented projects of our contemporaries. Owing such respect gives rise to a general duty not wilfully to destroy the inherited goods and the conditions that are constitutive of the persons' pursuit of future-oriented projects. In other words, it gives rise to a general duty not wilfully to destroy the social practices on whose existence the possibility of people pursuing future-oriented projects depends. We are under a general duty not to destroy the conditions of living in a society that is open to the future. The duty as stated neither obligates us to make good use of our predecessors' projects or to continue in the pursuit of the projects of our predecessors. Nor does the duty obligate us to do what we can in guaranteeing that future people will benefit from the projects we and our predecessors have been pursuing or that future people will continue in pursuing them. We as well as future people can be legitimate in not accepting what was bequeathed to us and in changing and replacing the goods we inherited, even if these goods might have been highly valuable to us. Rather, the duty obligates us to sustain opportunities for future people, such that they can benefit from their predecessors' efforts and continue to pursue the projects they choose.

CONCLUSION

I granted for the sake of the argument in this paper that rights-based considerations bear upon both "Same People Choices" and "Different People Choices." But, as I showed in section 1, considerations based on the rights of future people cannot or cannot fully account for all the concerns we might have for future people. Considerations based on rights of future people do not speak against our taking a decision to cause the cessation of human life on earth. Thus, we cannot prefer a future with people who all have lives far above the level of decency to a future with no people on the basis of such considerations. Considerations based on the rights of future people, furthermore, cannot guide us in choosing among policies that have different consequences with respect to the quality of life of future people when we do not violate their rights by choosing any of the alternative policies. Thus, considerations based on the rights of future people do not allow us to prefer a future with people whose lives greatly exceed the level of decency to a future with people whose lives barely exceed the level of decency.

In section 2, I suggested that the widely shared concerns about the continuation of human life on earth at a high level of well-being can, at least in part, be accounted for by a duty towards future people not to destroy the conditions of life in a society that is open to the future. We owe respect to highly valuable goods that our predecessors bequeathed to us as well as more remote future people, and we also owe respect to the highly valuable future-oriented projects of our contemporaries. Owing such respect gives rise to a general duty not wilfully to destroy the inherited goods and the conditions that are constitutive of persons' pursuit of future-oriented projects. In other words, owing such respect gives rise to a general duty not wilfully to destroy the social practices on whose existence the possibility of people pursuing future-oriented projects depends. This duty towards future people has no correlative in rights of future people against us. To inherit past generations' and our future-oriented projects and the benefits that are likely to accrue from them is beyond of what future people can be said to have a right to vis-á-vis us.[27]

NOTES

[1] For highly valuable comments and criticisms on a related paper I am grateful to Joseph Raz, Catherine Framm, David Heyd, Stanley L. Paulson, Thomas Pogge, Barbara Reiter, and H. Ph. Visser't Hooft.

[2] Whether (remote) future people can be said to have rights vis-à-vis us has been disputed for some time. See the early collection of papers, [47] and [33]; interesting recent contributions to the debate include [15], [34]. Some philosophers have argued that (remote) future people cannot be said to have rights vis-à-vis us. Most vehemently so [46] and [13].

[3] See David Heyd ([19], pp. 97-103), and Trudy Govier ([17], p. 106). While I rely on the distinction as introduced by Govier and Heyd, my wording differs from both. Govier distinguishes between 'epistemically possible people', and 'volitionally possible people'. She wants to stress that all future people are in an epistemic sense possible: we can only claim to have good reasons to believe that it is highly probable that there will be future people. Though this fact is of relevance with respect to both the types of rights we can attribute to future people as well as the weight we should give to these rights, I believe that the likelihood of there being people in the foreseeable future is so high that it is not

misleading to speak of actual future people as long as we keep in mind that we can know of future people only in terms of probability. Heyd distinguishes between 'actual future people' and 'potential future people'. In certain contexts foetuses have been called potential future people, relying on an Aristotelian concept of something developing into something else in the course of normal circumstances. Here I am not concerned with questions concerning the criteria for being a person.

[4] Contrary to the position Heyd put forward in ([19], p. 122) I have argued that the way in which he has characterized the distinction between actual and possible people permits us to explain not only that possible people cannot be said to have a right, against us, to existence, but also another widely held belief: All children have a right vis-à-vis their parents to the effect that their parents not act in a way likely to lead to their birth where the parents are in a position to know that the life of the child, should the child be born, will not be worth living. See [28] and [17], p. 111.

[5] However, studies on the climatic implications of a war in which weapons of mass extermination are used suggest that the possibility cannot be excluded that human decisions could lead to the termination of human life. See [27] and [51].

[6] Indeed, Ulrich Horstmann in [21] argues for a conscious collective decision to terminate the continuation of human life. Also, G. E. Moore states: "In order to prove that murder, if it were so universally adopted as to cause the speedy extermination of the race, would not be good as a means, we should have to disprove the main contention of pessimism--namely that the existence of human life is on the whole an evil. And the view of pessimism, however strongly we may be convinced of its truth or falsehood, is one which never has been either proved or refuted conclusively" ([29], p. 156).

[7] For an analysis and discussion of the special problems involved in weighing the interests (and rights claims) of actual future people against those of currently living people see [6], ([23], pp. 61-83), ([8], pp. 52-81), ([5], pp. 189-203), [12], [9].

[8] This reflects the dynamic character of rights. Rights "are not merely the grounds of existing duties. With changing circumstances they can generate new duties" ([39], p. 186, see p. 185); also ([15], p. 164).

[9] Indeed, as Wolf Biermann suggests in his song 'Der Hugenottenfriedhof' (1969) (The cemetery of the Huguenots) (text in ([7], pp. 215-17); recorded in *Warte nicht auf beßre Zeiten* (Don't wait for better times) (CBS Nr. 6753, 1973)) the sense of understanding oneself as standing in a tradition of past people's earlier endeavours can be a source of comfort particularly in times in which pursuing a project within the tradition is not acknowledged as valuable by many of one's own contemporaries. The refrain goes: "Wie nah sind uns manche Tote, doch wie tot sind uns manche, die leben." (How close we feel to some dead people but how dead are some who are alive.)

[10] In the ancient world, yields of olive trees offset the costs of planting them after only 15 to 19 years; good yields can only be expected every fifth year or so. Olive trees lived to be very old, often up to a couple of hundred years. Thus, olive tree plantations have been very valuable and, in the ancient world, cutting down olive trees belonged to the usual means of warfare. See, *e.g.*, Thucydides, *The Peloponnesian War*, Book 6, 99. The Torah includes a specific injunction against such means of warfare. See *Deuteronomy* 20, 19-20. For an interpretation of this and other intergenerational injunctions in the law of the Hebrew people, see [2], pp. 27-35. At the same time, the slowly growing olive tree has been regarded the appropriate symbol for a well-ordered, peace-loving society. See ([52], cols. 1998-2022, esp., 2011, 2014, 2021).

[11] Of course, I do not want to deny that investments of this kind have often been used as, *e.g.*, means of legitimation for a political system and its representatives. That is most clearly the case with the establishment of museums and the preservation of historical monuments as part of a conscious effort of constructing history in terms of the established political and economic order. But in such a case the instrumental value of these investments is, I suspect, dependent on their being seen as beneficial predominantly for future people. For the intricated politics of both GDR's and FRG's attempts at constructing a collective identity in post-war Germany by means of the preservation of monuments and the establishment of museums see [43].

[12] Is the expectation that future people are likely to continue to pursue these projects or that such projects might possibly have results beneficial to future people really constitutive of their meaning? When it comes to scientific projects that possibly will have results that could turn out to be beneficial to future people, one might observe that for the actual researchers involved the potential benefits to future

people are often of no relevance for their self-understanding in pursuing these projects. Granted, your being concerned about future people is likely not to have much of an impact on how you go about pursuing your research project on a day-to-day basis. Some people will even suspect that when scientists apply for the grants needed to do basic research, they tend to masquerade as being concerned about the future simply to improve their chances of succeeding in getting the grant. I do not want to comment on such a suspicion. Instead I only want to point out that pursuing scientific projects tends not to be the private matter of the researcher(s) involved. Rather, other people than the researchers take an active part in constituting the social meaning of scientific projects and, importantly so, those who make decisions on which projects are eligible for a grant. The instrumental value of appealing to the potential benefits to future people depends on its being acknowledged as a legitimate ground for pursuing these projects by those who make decisions on whether such projects are eligible for a grant. And that fact partly constitutes their meaning.

[13] As, e.g., [44].

[14] Though individuals can be excluded from the benefits by excluding them from the society to which they pertain.

[15] Of course, this non-competitiveness exists only within boundaries. E.g., in so far as pursuing such projects are resource-dependent, there is a limit to how many projects of the type from which mainly future people are expected to benefit can be undertaken within a society at a certain time while the society reproduces the conditions of its existence. On the other hand, being able to pursue future-oriented projects depends on the existence of specific social practices whose existence depends on a good number of people pursuing projects of the types in question. Also, as Thomas Pogge pointed out to me, people can pursue projects of shaping the future in the sense of replacing the existing set of social practices with a set of new ones. Obviously, different projects of that sort may be mutually exclusive and compete with each other.

[16] Here, I rely on the general definition of rights Raz offers in [38]. See also ([39], pp. 165-68).

[17] If the interest of no individual in the public good of living in a future-oriented society can be said to be sufficient by itself to justify holding another person subject to a duty, can individuals as members of a group be said to have a collective right to this public good since this right serves their interests as members of the group in the public good in question? I doubt it. People's interests in pursuing what I have called future-oriented projects typically arise not out of the fact that they are members of a particular group, but out of the fact that realizing such projects can be highly valuable to them as individuals of certain talents and abilities. In pursuing future-oriented projects, people often can make use of a particular community's practices on which the projects depend without being members of the community. While living in a society that is open to the future is a public good, it is not a collective good. Assuming that people can only have collective rights to collective goods, people cannot be said to have a collective right to living in a society of that quality. See ([25], esp., pp. 114 -15, 129-20).

[18] The Western model of welfare is not universalizable; it partly depends on an international economy that systematically disadvantages people living in other regions of the world; long-term sustainable development depends on Western countries changing their way of life rather dramatically. For empirically informed arguments to this effect see, e.g., ([53], esp., pp. 67-69); see also ([50], esp., pp. 215-18) (arguing that the Western countries have to change their model of welfare and to support a new economic world order in order to gain any credibility in their environmental policies towards the so-called Third World). For a critical and comparative review of these and other studies see [26].

[19] This is not to say that if the presently living were to pursue a modest life-style, future people could not have a right vis-à-vis them to pursuing some future-oriented projects. Given that resources are limited, the presently living might still be thought to be under an obligation to do research in the more efficient use of the known resources and in the possibility of gaining energy in not-yet-known ways. Thus justice might require of us to pursue and to continue to pursue some strongly future-oriented projects. See ([2], pp. 205-6).

[20] If I was correct in arguing (in, above, n. 17) that presently living people cannot be said to have a collective right to living in a future-oriented society, future people cannot be said to have a collective right in having the conditions of a future-oriented society preserved for them.

[21] As I hope to show in the following analysis, this general duty is not based on an extension of the notion of justice as reciprocity to the relations between generations. For a critique of such an account of the duty under consideration see ([4], pp. 232-34).

[22] Saying that we owe respect to past people's highly valuable activities and the conditions that are constitutive of them does not imply that we *harm* past people in our failing to show the proper respect for these goods. While an account of our wrongful failure has to include an account of the value of the goods worth preserving, such an account may not have to refer to a supposed harm done to past people. For the dispute of whether a person can be harmed or have her interests invaded after her death see [32], ([16], pp. 79-104), [36], [10].

[23] This is a general characteristic of duties. See ([40], p. 17), ([37], esp., pp. 223-24).

[24] The idea of duties to public goods cannot be accounted for in terms of the notion of duties always being owed to individual persons who have the corresponding right. Nor does the idea of duties to public goods comply with the notion of a duty always being to the disadvantage of its bearer and the corresponding right always being to the advantage of its bearer. Typically, individuals cannot be said to have a right to a public good. Those individuals who have duties to foster or preserve a public good are likely to be among those who benefit from the existence of the public good. See ([39], pp. 10-11).

[25] As I pointed out in above sec. 2.1, were we to face a choice between a future of people who all have lives worth living and a future of no people, considerations based on future people's rights could not guide us. While such rights-based considerations cannot restrain us from causing the cessation of human life, the respect we owe to highly valuable goods that our predecessors bequeathed to us as well as more remote future people gives us a reason for not bringing about the end of human life--unless we find ourselves in the direst circumstances in which neither we nor future people can benefit from what we inherited. While I certainly do not want to suggest that the respect we owe to the future-oriented projects of our predecessors can ground an individual duty to procreate, I do believe that such respect grounds a duty not willfully to risk or even to destroy the inherited goods and the conditions that are constitutive of future people continuing to pursue the future-oriented projects of our contemporaries and our predecessors. As Annette Baier puts it: "To end it all would not be the communal equivalent of suicide, since it would end not only our endeavors but those invested endeavors of all our predecessors" ([3], p.178).

[26] Here I discuss neither the special obligations we have towards the past victims of public evils we inherited as members of a political community nor the possibility of their being contemporary innocent victims of our disposing of a public evil.

[27] But see note 19 above.

BIBLIOGRAPHY

1.   Alexy, R.: 1989, 'Individual Rights and Collective Goods', in C. Nino (ed.), *Rights*, Dartmouth, Aldershot, 163-181.
2.   Auerbach, B. E.: 1995, *Unto the Thousandth Generation: Conceptualizing Intergenerational Justice*, Peter Lang, New York et.al.
3.   Baier, A.: 1981, 'The Rights of Past and Future Persons', in E. Partridge (ed.), *Responsibilities to Future Generations: Environmental Ethics*, Prometheus Books, New York, pp. 171-183.
4.   Barry, B.: 1979, 'Justice as Reciprocity', in E. Kamenka (ed.), *Ideas and Ideologies: Justice*, St. Martin's Press, New York, pp. 50-78, repr. in his: 1991, *Liberty and Justice: Essays in Political Theory 2* , Clarendon Press, Oxford, pp. 211-41.
5.   Barry, B.: 1989, *Theories of Justice: A Treatise on Social Justice (Vol. I)*, University of California Press, Berkeley.
6.   Bayles, M. D.: 1981, 'Famine or Food: Sacrificing for Future or Present Generations', in E. Partridge (ed.), *Responsibilities to Future Generations: Environmental Ethics*, Prometheus Books, New York, pp. 229-46.
7.   Biermann, W.: 1991, *Alle Lieder*, Kiepenheuer and Witsch, Köln.
8.   Birnbacher, D.: 1988, *Verantwortung für zukünftige Generationen*, Reclam, Stuttgart.
9.   Broome, J.: 1994, 'Discounting the Future', *Philosophy and Public Affairs* 23, 128-156.

10. Callahan, John C.: 1987, 'On Harming the Dead', *Ethics* 97, 341-352.
11. Conn, R. W. et al.: 1992, 'The International Thermonuclear Experimental Reactor', *Scientific American*, 75-82.
12. Cowen, T., and Parfit, D.: 1992, 'Against the Social Discount Rate', in P. Laslett and J. Fishkin (eds.), *Justice Between Age Groups and Generations*, Yale University Press, New Haven and London, pp. 144-161.
13. De George, R. T.: 1984, 'Do We Owe the Future Anything?', in J. P. Sterba (ed.), *Morality in Practice*, Wadsworth, Belmont CA, pp. 152-164.
14. De-Shalit, A.: 1995, *Why Posterity Matters: Environmental Policies and Future Generations*, Routledge, London and New York.
15. Elliot, R.: 1989, 'The Rights of Future People', *Journal of Applied Philosophy* 6, 159-169.
16. Feinberg, J.: 1984, *Harm to Others. The Moral Limits of the Criminal Law*, Vol. 1, Oxford University Press, New York.
17. Govier, T.: 1979, 'What Should We Do About Future People?', *American Philosophical Quarterly* 16, 105-113.
18. Hacker, P.M.S. and Raz, J. (eds.): 1977, *Law, Morality and Society: Essays in Honour of H. L. A. Hart*, Clarendon Press, Oxford.
19. Heyd, D.: 1992, *Genethics. Moral Issues in the Creation of People*, University of California Press, California.
20. Hoerster, N.: 1991, *Abtreibung im säkularen Staat. Argumente gegen den § 218*, Suhrkamp, Frankfurt.
21. Horstmann, U.: 1983, *Das Untier. Konturen einer Philosophie der Menschenflucht*, Medusa, Vienna and Berlin.
22. Hurka, T.: 1993, *Perfectionism*, Oxford University Press, New York and Oxford.
23. Jonas, H.: 1979, *Das Prinzip Verantwortung. Versuch einer Ethik für die technologische Zivilisation*, Insel Verlag, Franfurt.
24. Laslett, P. and Fishkin, J. S. (eds.): 1992, *Justice Between Age Groups and Generations*, Yale University Press, New Haven and London.
25. Margalit, A. and Raz, J.: 1990, 'National Self-Determination', *Journal of Philosophy* 87, 439-461, repr. in J. Raz, *Ethics in the Public Domain: Essays in the Morality of Law and Politics*, Clarendon Press, Oxford, 1994, pp. 110-130.
26. Marmora, L.: 1990, 'Ökologie als Leitbild der Nord-Süd-Beziehungen. Club of Rome—Brundtlandkommission—"Erdpolitik"', *Peripherie* 39/40, 100-126.
27. Marshall, E.: 1987, 'Armageddon Revisited. The Government's Latest Profile of World War III Fails to Consider Climatic Effects', *Science* 236, 1421-1422.
28. Meyer, L. H.: 1997, 'Can Actual Future People Have a Right to Non-Existence?' in R. Martin and G. Sprenger (eds.), *Rights* (Beiheft 67 of Archiv fur Rechts- und Sozialphilosophie), (forthcoming).
29. Moore, G. E.: 1903, *Principia Ethica*, Cambridge University Press, Cambridge.
30. Parfit, D.: 1984, *Reasons and Persons*, Clarendon Press, Oxford.
31. Parfit, D.: 1986, 'Overpopulation and the Quality of Life', in P. Singer (ed.), *Applied Ethics*, Oxford University Press, Oxford, pp. 145-164.
32. Partridge, E.: 1981, 'Posthumous Interest and Posthumous Respect', *Ethics* 91, 243-264.
33. Partridge, E. (ed.): 1981, *Responsibilities to Future Generations: Environmental Ethics*, Prometheus Books, New York.
34. Partridge, E: 1990, 'On the Rights of Future People', in D. Scherer (ed.), *Upstream/Downstream: Issues in Environmental Ethics*, Temple University Press, Philadelphia, pp. 40-66.
35. Pease, R. S.: 1987, 'The JET Project: Introduction and Background', *Philosophical Transactions of the Royal Society* A 322, 3-15.
36. Pitcher, G.: 1984, 'The Misfortunes of the Dead', *American Philosophical Quarterly* 21, 183-88.
37. Raz, J.: 1977, 'Promises and Obligations', in P. Hacker and J. Raz (eds.), *Law, Morality and Society: Essays in Honour of H.L.A. Hart*, Clarendon Press, Oxford, pp. 210-228.
38. Raz, J.: 1984, 'Legal Rights', *Oxford Journal of Legal Studies* 4, 1-21, repr. in J. Raz, *Ethics in the Public Domain: Essays in the Morality of Law and Politics*, Clarendon Press, Oxford, 1994, pp. 238-260.
39. Raz, J.: 1986, *The Morality of Freedom*, Clarendon Press, Oxford.

40. Raz, J.: 1989, 'Liberating Duties', *Law and Philosophy* 8, 3-21.
41. Raz, J.: 1994, *Ethics in the Public Domain: Essays in the Morality of Law and Politics*, Clarendon Press, Oxford.
42. Reaume, D.: 1988, 'Individuals, Groups, and Rights to Public Goods', *University of Toronto Law Review* 38, 1-27.
43. Reichel, P.: 1995, *Politik mit der Erinnerung. Gedächtnisorte im Streit um die nationalsozialistische Vergangenheit*, Carl Hanser Verlag, München and Wien.
44. Ritter, J. and Gründer, K. (eds.): 1971ff., *Historisches Wörterbuch der Philosophie*, Wissenschaftliche Buchgesellschaft, Darmstadt.
45. Scherer, D. (ed.): 1990, *Upstream/Downstream: Issues in Environmental Ethics*, Temple University Press, Philadelphia.
46. Schwartz, Th.: 1978, 'Obligations to Posterity', in R. Sikora and B. Barry (eds.), *Obligations to Future Generations*, Temple University Press, Philadelphia, pp. 3-13.
47. Sikora, R. I. and Barry, B. (eds.): 1978, *Obligations to Future Generations*, Temple University Press, Philadelphia.
48. Singer, P. (ed.): 1986, *Applied Ethics*, Oxford UP, Oxford.
49. Sterba, J. P. (ed.): 1984, *Morality in Practice*, Wadsworth, Belmont, CA.
50. Weizsäcker, Ernst U. v.: 1989, *Erdpolitik. Ökologische Realpolitik an der Schwelle zum Jahrhundert der Umwelt*, Wissenschaftliche Buchgesellschaft, Darmstadt.
51. Westing, A. H.: 1980, *Warfare in a Fragile World. Military Impact on the Human Environment*, Taylor and Francis, London.
52. Wissowa, G. et al. (eds.): 1937, *Pauly's Real-Encyclopädie der Classischen Altertumswissenschaft*, vol. xl, Metzlersche Verlagsbuchhandlung, Stuttgart.
53. World Commission on Environment and Development: 1987, *Our Common Future*, Oxford University Press, Oxford.

ROBERT ELLIOT

CONTINGENCY, COMMUNITY
AND INTERGENERATIONAL JUSTICE

THE NON-IDENTITY PROBLEM
AND OBLIGATIONS TO FUTURE PEOPLE

One psychologically powerful argument for the preservation and protection of the natural environment appeals to intergenerational justice. A variant appeals to the rights of future people: many, if not all, unjust acts can be reconceptualized as rights violations. So, it is often argued that present people ought to embrace environmentalism, and adopt green policies because they have certain obligations, deriving from justice or rights, to future people. For example, it might be claimed that present people ought not to pollute the oceans, since to do so would be to advantage themselves, unjustly, at the expense of future people. Or, in the language of rights, polluting activities by present people violate the rights of future people to something to which they are entitled, namely unpolluted oceans.

Appeals to intergenerational justice or to the rights of future people derive much of their psychological force from representing the actions of present people concerning future people in the same terms as the actions of present people concerning their contemporaries. Thus there is a swag of what might be called "upstream-downstream examples" in the environmental ethics literature, deployed in support of the view that present people have obligations to future people [1]. They are all basically variations of the following example. Imagine that two separate communities live beside a particular river. Each community is dependent on the ecological health of the river for its continued well-being. One community, however, is upstream of the other. The upstream community begins to engage in certain practices which, while improving their own quality of life, degrade the ecological health of the river, specifically that section of it on which the downstream community is dependent. Those actions which improve life for the upstream people, make life worse for the downstream people. The upstream people have no special claim to the river and its resources. They did not create it or in way contribute to its value. There is no sense in which they, more than the downstream people, are entitled to use it and to benefit from it. If we accept this, then it seems reasonable to represent the upstream people as behaving unjustly towards the downstream people, or to represent the upstream people as violating the rights of the downstream people. Next, it is urged that present people stand in relation to future people much as the upstream people stand in relation to the downstream people, with the biosphere playing the role of the river. So it might be said that our pollution of the air and of

Nick Fotion and Jan C. Heller (eds.), Contingent Future Persons, 157-170.
© 1997 *Kluwer Academic Publishers. Printed in the Netherlands.*

the oceans, our depletion of biodiversity and our degradation of the land, constitute an injustice to future people or a violation of their rights.

Unfortunately the analogy on which this argument for the preservation and protection of the natural environment depends turns out to be flawed. This is clear if we consider the following example. Jill and Jack plan to have a child. They would like to have a child sooner rather than later. They discover, though, that one of them has a passing disease, such that if they procreate now the resultant child will almost certainly be born with some life-long affliction. This affliction would by no means make the resultant child's life not worth living. The child could well have a life that was happy overall, but the affliction would condemn her or him to not infrequent bouts of severe pain. If Jill and Jack delay procreation for a few months, this outcome will be avoided. If they delay procreation the resultant child is likely to have a better life than the child who would result from an earlier procreative act; its life would likely be as rich and it would not be subject to bouts of severe pain ([6], pp. 355-361).

Do Jill and Jack have any obligation to delay conception? Some people might think that they do. In thinking this they might be moved by the thought that the earlier conception would be unjust to the child Jill and Jack would have were they not to delay or violate some right that it would have. This thought is challenged, though, once we press the questions as to whom the earlier conception would be unjust or whose rights would be violated. The obvious victim of the alleged injustice or rights violation is the child who would result from the earlier conception. But this thought is sustainable only if either one of two conditions is satisfied ([3], pp. 159-164). The first condition is that the child who would result from the earlier conception would himself or herself be better off were conception to be delayed. This condition is not satisfied. If we accept the view that time of conception is at least a partial determinant of identity, then the choice Jill and Jack face is not between having a particular child now or having that same child later but between having a particular child now and a quite different, distinct child later ([4], pp. 27-34, and [6], pp. 351-355). The second condition is that the life of the resultant child be not worth living. This condition is not satisfied either.

The point may be made more forcefully if we consider things from the point of view of the child who results from the earlier of the two possible procreative acts. Imagine that the child is born and grows into adulthood, living a happy life punctuated by severe bouts of pain. If we ask this person whether she is glad to have been born, whether she is glad that Jill and Jack did not delay conception, then the answer will be affirmative. The alternative is that she would not have existed at all. So, from her point of view as an actual being, things are better than they would otherwise have been. In the face of this person affirming that she is glad to have been born, it is difficult to think that the very act which brings her into existence could constitute an injustice to her or a violation of some right of hers. If we were to ask whether she wished that she did not suffer the bouts of pain she would doubtless answer in the affirmative. If, however, she knew that one necessary condition of her very existence is that she experience that pain, then she would agree that she is compensated for the pain by other, more joyful aspects of her existence.

Do these considerations entail that Jill and Jack have no obligation to delay conception? They do not. That obligation could have its basis in considerations other than justice concerning, or the rights of, the resultant child. For example, if Jill and Jack conceive now they might be imposing social costs on their community that they would not otherwise impose: they might be decreasing the well-being of other children they have: they might be limiting their own opportunities for a mutually fulfilling relationship. These examples highlight ways in which the choice to conceive earlier rather than later can adversely affect individuals other than the resultant child. These kinds of considerations are personal or person-regarding considerations; that is, they have as their focus the well-being of a particular, existing person. There are also impersonal considerations which might support the obligation to delay conception. For example, delaying conception might maximise the total amount of happiness in the universe or it might bring into existence a person who better exemplifies some ideal of human excellence. Delaying conception might bring more value into the world than would otherwise exist. Such considerations do not aim at what, intuitively, we might think of as making a particular person better off or protecting a particular person from harm. Rather they aim at adding to the total value of the world. It is like the difference between making some person happier than she or he currently is and bringing potentially happy people into existence in order to have a world in which there is more happiness. In this latter case we need to imagine that happiness is increased solely through the contribution of those potential people who come into existence: it is not a case of the already existing people becoming happier because the potential people are actualized. It is difficult, though, to connect these impersonal concerns to concerns about justice or rights violations, which seem to have to be understood in person-regarding terms.

Note that we might agree that some consideration weighs morally against the performance of some action without thinking that it generates an obligation not to perform that action. For example, that some action fails to increase value in the world to the same degree as an alternative action is a reason against performing it and for performing the alternative instead. While it might well be better from a moral point of view if the agent performs the alternative action, and while the agent herself might be deemed much more praiseworthy if she performs it than if she does not, it does not follow that there is an obligation to perform the alternative action. So, we might take the view that even though Jill and Jack have a moral reason for delaying conception they have no obligation because in conceiving now they do not act unjustly towards anyone and they violate no-one's rights.

The suggestion, then, is that in the case of Jill and Jack any obligation that they have to delay conception does not have its basis in considerations of justice or rights. And the case of Jill and Jack has implications for intergenerational justice. Jill and Jack stand to their potential children as present people stand to future people. For if we reflect on the matter, the particular individuals who constitute future generations, certainly those at several removes from this generation, are dependent on the choices we make now, in the same way that some particular child's existence is dependent on the choice that Jill and Jack make. For instance, consider the adoption of a policy designed to reduce pollution from exhaust emissions. Such a policy will certainly impact on the way that people live their lives, where they work, who they meet, how they spend their leisure time, when they sleep and whom they sleep with. Such a policy would quickly begin to affect the detail of people's lives. Patterns of travel might change as public transport was increasingly used, working hours might be rearranged to reduce the impact of peak hour traffic, there might be restructuring in the manufacturing sector and in the labour market as certain areas of production declined and others, for example those producing pollution inhibitors, expanded. Initially only a few lives would be affected but over time the effects would spread like a ripple on a pond. The adoption of a policy could thus make it the case that the particular individuals who constitute some future generation are different, distinct individuals from those who would otherwise at that future time have existed had a different policy been chosen. This is why the upstream/downstream examples are not sound analogies for intergenerational justice. The correct kind of analogy is instead exemplified by the case of Jill and Jack.

Where our choice between policies is also a choice between bringing into existence one of two separate, non-intersecting sets of future people, then, provided we are bringing into existence people whose lives are worth living, we are acting neither unjustly nor in violation of their rights.[1] Of course we could be acting unjustly towards, and in violation of the rights of, our contemporaries, both human and non-human. These latter considerations would strongly favour the non-polluting policy. There could be other compelling arguments, too, in favour of the non-polluting policy, that appeal to the value of ecosystems and species diversity.

Note that the so-called non-identity problem does not turn on the claim that it is impossible to identify particular future people, to get a fix on particular future people or to refer to particular future people. These things can in principle be done. For example, it is in principle possible to project forward along causal pathways from present actions to the particular people who come into existence as a result in the future ([7], pp. 27). This is a way of identifying them. Moreover it is possible to identify in this manner people who would have come into existence had some other course of action been pursued. The non-identity problem is really a problem to do with actuality rather than identity as such. In cases such as those we have been considering, some present action determines which of various sets of possible people are actual at some later point in time. The problem would arise even were we able to identify all of these possible people. What we cannot do prior to our choice of policy is identify those individuals who will be actual.

It is useful to retrace our steps. First, we noted that the view that we have obligations concerning future people, based on their rights and entitlement to just treatment, is a powerful argument for adopting green policies. Second, we accepted the metaphysical thesis that different origin entails different individual, and we accepted the biological thesis that altering the time of conception alters origin. Third, we saw that because the identity of future people can be determined by our present policy choices, the upstream/downstream examples do not provide the right analogy for representing the relationship of present people to future people. Fourth, we saw that only in one kind of circumstance could present choices be construed as constituting an injustice to, or a violation of the rights of, future people whose identities we affect, namely where those future people who come into existence have lives that are not worth living.[2]

Should the advocate of green policies accept this conclusion and advocate her or his policies on the basis of other, admittedly very compelling, arguments, or can she or he show how intergenerational justice or the rights of future plays a robust role? Ingmar Persson and Avner de-Shalit suggest ways in which the latter might be possible. Persson's suggestion is that person-regarding considerations do justify particular identity-determining choices outside the narrow range to which, it was earlier argued, they are restricted. Persson's suggestion does not amount straightforwardly to a re-introduction of considerations of justice or rights but it tends in that direction. For one thing, the force of talk in terms of justice and rights seems to derive in large part from the person-regarding nature of the associated normative principles ([1], p. 106). The focus of such principles is the impact of certain actions on particular people. The exclusion of future people from their scope is based on the claim that a significant category of actions concerning future people selects between different sets of potential people. Actions in this category do not affect some particular person and so are not restricted by the stringent normative requirements on actions that do affect particular people. Persson argues that the category is misconceived. De-Shalit, by contrast, explicitly appeals to justice. His suggestion is that a communitarian conception of intergenerational justice provides a basis for green policies. These suggestions are considered in turn.

PERSON-REGARDING REASONS
AND INTERGENERATIONAL JUSTICE

Persson believes that contingent future people fall within the scope of person-regarding principles. One plausible way of establishing this is to show that a person can be benefited by being brought into existence, since to say that someone is benefited by a particular action is to say that she or he is affected (positively) by it. Persson believes that advocates of the contrary view are moved by the principle: (P) "non-existent individuals, though sometimes identifiable, never fulfil the conditions for something's being of value to them" ([7], p. 28). To benefit someone, as Persson thinks advocates of P see it, is to make it the case that that person is better off than she or he would otherwise have been. The idea is that one and the same person should feature in each of two scenarios, and be better off in the one than in the other.

Consider Sally, who is deciding between doing a course in nursing and a course in computer science. The choice she makes will lead to one of two quite distinctively different futures. We might judge that Sally would be better off in the future that results from that choice than she would be in the future that results from the other choice. We might, therefore, encourage Sally to choose computer science. In so doing we would be moved by a person-regarding reason: we can see that a particular person, Sally, will be benefited. It is a mistake, though, to think that, if we accept that a person can be benefited by being brought into existence, we are commited to giving up P. It is not, as we shall see, the fact that a principle is person-regarding that provides the normative force associated with appeals to justice and rights but a quite different characteristic. It is this latter characteristic to which P gives expression. It is also a mistake, as Parfit has pointed out, to think that if a person could be benefited by being brought into existence that she or he would be harmed by not being brought into existence ([6], pp. 487-490).

Persson is correct in claiming that person-regarding reasons require, minimally, that "(i) there must be an alternative to the relevant person's being in a particular condition, and (ii) an evaluative ranking between the alternatives must be possible" ([7], p. 27). He is likewise correct in making the qualification that the evaluative ranking must be possible from that person's point of view. Consider the claim that bringing Simon into existence would benefit Simon. The alternatives to be evaluatively ranked are Simon's existing and some state of affairs in which Simon does not exist. And, on Persson's account, these alternatives are to be evaluatively ranked from Simon's point of view. Can Simon's existence be thus ranked, from Simon's point of view, against Simon's non-existence? Persson apparently thinks it can be. He thinks that Simon's non-existence is, to Simon, a value-less state. Persson would say that Simon would, in that alternative in which he does not exist, be "in a state in which everything is genuinely valueless to" him. ([7], p. 29). Persson thinks that this value-less state can be ranked against states of positive value, states of negative value or states of indifference. In particular, he thinks that Simon's non-existence would be equal in value to Simon's existing in a state of indifference.

The initial appeal of Persson's suggestion erodes once we focus on one crucial feature. The evaluative ranking, of Simon's non-existence against his existence, is supposedly an evaluation from Simon's point of view. But in the situation in which Simon does not come into existence there is no actual point of view that can be specified as his point of view and from which his non-existence can be evaluatively ranked against his existence. Moreover, it is not that Simon will definitely come to have a point of view, since, we are supposing, it is an open question whether or not he will come into existence. Whether Simon comes into existence or some other person comes into existence or no-one comes into existence is entirely dependent on our procreative choices, which are influenced by social policies. The state of affairs which Persson wants to say is valueless from Simon's point of view can be so only if Simon's point of view comes to exist. Only if he does come to exist, can he rank his non-existence relative to his existence. He can say, for example: "It is better, from my point of view, that I exist, than that I never existed. My life has been, and is likely to continue to be, a happy one." Or he can say: 'It is worse, from my point of view, that I exist than that I had never come into existence, for my life has been completely miserable." In these cases Simon does not regard the state which does not eventuate as valueless, rather he regards it as having negative value or positive value. However, in possible worlds realizing the state of affairs of Simon's non-existence, that state of affairs is neither of positive, indifferent nor negative value, nor valueless, from Simon's point of view. In those worlds Simon does not have a point of view. If our world, the actual world, is one such world, then Simon's non-existence does not get evaluatively ranked from Simon's point of view, in this, the actual, world. Where Persson is inclined to say ([7] p. 29) that in those worlds in which Simon does not exist he "is in a state in which everything is genuinely valueless to" him, we can properly reply that he is in no state at all. It does not make sense to suggest that Simon's non-existence can be evaluated from Simon's point of view, except in those states of affairs in which Simon exists.

Persson's discussion of these matters seems inadequately to distinguish between two claims. The first, which is true, is that Simon's non-existence can be evaluated from Simon's point of view in that state of affairs in which Simon exists. The second, which is false, is that Simon's non-existence can be evaluated from Simon's point of view in that state of affairs in which Simon does not exist. Both claims must be true if P, the principle that "non-existent individuals, though sometimes identifiable, never fulfil the conditions for something's being of value to them", is to be defeated. Moreover, in most cases where Simon does evaluate his non-existence, he will say that it has positive value rather than value equal to indifference. And where Simon does not exist, others may rank his non-existence as equivalent to the value of a life which, if it were Simon's life, Simon would rank as indifferent.

Another way of eliciting the problem inherent in Persson's position is to emphasize a modal difference between, say, Sally's situation in the earlier example and Simon's situation in the scenarios just discussed. In the former, an actual individual, Sally, is able prospectively to evaluate two possible futures in which she features. Sally is so placed that she herself can choose between two futures. In Simon's case, though, no such prospective evaluation is possible. Furthermore, no evaluation, prospective or retrospective, is possible from Simon's point of view, unless that course of action is adopted which brings him into existence. This is, arguably, really what strikes the advocates of the primacy of person-regarding principles as normatively salient. This feature is not, however, indicated by the mere fact that Sally can be benefited by her choice. There is indeed a sense in which bringing Simon into existence benefits him. If we think of benefiting someone as making it the case that things are more as they prefer than they disprefer, then we do benefit Simon by bringing him into existence. If Simon is brought into existence, then most likely he ranks his existence higher than his non-existence. Leastways, he would likely value, if not his existence as such, then the experiences which his existence makes possible. While Simon can be benefited by being brought into existence, it is significant that if he is not brought into existence there is no actual person for whom things are not as good (or bad) as they could otherwise have been. This is the modal difference between the case of Simon and the case of Sally.

So, (i), which says that "there must be an alternative to the relevant person's being in a particular condition", and (ii), which says that "an evaluative ranking between the alternatives must be possible", do not exhaust the requirements implicit in P. There is a further requirement: (iii) the choice between the alternatives cannot affect the actuality of A, cannot itself make the difference between A's being actual and A's being merely possible. Advocates of P think that it is normatively more significant or important to benefit an individual who is actual, independently of their present choices, than it is to benefit an individual by making her or him actual. Some might argue that this actualism is discriminatory in the fashion of sexism and speciesism. This is difficult to accept. For consider a case where we might choose between curing someone of a continuing, painful affliction and bringing someone into existence. The choice is "revenue neutral" in terms of maximizing total well-being, each option resulting in the same net increase in total well-being. There is reason though to choose the former option. It makes a significant normative difference that the first option benefits an actual person. Moreover, there is a striking disanalogy between discounting which favours actual persons and discounting which favours members of one's own race, sex, nation, species, class or the like. In these latter cases the discounting discriminates between actual people on the basis of some property they exemplify. In the former case the "discrimination" is against no-one, since, if it is practised, no-one is unjustly treated or harmed.

These considerations should move us to distinguish between two senses of "benefiting"; one which incorporates actualism and one which does not. We might reflect this in a further distinction between person-affecting reasons and person-regarding reasons. Benefiting in the second sense aligns directly with an impersonal consequentialism. This alignment results from treating all possible people as capable of benefiting and so the consequentialist principle—Persson appears to endorse a maximizing consequentialism—is applied over the entire range of possible persons. This consequentialism may represent itself as person-regarding, and so it is if that notion is tied to the wider sense of "benefiting". It is person-regarding in that it strives to maximize value through a consideration of the effects of actions on each possible person, each of whom in principle can be benefited by being brought into existence. To try, however, to distinguish this person-regarding consequentialism from impersonal consequentialism is to make a distinction without a difference. The difference emerges only if P is characterized in terms of (i), (ii) and (iii) as well.

Let us make a connection with the issues of the first section. The chief claim there was that appeal to rights and justice concerning future people cannot play the role advocates of green policies typically assign them. This is because in selecting between two sets of future people there is no obligation to bring into existence the set with the higher level of well-being, provided that the set which is brought into existence is made up of people with lives that are worth living. Persson's argument threatened this position; firstly, by suggesting that its motivating norm has to do with the salience of person-regarding reasons, and, second, by suggesting that there are person-regarding reasons for bringing potential people into existence. If Policy X will bring into existence a happier group of future people than Policy Y, then Persson would say that there is an obligation to choose X rather than Y. His reason is that in so doing we would be benefiting people to a greater extent than if we chose Y.

Note that, even if Persson is right so far, it would not straightfowardly follow that it would be unjust or a violation of rights to chose Y rather than X. One has only to consider cases involving our contemporaries in order to see this. For example, I might choose to benefit one group of people quite significantly or choose to benefit another group to a lesser extent. It would not follow that, in failing to confer the larger benefit, I have acted unjustly or in violation of anybody's rights. Instead, I am, on the face of it, morally free to choose which group I benefit. Of course there could be special circumstances that would entail that my failure to confer the larger benefit is unjust or a violation of rights. This would be so if, for instance, I had contracted or promised to benefit the first group, or if the first group, but not the second, are in their dispreferred state because of some past unjust act of mine. The more general entailment is only secured if a maximizing consequentialism is established; that is, a consequentialism that reduces questions of justice and rights to considerations of utility or, more broadly, value, and that enjoins us to maximize utility or value.

This quibble aside, the import of Persson's argument is to call into question one plausible account of the distinction between person-regarding reasons and impersonal reasons. If person-regarding reasons are reasons for acting which focus on the potential of the act to benefit, then there are person-regarding reasons for bringing into existence potential future persons. Moreover, if we accept this view, then the very distinction between person-regarding reasons and impersonal reasons is blurred. Recall the upstream/downstream example involving contemporaries. Plausibly our judgement that justice requires the upstream community to refrain from polluting the river is tightly connected with the fact that refraining from polluting the river benefits the downstream people. Persson shows that we can, likewise, have person-regarding reasons for bringing someone into existence. But it is not the mere fact that an action is person-regarding that gives it the special normative salience associated with justice and rights. What is, in addition, relevant is that the action benefits people whose existence or actuality is independent of the action in question.

It is helpful to look at the question of actualizing potential people from the perspective of harming. While failing to benefit someone is a way of harming someone, this is not possible in the case of contingent future people. If we refrain from bringing someone into existence who, had we brought them into existence, would have been happy and so benefited, we do not thereby harm that person. It gets back to the point, already made several times, that there would, in that case, be no-one to harm. Consider again the case of Jill and Jack. If they procreate now, then they would confer a benefit on a person which is less than the benefit they would confer were they to postpone procreation. But in failing to postpone procreation they harm no-one, indirect harms aside. Likewise those future people who come into being as a result of our adoption of the polluting policy are not thereby harmed. In fact, provided their lives are worth living, they are, on Persson's own argument, benefited. By contrast, the members of the downstream community are harmed by the polluting activities of the upstream people because the quality of their lives is made less than it would otherwise have been. We could say that the distinguishing feature of person-regarding reasons is not the possibility of benefiting but the possibility of harming. An action only harms if it makes someone worse off than they would otherwise be or makes their life worse than indifferent.

COMMUNITARIAN INTERGENERATIONAL JUSTICE

De-Shalit believes that his communitarian conception of intergenerational justice avoids the problems of individualistic conceptions of justice. According to the communitarian theory, justice and rights have a special significance within communities. While accepting that there are, for example, human rights, which generate strong obligations towards all humans irrespective of whether they are members of one's own community, De-Shalit thinks that there are special obligations, expressible in the language of rights and justice, that extend only to, or at least more weightily to, members of one's own community. Let us accept this basic framework and see whether it provides an account of obligations to future people which eludes the non-identity problem.

As with a community of contemporaries, the intergenerational community is built around a commonality of core values. And the community, thus understood, is supposed to constitute a self, with which one can identify, and which extends beyond one's own generation into the future. The thought is that many of one's most important or salient preferences are directed not so much to how things are for oneself as towards how things are for that collection of people, whomever they might be, with whom one has a commonality of values. It is by way of such preferences that the focus of the self can be widened, from a narrowly-defined, individualistic conception, to a more inclusive, communitarian conception. De-Shalit says: "...one's self-awareness is related to one's community, both in the present and in the future, ie. in relation to the aims, desires, dreams, and values of the transgenerational community" ([2], p. 124 and [5], pp. 45-51). Later he says: "I ...develop a strong intense relationship towards the ideas I believe in, fight for, and so on. I regard them as part of me, of what I am" ([2], p. 125).

The key mechanism of cohesion within a community is, on de-Shalit's account, moral similarity, which is distinct from "unanimous agreement on moral and political questions" and which "co-exists happily with pluralism" ([2], p. 26). The phenomenon of moral similarity combines with the psychological fact of the desire by most people for "self-transcendence" to produce an intergenerational community ([2], p. 34). Such cohesion will be a matter of degree and so the boundaries of communities would be vague. De-Shalit also thinks that the transgenerational community of which we are members will fade away over time as the common value-based bonds are loosened ([2], p. 125). Finally, we should note that it is possible that our transgenerational community could be punctuated: central components of our culture might disappear and later reappear.

Communitarian intergenerational justice is not going to tie us to all future generations, even at any given time in the future, just as the analogous conception of intragenerational justice will not tie us to all of our contemporaries. Our advocacy of green policies, based on the communitarian conception of intergenerational justice, is only indirectly non-discriminatory as between different transgenerational communities. Thus, if we could be sure that some policy advantaged future members of our community but not future members of another community, then we would perhaps be at liberty, leastways in terms of communitarian justice, to choose it in preference to a policy which equally advantaged members of all transgenerational communities. Now De-Shalit points out that there are human rights that are not weighted in favour of members of one's own community, that will prohibit certain acts which are harmful to one's contemporaries. They are however severely limited in the scope of their intergenerational application by the fact of the non-identity problem.

Even if we restrict our considerations to justice within the transgenerational community, a variant of the non-identity problem arises. For the choices we make in the present determine whether future people are members of our transgenerational community. It is plausibly the case that our values are a function of our state of economic and technological development. Thus it is easy to imagine that increased resource scarcity in the future will erode, say, commitment to liberal democratic norms. A consequence might be that those people inhabiting that future will not be members of our own intergenerational community. So, our choices now can determine the temporal range of the community to which we belong. In particular, we may elude any requirement of communitarian justice to the further future by making choices that ensure that the people in that future are not members of our intergenerational community.

One response here is to insist that we could never be sure that inhabitants of the further future were or were not members of our community. It might be suggested that we should respond to this contingency by ensuring, as far as it is in our power, that the further future is an hospitable environment. This response is misconceived. Imagine that there are three policies, P, Q and R, from which we might now choose. If we choose P then people in the further future would likely be both well-off and members of our intergenerational community. If we choose Q, then people in the further future would likely be only modestly well-off and would possibly be members of our intergenerational community. If we chose R, then people in the further future would be poorly off and would not be members of our intergenerational community. Which policy does communitarian justice require us to chose? The answer is: any one of them. If we choose P we do not make it the case that some particular members of our community are better off than they otherwise would be. Rather we make it the case that a quite different set of people would exist than would otherwise exist. We do not somehow better provide for particular members of our community than we would otherwise do, since, had we chosen Q, those particular people would not come to exist. And if we chose R, then provided R left people in the further future with lives worth living, then we would have committed no injustice, since those people would not be members of our intergenerational community. The non-identity problem is no less a problem for those who subscribe to communitarian intergenerational justice, than it is for individualistic conceptions. A communitarian theory of intergenerational justice does not rehabilitate the upstream/downstream analogy as an accurate representation of the relationship between present people and future people, or provide the basis for the correct account of the obligations, deriving from justice or rights, which present people have to future people.

De-Shalit's view, however, made reference not just to communitarian justice but also to the idea of transgenerational identity. The idea is that the individual identifies with the values that are constitutive of her or his community—the values are an expression of the self—and she or he wants the values in question to continue into the future ([5], pp. 41-43). The desire that there be a transgenerational community is not completely remote from the desire for self-preservation, except that the self is preserved not through the continuation of a particular biological life but through the flourishing of a whole way of life. This is all well and good but it does not seem to have much to do with justice or rights; it exhibits instead something of the flavour of egoism or of a duty to self. Maybe this is what de-Shalit signals when he says that the communitarian theory "relies on contemporaries to do the entire job" and "follows…a model in which the self is not totally confined within the barriers of its own physical existence" ([2], p. 125). De-Shalit does not explicitly endorse an extended egoism: he strives to keep the focus on concern for others. Thus he says: "by extending the community to include future generations…obligations are directly owed to them" ([2], p. 125).

The issue comes better into focus if we compare communitarian intragenerational justice with communitarian intergenerational justice. In the former case we are alleged to have additional or more compelling obligations to those of our contemporaries who are members of our community than we have to others. This has to do with our sharing with the former central values, desires, *etc.* But presumably we are meant to feel for these people as individuals and not merely as cyphers through which a particular kind of social, political and cultural life is exemplified. Leastways the focus would seem to be on them as individuals who have special rights, to whom special obligations are owed, in virtue of their sharing, *qua* the particular people they are, a way of life with us. We do not simply think of them as extensions of our selves, as worthy of distinctive treatment merely because they are elements in the expression of a form of life that is somehow constitutive of our own identity. Surely we do not strive to improve their lot or protect them from harms because we want it to be the case that the way of life with which we identify is exemplified by some set of people who are well-off. Rather we want the particular people, the very people, with whom we participate in a shared way of life to be well-off. When attention is switched to the intergenerational case, though, the non-identity problem makes no space for concern for particular people. Our concern loses its particularity because our choices select between different sets of future people who, with us, will be joined in our transgenerational community.

De-Shalit's theory of intergenerational justice has been so far characterised as egoistic. Perhaps this is somewhat unfair; for two reasons. First, there is the point that communitarian justice or rights rooted in community do not exhaust considerations of justice and rights. Second, and more interestingly, it is possible to give de-Shalit's theory a consequentialist gloss. So, we might ask the question: why should we be concerned how things are in the future? One answer, the vaguely egoist one, is that in making choices for future people "we can...and should immortalize the creative part of us" ([2], p. 38). We can do this by choosing present policies which are more likely than not to ensure the continuance of our community, characterized by the values, *etc.* that partly constitute our selves. If, however, we shift the focus of our concern from self-immortalization to the preservation of a robust, critically reflective way of life, then we might emerge looking less like egoists and more like ideal utilitarians. Ideal utilitarianism offers an answer to the earlier question: it says that we should be concerned about how things are in the future because certain ways of life are better, have more value, than others.

So, if we choose a resource depleting policy we might be reasonably sure that many people in the future, whoever they might be, are unjustly treated by their contemporaries. If we choose a resource conserving policy we might be reasonably sure that fewer future people will be unjustly treated by their contemporaries. Here we are dealing with different sets of future people. Our concern about the frequency of unjust acts is not a concern that members of one specific set of people are treated unjustly less often than they would otherwise be. Our concern is that a certain ideal of just treatment should characterize a future state of affairs irrespective of the identity of its inhabitants. Generalising, it is possible to see how a present desire to produce future people who will advance present social, cultural and intellectual projects, can be seen as a desire to ensure that certain ideals of excellence are realised. The redistribution of resources from the present to the future, for example through the adoption of resource conserving policies, is a means of realizing the ideal. It is not, however, a redistribution that is at all clearly driven by a desire for more just treatment of particular people. It does not matter who the people are, who are the means through which the ideal is realized. For this reason it seems more accurate to think of de-Shalit's communitarian theory as a sophisticated consequentialism or ideal utilitarianism. The reason why, on the theory, there is no need "to identify future people before constructing a theory of obligations towards them" ([2], p. 128) is that the theory is best represented either as a variant of egoism or of ideal utilitarianism.

CONCLUSION

In the first section we considered the non-identity problem and its implications for intergenerational justice. It was argued that appeals to intergenerational justice were less easily able to justify green policies than many advocates of such policies are inclined to think. Two responses to the non-identity problem, Persson's and de-Shalit's, were considered. Neither transparently succeeds it showing how straightforward notions of justice or rights can elude the constraints of the non-identity problem. The views outlined in their responses underwrite green policies, only to the extent that they are either species of consequentialism or of egoism. It is simply not obvious that justice and rights in anything like their normal sense enter into the picture.

NOTES

[1] This has a curious implication. Some not insignificant proportion of people who come into existence will have lives that are not worth living. In many cases this is not because of contingencies befalling them during their lives but as a direct result of the circumstances of their conception. It might be thought that this is analogous to a situation in which harm or suffering is distributed by lot. To subject unconsenting people to such a lottery would be unjust, even though the chances of any particular person "winning" the lottery might be small. If the analogy holds, then procreation is inevitably unjust or inevitably violates rights. Perhaps the positive value that procreation yields excuses this. This issue is not pursued here.

[2] See also the discussion of booby-trapped time-capsule in ([3], pp. 162-164).

BIBLIOGRAPHY

1. De-Shalit, A.: 1992, 'Community and the Rights of Future Generations: a Reply to Robert Elliot', *Journal of Applied Philosophy* 9, 105-115.
2. De-Shalit, A.: 1995, *Why Posterity Matters: Environmental Policies and Future Generations*, Routledge, London.
3. Elliot, R.: 1989, 'The Rights of Future People', *Journal of Applied Philosophy* 6, 59-171.
4. Elliot, R.: 1993, 'Identity and the Ethics of Gene Therapy', *Bioethics* 7, 27-40.
5. O'Neill, J.: 1993, 'Future Generations: Present Harms', *Philosophy* 68, 35-51.
6. Parfit, D.: 1984, *Reasons and Persons*, Clarendon Press, Oxford.
7. Persson, I.: 1995, 'Genetic Therapy, Identity and the Person-Regarding Reasons', *Bioethics* 9, 16-31.
8. Routley, R. and Routley, V.: 1978, 'Nuclear Energy and Obligations to Future Generations', *Inquiry* 21, 133-179.

CAROL A. TAUER

BRINGING EMBRYOS INTO EXISTENCE FOR RESEARCH PURPOSES

The new reproductive technologies provide a new context for asking questions about existence, number, and identity. Procedures such as in vitro fertilization (IVF) make it possible for new human life to be created in the laboratory under the supervision of scientists, rather than through sexual intercourse. In this situation, decisions must be made as to how many oocytes will be fertilized, how many zygotes (fertilized eggs) will be supported in their continued development, which cleavage-stage embryos will be transferred to a woman, and what will be the fate of the others. Each step of the process involves decisions about the existence, number, and identity of future persons.

An additional set of questions related to the genesis of human persons arises when scientists undertake research involving IVF and the embryos that result from IVF.[1] Is it wrong to bring a human embryo into existence solely for purposes of a research program? Does one's intention in generating an embryo make the act right or wrong, good or bad? Are the zygote, morula, and blastocyst in the laboratory caught in a shadowland between nonexistence and existence as human beings?[2] What does one owe a human entity in this situation?

THE EMBRYO RESEARCH CONTROVERSY

Countries that provide advanced clinical programs in reproductive technology vary widely in their support for IVF and embryo research ([4], pp. 65-163; [39], pp. 227-236; [25], p. 40; [36], pp. 607-659). In the United States, this research has been conducted entirely under private auspices because of a de facto ban on federal sponsorship and funding. An Ethics Advisory Board report in 1979 approved federal funding as ethically acceptable, but this report was never implemented. In 1993 Congress charged the National Institutes of Health (NIH) to become involved in research on human infertility and reproductive techniques. In doing so, Congress opened the door to NIH sponsorship of research with preimplantation human embryos[3] ([24], pp. 1-2).

Before actually funding any research proposals, NIH officials appointed a panel of 19 individuals with expertise in a variety of fields to develop ethical guidelines. This group, the NIH Human Embryo Research Panel, submitted its final report in September 1994; it was unanimously approved by the NIH's Advisory Committee to the Director on December 2, 1994. Both at the initial publication of the report and at the time of Advisory Committee approval, intense public controversy erupted.

171

Nick Fotion and Jan C. Heller (eds.), Contingent Future Persons, 171-189.
© 1997 *Kluwer Academic Publishers. Printed in the Netherlands.*

While many points in the report were heatedly debated, the most intense controversy focused on one recommendation of the panel: That under carefully delineated circumstances, it was ethically acceptable to fertilize oocytes in the laboratory solely for purposes of research ([20]; [7], pp. 13-14; [24], pp. xi-xii, 41-45).

This issue, whether it is permissible to develop embryos purely for research, that is, "research embryos," or whether all research must rely on embryos remaining from infertility treatment, that is, "surplus" or "spare" embryos, was one of the most difficult for the panel.[4] While attempting to consider both sides, members acknowledged the difficulty of developing adequate philosophical arguments to ground their deliberations ([24], pp. 41-45, 50; [26]).

In this article I will attempt to further the debate on these questions: Is it morally wrong to bring a human zygote into existence without any intent that it become a future person, but in order to gain knowledge about human reproduction and fertilization, developmental failure and birth defects, genetic diseases and chromosomal abnormalities? Is there a morally relevant distinction between fertilizing oocytes (creating embryos) that are destined to be used only in research, versus fertilizing oocytes for infertility treatment and then permitting embryos not needed to achieve pregnancy to be donated for research? In other words, may one develop embryos for use in research, or may one use only discarded embryos that remain after the completion of infertility treatment? Or is it equally wrong to use both types of embryos?

RESEARCH EMBRYOS AND SURPLUS EMBRYOS

The central question is whether there is a morally relevant distinction between the use of research embryos (created specifically for research) and the use of surplus embryos that result from infertility treatment. I will examine this question under three different assumptions: (1) that the preimplantation embryo is not yet a human being or person but is a human entity at an earlier developmental stage; (2) that the life of the human being begins at fertilization, so that once conceived, the preimplantation embryo is a fully human subject; (3) that the preimplantation embryo in the laboratory (though not in normal procreation) is still a merely possible person, in the sense that its existence as a future person depends on decisions and actions yet to be taken. Only the third assumption treats the in vitro situation as unique from a moral perspective.

Assumption (1): A Developing Form of Human Life

The Human Embryo Research Panel argued for assumption (1) and used it as a rationale for its ethical recommendations. It described the preimplantation embryo as a "developing form of human life" that "does not have the same moral status as an infant or child" ([24], pp. x, 35-40, 45-48). Extensive data on the development of the early embryo have led many scholars, including some prominent Roman Catholic authors, to conclude that a human being or person could not possibly be present before 14 days' developmental age[5] ([17]; [29]; [11]; [2]). The Human Embryo Research Panel followed these scholars in arguing that the preimplantation embryo is not a full human subject, and thus does not have the same rights or require the same treatment as an infant or child ([24], pp. x, 36-39, 45-48).

A surprising number of critics of the panel's conclusions agree with its assessment of the ontological and moral status of the preimplantation embryo itself. Many critics who acknowledge that the preimplantation embryo is not yet a human being or person, express opposition to the creation of embryos purely for research. While accepting the use of "spare" embryos, they regard the development of research embryos as "unconscionable," "alarming," morally problematic, and unworthy of federal support ([49]; [6]; [3], p. 1331).

But if one focuses on the ontology of the embryo itself, then "spare" embryos and embryos developed for research have the same status at a comparable developmental stage. If rights and obligations derive from the status of the embryo, then two embryos, one in the laboratory because it was fertilized for research purposes, the other because it is no longer needed for infertility treatment, have the same moral status at this time. Two authors who have considered this issue, Nicole Gerrand and Dena Davis, have provided extensive arguments in support of such moral equivalence ([19], pp. 176-179; [12], pp. 344-350). Their arguments imply that if it is permissible to use a surplus embryo for research, then it is permissible to use a specially created embryo at a similar developmental stage.

However, the objections of those who would prohibit the creation of research embryos are not necessarily based on the ontological status of the embryos themselves. Critics have identified other concerns that, in their view, ought to preclude creating research embryos while allowing research with already existing and available embryos.

Respect and Symbolism

An intuitive sense that the human zygote should be treated in some way differently from the way gametes are treated has led to conceptualizations like "respect." The Ethics Advisory Board in 1979 said that the human embryo was "entitled to profound respect" ([14], p. 35056), while the 1994 panel spoke of "respect for the special character of the preimplantation human embryo" ([24], p. xi). Attempts to delineate precisely what this "respect" entails lead to agreement on only one point: that there should be some restrictions on what can be done with human embryos that go beyond constraints on the study of human gametes or animal embryos. In other words, a line must be drawn.

The Human Embryo Research Panel drew a line that combined many elements, for example, the purpose and importance of the research, the lack of alternative methods such as animal models, the number of embryos to be studied, and the length of time for which embryos would be sustained. In particular, it limited the use of specially created embryos to research that is not only of great importance, but that either cannot be conducted at all, or that cannot be conducted validly, without allowing some fertilization of eggs in the research context ([24], pp. 69-70).

Opponents of any development of research embryos seem to regard the line separating "spare" embryos from specially created embryos as the crucial line. For example, an influential *Washington Post* editorial opposing the development of research embryos had the title, 'Embryos: Drawing the Line' [49].

But if the line is not based on ontological characteristics that differentiate "spare" from research embryos, but is our expression of the "respect" we wish to show human embryonic life, then the line could be drawn at many other places. We could, for example, allow research only up to 5 days or 7 days; we could more stringently restrict the use of all embryos; or we could allow research embryos to be studied only to the point of syngamy (the final stage of fertilization when the male and female chromosomes unite). While it seems intuitively clear that *some* line should be drawn (unless one wishes to regard even the most bizarre research as ethically unproblematic), there are essentially no criteria for drawing a line that simply expresses "respect."

John Robertson describes the line as a symbol of the value we place on human life; for many, choosing to use only "spare" embryos in research communicates "a clear symbolic meaning" ([35], pp. 37-38). In drawing the line at creating embryos for research "we [reaffirm] a commitment to the value of human life" ([35], p. 38). Yet Robertson notes that "strictly limiting" the creation of research embryos to certain well-defined purposes, such as the study of the process of fertilization itself, could affirm a similar commitment.

A "respect" which imposes no clear duties but is affirmed and expressed through drawing symbolic lines, admits of an infinity of different embodiments. In Robertson's words, "Symbolic meanings are so personal and variable" that a line which seems overly permissive to one person will appear rigidly restrictive to another ([35], p. 38). Robertson himself found the Human Embryo Research Panel's recommendations "quite conservative," and advised academic and research institutions not to feel bound by them in non-federally-funded research ([34], p. B2).

There is no logical reason why the line must be drawn just precisely between the use of "spare" embryos and the use of research embryos. While this may be the line we choose to adopt, it is only as valid in expressing "respect" as its interpreters find it to be.

Procreative Ends

Another line of reasoning stresses the centrality of procreative purpose, beginning with the assumption that embryos ought to be brought into existence only for procreative purposes, and that it is unethical to create human life for any other reason. However, once the procreative purpose(s) of a couple have been achieved, if there are embryos remaining that they no longer need or desire, then the couple may donate these surplus embryos for research. It is then ethically acceptable to use them for study and research ([3], pp. 1330-1331).

In this argument it is unclear what grounds there are for the assumption that a zygote may be brought into existence only for a procreative purpose, that is, with the intent that it become an actual person. Before the zygote existed, it had no right or claim to exist (for any purpose), nor not to exist (for any purpose). David Heyd seems correct in arguing that "coming to life is neither a harm nor a gift," even in the case of those who eventually become actual persons ([22], p. 109). Moreover, a zygote brought into existence for research purposes will exist for only a small number of days, and will perish before it can have even the lowest level of experience. Hence it cannot experience any harm from the research. Since it will neither have rights violated, nor be harmed, nor be deprived of benefit by being brought into existence as a research embryo, it is unclear why bringing it into existence for this purpose is unethical.

Possibly some sort of natural law argument is at work here. For example, the Roman Catholic version of natural law theory would maintain that egg and sperm may be joined only with a view to their "natural end" or *telos* of developing into a fetus and then a person. But Catholic teaching would not permit any joining of eggs and sperm in the "unnatural" setting of the laboratory, separated from the act of sexual intercourse [37]. Hence according to this view of natural law morality, the presence of any embryos in the laboratory, even those intended for transfer, represents a violation of the moral law.

In an extended discussion of the significance of procreative purpose, George Annas, Arthur Caplan, and Sherman Elias claim:

An embryo has moral standing not so much for what it is…, but because it is the result of procreative activity…. People have a direct interest in the status and fate of every embryo formed from their gametes, because such embryos carry their genes and can potentially become their children ([3], p. 1330).

Taken at face value, the first sentence appears preposterous; in normal sexual intercourse, many conceptions do not result from any explicit procreative intention. Some conceptions occur even when there is deliberate nonprocreative intention and activity, such as use of a contraceptive method. To suggest that the moral status of an embryo depends on the nature and intent of the activity within which it is conceived seems intuitively absurd.

Furthermore, the passage raises questions about the authors' support for the use of "spare" embryos in research. If gamete providers have a "direct interest in the . . . fate of *every* embryo formed from their gametes," then what would lead them to renounce this interest by consenting to research use of any of their embryos? If Annas *et al.* are correct about this felt interest of the gamete providers, it would seem to be impinged on more through their donating a specific embryo with a specific genetic constitution than by their donating eggs or sperm when the fertilization is as yet indeterminate.

Later Annas, Caplan, and Elias state their underlying assumption in a less ambiguous way: "For most people it is the intention to create a child that makes the creation of an embryo a moral act" ([3], p. 1331). But as long as one originally intended procreation, then surplus embryos may be used for research. However, this line of reasoning begs the question at issue: If it is not wrong to use a preimplantation embryo in research, then how can it be wrong to intend this use at the time of fertilization? In Gerrand's words, "To argue that an *intention to do X* is immoral, presupposes that *doing X* is immoral" ([19], p. 180). If it it wrong to *intend* to use embryos for research at the time of fertilization, then how can it later be permissible to *use* them for research?

The proliferation of references to "intent" suggests that some version of the double effect principle is operating in this argument.[6] When in vitro fertilization is undertaken, the usual scenario is to induce hyperovulation in the woman, to recover and fertilize as many eggs as possible, and to transfer several back to the woman. The remainder may be frozen to await a possible future transfer. The "good effect" of the act of fertilizing a number of eggs is achieving a pregnancy, and this is the directly intended effect at the time of fertilization. Presumably the "bad effect" is a collection of leftover embryos, in culture or frozen. While this effect is most likely foreseen from the beginning, it is presumably not the explicit intent of either the prospective parents or the clinicians.

Thus one might argue that the existence of "spare" embryos is an unintended, indirect effect of the attempt to achieve pregnancy and the birth of at least one child. Of course, there are other alternatives for the surplus embryos besides entering them into a research protocol. But if they otherwise would have been discarded or left in storage indefinitely, then to study them in research might be regarded as the least bad of the available choices. Faced with an unintended and undesirable situation, one makes the best of it and reaps what good one can.

A related argument makes use of the Kantian dictum that we ought never to treat others merely as means to our own ends. Davis imagines how this dictum might be applied:

One could argue that "spare" embryos are created as part of a process that is aimed at the creation of a...baby who will be valued for its own sake as well as for the happiness it will bring its parents. Thus the spare embryo is the "fallout" of a process that at least begins by treating it as an end. In contrast, [quoting King], "The fertilization of human oocytes is unnerving because human life is being created solely for human *use*" ([12], p. 349).

The initial procreative purpose is supposed to insure that no embryo is treated solely as a means to the ends of others.

In Davis' view, the typical IVF scenario belies this interpretation. When a large number of ova are retrieved and fertilized in the hope that one will implant after transfer, then most of the fertilized eggs do seem to have the role of means to the future development of one or two others. "A scenario in which the goal of a born child almost always depends upon the destruction of a number of embryos along the way is hardly one in which each embryo is treated as an end in itself" ([12], p. 350).

The essential double effect distinction between what is intended and what is merely foreseen appears to break down in this scenario. When 10 to 15 eggs are fertilized, there surely is no intent to achieve 10 to 15 live births. The intent probably is to achieve one, two, or three pregnancies and births, ideally one at a time. If the clinicians are interested in research, they may even choose to fertilize a large number of oocytes in the hope that some will be "left over" for research. Thus, the availability of "spare" embryos for research may be part of their initial direct intention.

Since there is some randomness in the IVF process, one could claim that each individual embryo initially has a fair (equal) chance to develop into a person. Cleavage-state embryos are selected for transfer fairly randomly as there is no reliable way to select those with the best developmental potential ([48], pp. 9-16), and after transfer the one(s) that implant(s) are selected by a natural lottery. Embryos that eventually perish or become "spare" embryos presumably had a fair chance of survival in the original lottery. None was initially identified simply to be used as a means in research.

However, if the preimplantation embryo were an actual human being, the sort of entity to which the Kantian maxim properly applies, then no destructive research with it would be permissible. Merely being given a statistical chance to be treated as an end in itself would not be sufficient. Each individual embryo would have to be given the best possible opportunity to continue its development, perhaps by transferring embryos one by one until all had been transferred, or perhaps by fertilizing only one oocyte at a time. There could be no such thing as a surplus embryo made available for research.

In invoking a distorted form of double effect reasoning, authors may even be suggesting to clinicians and researchers that bad faith practices are ethically acceptable. If the only way to develop embryos for research is to make sure that "spare" embryos will exist, then clinician-researchers can easily recommend the fertilization of many more oocytes than will (on average) be needed to satisfy their clients' needs. In this way the researchers can maintain that all were fertilized for a procreative goal, while knowing that a significant proportion of IVF embryos were actually fertilized to become research embryos.

Recently David Heyd has even called into question whether the decision to procreate, or to bring an actual child into existence, treats the child as an end in itself. He asserts that the decision to cause a child to exist "is the only one in which the child is treated purely as a means (usually to the parents' satisfaction, wishes, and ideals)!" ([22], p. 52). For him, genesis (existence) choices are always egocentric:

People produce children for a variety of reasons.... None of these reasons or motives refers to the welfare of the child; none takes the child as an end in itself ([22], pp. 108-109).

Since Heyd sees the decision to bring a child into existence as one of the most self-interested of human choices ([22], p. 199), he might argue that to use one's gametes to create one's own genetic child is more egocentered than to donate gametes for the creation of research embryos that would benefit all of humankind.

Heyd's assertions cast doubt on the assumption that procreative intent is morally pure and other intentions are morally suspect. However, his claim that procreation treats a child purely as means seems exaggerated. There is truth in what Heyd says, but there is also truth in an opposing view.

Summary

In this section I have examined arguments presented under the assumption that the preimplantation embryo is not yet a human being or person but is a human entity at an earlier developmental stage. I have asked why authors who hold this view may believe it is morally unacceptable to develop human embryos for research, while they find it acceptable to use surplus embryos remaining from infertility treatment.

Since no innate ontological characteristics distinguish research embryos from "spare" embryos, authors have invoked other grounds for making a moral distinction. Some authors regard the line separating use of "spare" embryos from creation of research embryos as a significant symbolic expression of our commitment to the value of life; others base the distinction on the belief that embryos may morally be created only for a procreative purpose, although unneeded embryos may later be used for research. I have shown that their arguments are not convincing. Under assumption (1), there appears to be no valid reason for prohibiting the development of embryos for research while allowing research use of "spare" embryos.

Assumption (2): A Fully Human Subject

The view that the life of each individual human being begins at conception or fertilization is widely espoused, and is perhaps the most commonly held view. Some of its adherents accept abortion as a legitimate moral choice in tragic circumstances, while others believe all abortions are morally wrong and should be legally prohibited. Similarly, some adherents consider the use of "spare" embryos in research to be morally acceptable, or at least find this use less troubling than the creation of embryos for research; others, most notably the Catholic Church, oppose all forms of embryo research equally (unless expected to be directly therapeutic to the embryo) ([31]; [32]; [33]; [37]; [50]). Under assumption (2), is it coherent to distinguish between the use of "spare" and research embryos, and if so, on what might this distinction be based?

Consider two oocytes, A and B. Oocyte A is fertilized as part of a research project to compare methods for maturing eggs in the laboratory (rather than through hormonal stimulation of a woman). For three days after fertilization, embryo A is studied to determine whether it cleaves normally, has chromosomal abnormalities, etc. Because of uncertainty about its potential for normal development, there is never any intent to transfer embryo A to a woman, and no effort is made to support its survival in culture beyond three days.

Oocyte B is fertilized along with 15 others as part of an effort to achieve pregnancy for the gamete providers. Although embryo B has no sign of abnormality, it is not selected for transfer. Its progenitors eventually have two children and decide not to have more, so they donate embryo B for research. By now embryo B, which was frozen at the 16-cell stage several days after fertilization, has been frozen for four years. Upon thawing it appears normal and is studied to see how far it can be made to develop in culture. When it reaches the blastocyst stage at the equivalent of 8 days' development, it progresses no further.

Critics of all creation of research embryos would argue that embryo A should never have been brought into existence. But why would some of these critics permit research involving "spare" embryo B? Under the assumption that both A and B are existing full human beings, if is difficult to understand how it could be justifiable to use either A or B in research that will result in an end to its life.

Those who wish to distinguish A from B may invoke an analogy with the use of tissue from aborted fetuses for research. They may accept the use of tissue from an aborted fetus although they "would be horrified at the idea that a woman could become pregnant for the sole purpose of having an abortion to produce fetal tissue for research purposes" ([3], p. 1331). But this analogy fails.

The aborted fetus thought to be analogous to the "spare" embryo is not in a remotely comparable situation. The aborted fetus is, after all, dead, and has no possibility whatsoever to develop into a future person. The choice of its fate has already been irrevocably made. On the other hand, the preimplantation embryo that is no longer needed for infertility treatment, assuming it is not damaged, presumably does have the capacity to continue its life and development. It only needs a womb to which it can be transferred.

Those who believe that the embryo's life as a human being begins at fertilization cannot regard the "spare" embryo as doomed. Its fate is not inevitably death, and that claim cannot be used to justify its use in destructive research.

The only argument that might carry weight is one that gives moral precedence to the choices of the genetic parents. Suppose that the progenitors of embryo B do not want to have any more children, nor do they want their surplus embryos "adopted" by other couples. As Annas, Caplan, and Elias assert, they "have a direct interest in the status and fate of every embryo formed from their gametes" ([3], p. 1330), and thus are unwilling to have their genetic child gestated and raised by unknown parents. We cannot morally coerce these progenitors to have more children, nor to donate their embryos for transfer to another woman. Such coercion would seriously violate both their reproductive rights and their right of informed consent in the medical context.

All other alternatives necessarily result in the end of the existence of embryos like B. Given the choice of B's parents not to allow B to survive, one might claim they have chosen the equivalent of an abortion, and so researchers can agree to reap some benefit from the inevitable end of B's existence by using B for study.

Once again, however, such reasoning appears to encourage bad faith among researchers. After all, the couple presenting for services could have been told that all embryos that appear capable of development must eventually be transferred, either to them or to another couple. Under the assumption that a human life begins at fertilization, this constraint seems required at the very beginning of the treatment process. Otherwise it appears that clinician-researchers are permitting careless proliferation of embryos in order to end up in the situation where "spare" embryos are available for research, with the justification that the progenitors refuse to allow them to be transferred. One should have faced this predictable outcome at the beginning, not at the point where there are only bad choices.

Assumption (3): A Merely Possible Person

The issue of whether it is ethical to develop research embryos can be examined under still a third assumption, which capitalizes on the distinction between the preimplantation embryo in vivo and in vitro. In normal conception, although many embryos may be lost in the period between fertilization and implantation, no further decisions need be taken by moral agents in order for implantation to occur. The opposite is true in the laboratory, where every step requires a decision: what culture medium will be used and what growth factors will be added to it, at what stage will transfer be done, how many embryos and which ones will be transferred, what will be done with the remaining embryos? At any of these steps, the developmental process may be brought to a halt through the choice that is made.

This difference suggests that what entities we identify as merely possible persons, and which we identify as likely future persons, may differ between the in vivo and in vitro situations. Thus David Heyd's analysis of our duties to possible persons may apply in the IVF context. Heyd characterizes a possible person as a person whose existence depends on decisions yet to be made. He argues that possible persons have no moral status whatsoever, since their existence is logically dependent on whether we decide to bring them into existence ([22], p. 99). In his view, a being is not benefitted by being brought into existence, nor harmed by not being brought into existence:

Existence is not a moral predicate; to be cannot in itself be either good or bad, a subject of duty or prohibition, a right or a wrong ([22], p. 124).

A possible person in this sense is sometimes called a potential person, and Heyd appears to use the terms interchangeably ([22], pp. 97-103). However, I believe this usage is confusing. The concept of *potential*, hence potential personhood, has a long philosophical history. In the Aristotelian-Thomistic tradition, potentiality is a teleological concept that refers to a being's ability to actualize itself through an inner principle it possesses. A standard definition of *potential person* is: a being that will become a person in the normal course of its development ([46], p. 79; [13], pp.

94-100; [27], p. 25). It is reasonable to regard a human embryo in vivo as a potential person from the time of conception.

Potential may also refer to probabilities. In this sense, the potential of an entity to develop into a person is the probability that it will do so in the normal course of its development. The probability that an unfertilized egg will develop into a person is zero. But the probability that a fertilized egg in vivo will spontaneously develop into a person is substantial, perhaps 25 to 30 percent. The total natural pregnancy loss rate is uncertain, but certainly a good proportion of conceptions do develop into persons ([40], p. 86).

The teleological and statistical senses of *potential* are closely related. In Edward Langerak's words:

If the natural end of (a) is to become (A) then it is highly probable that, without interference, (a) will become (A) ([27], p. 28, n.4).

I will follow this usage and reserve the term *potential person* for an entity that is likely to become a person in the normal course of its development, or if its normal development is not interfered with.

The term *possible person* will refer to a person whose existence depends on decisions yet to be made and actions yet to be taken. A standard definition of *possible person* is: a being that could, under certain causally possible conditions, become an actual person ([27], p. 25; [43], pp. 297-305; [44]). An unfertilized ovum represents a possible person; by making decisions to fertilize it, to maintain it, and to transfer it to a woman, we choose the interventions that give it the potential to develop into an actual person.

The IVF embryo in the laboratory is also a merely possible person. Whether it acquires the potential to become an actual person or not depends entirely on a series of decisions we make with respect to it. Since we have no obligation to bring this nonexistent person into existence, our decisions are not constrained by its rights or our duties. As Singer and Dawson note, the embryo in the woman's body has a definite chance of developing into a child "unless a deliberate human act interrupts its growth," whereas in the laboratory setting, deliberate human acts are needed if it is to develop at all. In the laboratory, "everything depends on our knowledge and skills, and on what we decide to do" ([40], p. 77).

I would argue that although there may be moral obligations with regard to potential persons, such as not interfering with their development into actual persons unless there is a morally justifying reason, there is no corresponding obligation regarding possible persons. One has no obligation to bring them into existence. With IVF embryos in the laboratory, one has no obligation to bring any of the possible persons they represent into actual existence.

While I believe this argument has theoretical coherence, it does not seem to be appealing to most people. Some have said that it appears to put too much weight on the location of the embryo, whether in the woman or in the laboratory. Singer and Dawson hold that one cannot talk meaningfully of the potential of an entity "independently of the context in which that entity exists" ([40], p. 77). And yet, should an entity's status as merely possible or as future actual depend on whether it is in the laboratory or inside a woman?

A thought experiment may make this distinction more plausible, by putting the focus back on the human decisions to be made rather than on location. Suppose an IVF embryo at the 8-cell stage is in the laboratory in preparation for transfer. It appears to be developing well, and scientists believe it could be separated into two 4-celled embryos that would both have a good chance of implanting. Even if one thinks that the 8-cell embryo is more than just a possible person, surely the existence of a second (genetically identical) person is merely possible, and represents only a possible person. No one would claim that there is any obligation to bring this second possible person into existence; some would even argue that it would be wrong to make an identical twin exist, citing concerns about uniqueness and identity. The fact that four existing cells could be separated from the original embryo and nurtured to develop into a person puts us under no obligation to take the steps that would accomplish this.

This example shows that there clearly are entities in the laboratory setting that have a complete human genetic constitution but are merely possible persons. Analogously, the earlier claim that the in vitro embryo itself represents a merely possible person should not be lightly dismissed. This embryo is also a simple collection of cells that will never develop into a person unless specific decisions and actions are taken.

If one sees the in vitro embryo as a merely possible person, then the distinction between research and "spare" embryos is irrelevant. Neither the research embryo nor the "spare" embryo is a future actual person, since the decision to transfer for implantation has not been made in either case. The decision to fertilize an oocyte is just the first in a series of choices that have to be made in order for a person to come into existence. Until the decision to transfer is made, the existence of a person with the particular genetic identity of a specific IVF embryo is still the existence of a possible person.

CONSEQUENCES FOR ACTUAL PERSONS

I have shown that arguments intended to make a moral distinction between research use of "spare" embryos and the development of research embryos are seriously flawed. These arguments fail under each of three possible assumptions regarding the ontological and moral status of the ex utero preimplantation embryo.

So far, however, I have not explicitly considered the consequences that might follow from a failure to distinguish research embryos from "spare" embryos. In considering consequences, I will assume a "person-affecting" rather than an "impersonal value" view of consequences ([22], pp. 80-90). In a "person-affecting" approach, the moral rightness or wrongness of a choice depends on the effects on actual persons, either those who actually exist now or those we predict will exist in the future.

Possible Bad Consequences

Opponents of the development of research embryos sometimes cite alarming possible long-term outcomes such as "learning how to grow embryos and fetuses entirely outside the human body" [6]. While such things hypothetically could happen, I will focus on more immediate and more likely consequences. The most frequently-cited concerns are these: The opportunity to create research embryos may lead to the commodification of eggs and embryos, to buying and selling them at a market price. This market may involve clinician-researchers in conflict of interest situations, which may also occur if researchers are invested in profit-making ventures that utilize the results of their work. Both healthy egg donors and infertile women could be exploited in this market, which may offer them significant financial or other compensation for providing eggs for fertilization at risk to themselves. If eggs become easily available, it may become routine to fertilize them for research purposes. As a result, they could be used for toxicity testing and other routine studies. It might be convenient to have a store of research embryos of a great variety of genetic heritages, leading to embryo "banks" or "libraries" ([3], p. 1331; [21], pp. 611-613; [1], pp. 40-44; and [19], pp. 182-186).

Some of these predicted consequences directly affect existing persons: infertile women who are asked to contribute some of their eggs for research, healthy young women who are enticed to accept risks to their health or future fertility to provide eggs, and infertile couples who may be unaware of a conflict of interest on the part of those who are treating them. Such consequences can be prevented by not permitting the practices that cause them. The Human Embryo Research Panel insisted that neither eggs, sperm, nor embryos could be bought or sold ([24], pp. 54-55); that only women who were undergoing surgery for their own health or treatment could donate eggs ([24], pp. 56-59); and that researchers must disclose to donors and research participants if they had a financial interest in the research ([24], pp. 53-54, 66-67). These recommendations, if adopted by NIH, would explicitly apply only to federally-funded research, though the panel hoped that NIH standards would be generally adopted by researchers and professional organizations ([24], p. x).

Other consequences, those related to the proliferation of research embryos, affect actual persons in different ways depending on their own perceptions. Alta Charo has called attention to the fact that the deep offense and outrage expressed by opponents of embryo research is a consequence that must be taken into account ([7], pp. 21-23). Most people appear to be disturbed by the prospect of routinely creating embryos, using them for standard toxicity testing, or banking them as convenient sources of research material. The Human Embryo Research Panel specifically ruled out such practices ([24], pp. 44-45).

There are ways to prevent the projected bad consequences of the use of research embryos. But is there sufficient positive reason for venturing into this unknown and controversial territory? What good consequences can be predicted from the use of research embryos that could not be achieved with surplus embryos?

Projected Good Consequences

All scientific research is justified by recounting the good consequences that are expected to result from the research. When research is ethically sensitive, additional justification is usually expected. For example, if human subjects are put at risk, then there must be an expectation of therapeutic benefit, either to them or to others, to justify this risk. In the case of embryo research, specifically the creation of research embryos, it is reasonable to require that the expected benefit from research be significant. Three types of beneficial consequences can be cited: (1) already achieved benefits; (2) projected benefits; and (3) avoidance of harms that are likely in the absence of research.

In the category of already-achieved benefits is, first of all, in vitro fertilization itself. Those who support research use of "spare" embryos but not the fertilization of research embryos seem to forget that IVF succeeded only after many years of research on laboratory fertilization. Animal work proceeded as far as it was productive, and eventually a human oocyte was exposed to human sperm in the laboratory. While the hope was an eventual pregnancy and the birth of a child, surely no one thought the first attempt at fertilization would lead to this result. Decades of work, hundreds of attempted fertilizations, observation to determine whether viable embryos had been produced, all preceded the first transfers of IVF embryos to women ([16]; [15], pp. 44-45).

Even so, many scientist-clinicians believed that the process moved too quickly, and that not enough study was done to insure the safety of the process before it was recommended to infertile couples ([41]; [42]). How much laboratory work is needed before clinical application is initiated is, of course, debatable. But surely some laboratory study of a new reproductive technique is ethically prerequisite to its use with prospective parents. Some fertilization in the laboratory context, without intent to do the transfer that could lead to pregnancy, is essential if IVF and its variants are to be developed at all.

Although IVF is now in wide use in a large number of countries, success rates remain low. There is also evidence that some aspects of the procedure are not as safe as they could or should be ([10], pp. 19-21; [38]). Many scientists believe that significant improvements could be made, and that the lack of progress is partly attributable to the fact that there has not been a coordinated research program that includes basic research ([48], pp. 3-17). In the U.S. this is largely due to the complete absence of federal funding.

The Human Embryo Research Panel's report devoted 27 pages to description of the benefits that could be anticipated from IVF and embryo research ([24], pp. 7-33). In its consideration of the moral debate on the creation of research embryos, it specifically identified advances that could not be made without allowing some fertilization in the research context ([24], pp. 42-45). In many of these studies fertilization would be the endpoint of the research protocol: the study of ovum maturation in the laboratory, the study of ovum freezing, the development of new contraceptives. The ovum studies would be of great benefit to infertile women who might not have to undergo hormonal stimulation to bring the eggs to maturation, to women with medical conditions that preclude such stimulation, and to women who need cancer treatments that would damage eggs left within their bodies ([23], p. 2). Research on innovative and more effective contraceptive methods has been on hold for years, a fact recently called to our attention by a 1996 Institute of Medicine report [28].

Critics argue, however, that prospective benefits cannot provide justification for research that is itself immoral. Some commentators suggest that by invoking prospective benefits one is allowing a "scientific imperative" or "research imperative" to override ethical considerations ([5], pp. 39-40).

It may well be true that research is not ethically required: we are not obligated to advance scientific knowledge nor to offer new benefits to humankind. Perhaps even the cure of disease is not ethically mandatory, much less the overcoming of infertility. Assuming that all these ends are optional, it is plausible to suggest that they may be sought only through ethically unquestionable methods. Moreover, the status of IVF and its various applications is relevantly different from that of most medical advances. In offering IVF to infertile couples, clinicians are not attempting to remedy the physiological causes of infertility. Rather, they are offering to bypass these conditions and to achieve a pregnancy *without* remedying the underlying functional deficiencies. Thus they are performing procedures that often involve risks, and may cause harms, in order to give the infertile couple a child, not in hopes of curing a disease or correcting an anomaly.

This point is morally relevant because the clincans may be causing harms in the course of providing a purely elective procedure. One could argue, as Cynthia Cohen has, that if reproductive technologies cause harms, then they should not be used, even though some children will then not exist [10]. Many of these harms could be avoided if the necessary research were done before a new procedure was offered clinically. Scientist Alan Trounson describes a striking example:

I argued strongly that the risks of serious chromosomal abnormalities arising from the freezing of unfertilized eggs did not warrant the introduction of this technique into clinical IVF. The frozen-thawed human eggs should first be evaluated as pronuclear eggs or pre-embryos before the technique was considered for use clinically. Others did not agree and went ahead and introduced the technique into clinical IVF. . . . Many publications have subsequently identified genetic and developmental problems in the freezing of unfertilized eggs ([47], p. 15).

A second example cited by Trounson is the fertilization of eggs by injecting one sperm under the zona pellucida (shell). Although this process is already in wide use in Australia and the United States, Trounson argues that clinical studies needed for safety have not been conducted ([47], p. 16). A third example is zona removal ("assisted hatching") for fertilized eggs that have shown an inadequacy to achieve this naturally. The prospect of contamination of an unprotected fertilized egg through exposure to the various components added to the culture medium is real but unknown ([48], p. 10).

Some authors maintain that it is not wrong to use untested reproductive technologies that might cause harm to embryos intended to develop into children, since without such procedures these children would not exist at all. Even if such a claim could be upheld, one would also be risking serious harm to already existing persons, particularly women. No infertile couple presents for treatment in the expectation that they will have a seriously damaged child. While that is always a possibility in any pregnancy, in this situation it is the technology used to achieve pregnancy that may cause the damage. It is one thing to accept this risk when it is the best that can be offered; it is another to accept the risk when "the embryo may be defective as a result of the lack of adequate prior research" ([18], p. 122).

Thus one might argue that the harms likely to be caused through offering untested therapies are actual harms to actual persons, while the disvalue of creating embryos for research, provided that the practice is carefully regulated, is largely hypothetical. In balancing these two sides, one might conclude that the side favoring research carries heavier weight, and that such research is at least permissible and possibly mandatory.

But another alternative exists that is often forgotten. All of the high-tech reproductive techniques are purely elective; we do not have to use any of them. In an essay in *Embryo Experimentation*, the alternatives are starkly enunciated:

Cease using these techniques (even though they could become validated if proper testing were permitted) or do the necessary embryo research to validate procedures before transferring embryos created in that way to women ([18], p. 122).

If the choice were presented this way to politicians and the public, I believe their reaction would be different from what it is currently. Rather than a moratorium on federal funding of IVF research, we would have a moratorium on clinical use of high-tech infertility treatments, or at least a moratorium on every procedure that goes beyond basic IVF (using an unstimulated hormonal cycle, partner gametes, and one embryo transferred at a time). While success rates and qualifying candidates for this basic procedure may be low, the unknown risks and harms of other protocols would be avoided until appropriate studies of safety and effectiveness could be conducted.

Moreover, one could argue that persons who are opposed to all creation of embryos in research should forgo even simple IVF. Since IVF was developed as a result of research on the fertilization of oocytes, in using IVF these persons are benefitting from research that they believe to be seriously morally wrong. Whether it is morally justifiable to profit from such research after the fact is at least debatable.

CONCLUSION

In this paper I have argued that, regardless of the position one takes on the moral status of the preimplantation embryo, there are no convincing moral arguments to distinguish research use of surplus embryos from development of embryos explicitly for research. Either both practices are morally permissible, or neither is morally permissible.

I have also argued that if public policy decisions prohibit or curtail research on the safety and efficacy of new reproductive techniques, then this restriction should be accompanied by equally stringent restriction on the clinical use of these techniques. It is not morally permissible to put persons at risk of harm by offering unvalidated medical procedures, particularly in situations where treatment is purely elective.

NOTES

[1] The term "preembryo" has come into use to denote the embryo during the first 14 days after fertilization. I will, however, follow the more standard scientific usage and refer to the human conceptus as an "embryo" from fertilization until 8 weeks' developmental age.

[2] Note Derek Parfit's suggestion that "a person is not...a being whose existence must be all-or-nothing." In his view, personal identity is an indeterminate concept which is not of great importance either metaphysically or ethically ([30], pp. 274-282). In contrast, note the position of Roderick Chisholm, who identifies personal identity and existence as a uniquely determinate kind of existence. While the identities of other sorts of things (ships, tables, clubs, nations) may depend on our stipulations and constructs, the identity (existence) of a particular person does not ([8], pp. 136-137; [9]).

[3] The NIH Human Embryo Research Panel defined the "ex utero preimplantation embryo" or "preimplantation embryo" as a fertilized ovum in vitro that has never been transferred to or implanted in a uterus ([24], p. ix).

[4] The Human Embryo Research Panel consistently used the terminology "embryos remaining from infertility treatment," and avoided referring to these embryos as "surplus" or "spare." However, since the latter terminology is common in the literature, I will often use it as a shorthand for "embryos remaining from infertility treatment."

[5] Such data include the following: Because of the possibility that both twinning and the reaggregation of cleavage-stage embryos can occur, the embryo at this stage is not yet a distinct individual, or is not individuated. It has the characteristics of a cellular-stage entity and lacks the differentiation and organization required for a human organism. The primitive streak which gives orientation to the embryo and marks the beginning of tissue and organ differentiation appears only around 14 days in vivo, and probably later in vitro. Only after the appearance of the primitive streak does neurulation, the development of the nervous system, begin.

[6] I owe this suggestion to Ronald Green.

BIBLIOGRAPHY

1. Alpers, A., and Lo, B.: 1995, 'Commodification and Commercialization in Human Embryo Research', *Stanford Law and Policy Review* 6, 39-45.
2. American College of Obstetricians and Gynecologists, Committee on Ethics: 1994, *Preembryo Research: History, Scientific Background, and Ethical Considerations*, Committee Opinion No. 136, Washington, D.C.

3.   Annas, G.J., Caplan, A., and Elias, S.: 1996, 'The Politics of Human-Embryo Research—Avoiding Ethical Gridlock', *New England Journal of Medicine* 334, 1329-1332.
4.   Andrews, L.: 1994, 'Appendix A: Country-by-Country Analysis', in *Papers Commissioned for the Human Embryo Research Panel*, vol. 2, National Institutes of Health, Washington, D.C., pp. 65-153.
5.   Callahan, D.: 1995, 'The Puzzle of Profound Respect', *Hastings Center Report* 25(1), 39-40.
6.   Caplan, A.: 1994, 'Congress, NIH Should Move Cautiously on Embryo Research', *St. Paul Pioneer Press*, October 13.
7.   Charo, R.A.: 1995, 'The Hunting of the Snark: The Moral Status of Embryos, Right-to-Lifers, and Third World Women', *Stanford Law and Policy Review* 6, 11-37.
8.   Chisholm, R.M.: 1976, *Person and Object: A Metaphysical Study*, Open Court, LaSalle, IL.
9.   Chisholm, R.M.: 1977, 'Coming into Being and Passing Away: Can the Metaphysician Help?', in S.F. Spicker and H.T. Engelhardt, Jr. (eds.), *Philosophical Medical Ethics*, D. Reidel, Dordrecht, Holland, pp. 169-182.
10. Cohen, C.B.: 1996, '"Give Me Children or I Shall Die!": New Reproductive Technologies and Harm to Children', *Hastings Center Report* 26(2), 19-27.
11. Curran, C.E.: 1973, 'Abortion: Law and Morality in Contemporary Catholic Theology', *Jurist* 33, 162-183.
12. Davis, D.S.: 1995, 'Embryos Created for Research Purposes', *Kennedy Institute of Ethics Journal* 5, 343-354.
13. Devine, P.E.: 1978, *The Ethics of Homicide*, Cornell University Press, Ithaca, NY.
14. Ethics Advisory Board: 1979, 'Report and Conclusions: HEW Support of Research Involving Human In Vitro Fertilization and Embryo Transfer', *Federal Register* 44, 35033-35058.
15. Edwards, R.: 1990, 'Ethics and Embryology: The Case for Experimentation', in A. Dyson and J. Harris (eds.), *Experiments on Embryos*, Routledge, London, pp. 42-54.
16. Edwards, R., and Steptoe, P.: 1980, *A Matter of Life: The Story of a Medical Breakthrough*, William Morrow and Co., New York.
17. Ford, N.M.: 1989, *When Did I Begin?*, Cambridge University Press, Cambridge.
18. Gaze, B., and Dawson, K.: 1990, 'Who Is the Subject of Research?', in P. Singer *et al.* (eds.), *Embryo Experimentation: Ethical, Legal and Social Issues*, Cambridge University Press, Cambridge, pp. 109-124.
19. Gerrand, N.: 1993, 'Creating Embryos for Research', *Journal of Applied Philosophy* 10, 175-187.
20. Green, R.M.: 1994, 'At the Vortex of Controversy: Developing Guidelines for Human Embryo Research', *Kennedy Institute of Ethics Journal* 4, 345-356.
21. Healy, B.P., and Berner, L.S.: 1995, 'A Position Against Federal Funding for Human Embryo Research: Words of Caution for Women, for Science, and for Society', *Journal of Women's Health* 4, 609-613.
22. Heyd, D.: 1992, *Genethics: Moral Issues in the Creation of People*, University of California Press, Berkeley.
23. Hogan, B.L., and Green, R.M.: 1995, 'Embryo Research Revisited', *Hastings Center Report* 25(3), 2-4.
24. Human Embryo Research Panel: 1994, *Report of the Human Embryo Research Panel*, vol. 1, National Institutes of Health, Washington, D.C.
25. Human Fertilisation and Embryology Authority: 1993, *Code of Practice*, rev.ed., Human Fertilisation and Embryology Authority, London.
26. King, P.A.: 1994, 'Statement of Patricia A. King: Concurring in Part and Dissenting in Part', in *Report of the Human Embryo Research Panel*, vol. 1, National Institutes of Health, Washington, D.C., pp. A3-A4.
27. Langerak, E.A.: 1979, 'Abortion: Listening to the Middle', *Hastings Center Report* 9(5), 24-28.
28. Leary, W.: 1996, 'Obstacles Are Said to Block New Kinds of Contraceptives', *New York Times*, May 29.
29. McCormick, R.A.: 1991, 'Who or What Is the Preembryo?', *Kennedy Institute of Ethics Journal* 1, 1-15.
30. Parfit, D.: 1985, *Reasons and Persons*, Oxford University Press, Oxford.
31. Pellegrino, E.D.: 1994, Letter to the NIH Human Embryo Research Panel, October 31.
32. Pellegrino, E.D.: 1995, 'Ethics', *Journal of the American Medical Association* 273, 1674-1676.

33. Ramsey Colloquium: 1995, 'The Inhuman Use of Human Beings: A Statement on Embryo Research by the Ramsey Colloquium', *First Things*, January, pp. 17-21.
34. Robertson, J.A.: 1994, 'Institutional Autonomy and Embryo Research', *Chronicle of Higher Education*, November 9, pp. B1-B2.
35. Robertson, J.A.: 1995, 'Symbolic Issues in Embryo Research', *Hastings Center Report* 25(1), 37-38.
36. Royal Commission on New Reproductive Technologies: 1993, *Proceed with Care*, vol. 1, Report of the Royal Commission, Ottawa, Canada.
37. Sacred Congregation for the Doctrine of the Faith: 1987, *Instruction on Respect for Human Life in Its Origin and on the Dignity of Procreation*, Vatican Polyglot Press, Vatican City.
38. Schenker, J.G., and Ezra, Y.: 1994, 'Complications of Assisted Reproductive Techniques', *Fertility and Sterility* 61, 411-422.
39. Singer, P., *et al.* (eds.): 1990, *Embryo Experimentation: Ethical, Legal and Social Issues*, Cambridge University Press, Cambridge.
40. Singer, P., and Dawson, K.: 1990, 'Embryo Experimentation and the Argument from Potential', in P. Singer, *et al.* (eds.), *Embryo Experimentation: Ethical, Legal and Social Issues*, Cambridge University Press, Cambridge, pp. 76-89.
41. Soupart, P.: 1978, 'Cytogenetics of Human Preimplantation Embryos', research proposal presented to the Ethics Advisory Board, September 15.
42. Soupart, P.: 1984, personal communication, April 3.
43. Tauer, C.A.: 1982, *The Moral Status of the Prenatal Human Subject of Research*, University Microfilms International, Ann Arbor, MI.
44. Tauer, C.A.: 1984, 'Laboratory-Fertilized Embryos: Potential Persons?', unpublished paper.
45. Tauer, C.A.: 1995, 'Preimplantation Embryos, Research Ethics, and Public Policy', *Bioethics Forum* 11(3), 30-37.
46. Tooley, M.: 1972, 'A Defense of Abortion and Infanticide', in J. Feinberg (ed.), *The Problem of Abortion*, Wadsworth, Belmont, CA, pp. 51-91.
47. Trounson, A.: 1990, 'Why Do Research on Human Pre-Embryos?', in P. Singer, *et al.* (eds.), *Embryo Experimentation: Ethical, Legal and Social Issues*, Cambridge University Press, Cambridge, pp. 14-25.
48. Van Blerkom, J.: 1994, "The History, Current Status and Future Direction of Research Involving Human Embryos', in *Papers Commissioned by the Human Embryo Research Panel*, vol. 2, National Institutes of Health, Washington, D.C., pp. 1-25.
49. *Washington Post* Editorial Staff: 1994, 'Embryos: Drawing the Line', *Washington Post*, October 2.
50. Weigel, G.: 1994, 'Creating Life to Study, then Kill', *Star Tribune* (Minneapolis), December 13.

WILLIAM P. GEORGE

ANTICIPATING POSTERITY: A LONERGANIAN
APPROACH TO THE PROBLEM OF CONTINGENT FUTURE PERSONS

Those inviting contributions to this volume have emphasized that the problem of contingent future persons (CFPs) poses theoretical and normative challenges to both philosophers and theologians. I understand the central question in this discussion to be whether one can reasonably speak of harm or benefit to persons whose existence is dependent upon certain types of action, such as the timing of conception. Apparently, such persons cannot be said to be harmed or benefited by any choice or action on which their existence depends because any other choice and action would mean that some *other* human being would come into existence. The persons actually born as a result of the choice and action are neither "better off" nor "worse off" than they would have been otherwise, for to say that contingent persons would be better or worse off would seem to require comparing their existence with some state prior to their existence. But comparison with a non-existent state seems impossible. And if it is unreasonable to speak of harm or benefit to future persons whose existence is contingent on our choices, then moral constraints on those choices would seem to evaporate ([9], pp. 3-7).

In my view, the challenges posed by this problem may be misplaced because the problem itself has been so narrowly construed. For instance, the problem, as it is laid out, seems to assume that the only morally significant comparison is between the later and earlier existence of one and the same person. But "better" or "worse" are relational concepts that just as surely involve comparing the existent or possible state of one person or community with the existent or possible state of another person or community. There is nothing unreasonable in saying that children being abused this very moment are worse off than other children now receiving loving care, or that *this* abusive situation is worse than *that* caring one. The reticence to envision comparisons of this kind when formulating the problem may signal a highly individualistic or atomistic understanding of personhood and of society.

It may turn out, in fact, that *given its initial formulation*, the problem of CFPs is insoluable in the way that certain puzzles or brain-teasers are insoluable: the proper answer is that there is no answer ([12], pp. 19-25). Such may be the case here. In seeking to make sense of benefit and harm within the "rules" of the problem as stated, the mind flits back and forth—"but if things had been otherwise..."—and the very future persons one is supposedly asking about keep disappearing. In such instances it may be best to give up the chase, at least momentarily, and pursue alternative lines of inquiry.

That is perhaps the most this essay can offer. I do not claim to have solved the problem of CFPs as stated. Nor do I propose to offer detailed prescriptive judgments

Nick Fotion and Jan C. Heller (eds.), Contingent Future Persons, 191-208.

on specific cases (e.g., embryo transfer, genetic counseling, etc.). Finally, I barely touch on the many theological issues that accompany considerations of the future. Rather, I am stepping back, or turning aside, to implicitly question the particular manner in which the problem is posed. This line of inquiry should, however, begin to respond to concerns of those who have posed the problem of CFPs. That is, I do want to show why and how, in the practical order wherein decisions are contemplated and made, it still makes sense to consider benefit and/or harm to future persons—the very point that the problem of CFPs calls into question.

By turning to philosopher and theologian Bernard J.F. Lonergan (1904-1984), I suggest ways of approaching the problem of CFPs that are rooted, and may thus be identified, in our own experience—that is, in the operations of our conscious intentionality (e.g., attending to data, raising questions, getting insights, testing those insights and resultant hypotheses in acts of judgment, apprehending value through feelings, making value judgments, deciding to act) ([12], passim; [11]). It is in the subject's heuristic or questioning attitude, which includes within itself immanent norms, or "transcendental precepts," that the basis for moral constraint and direction regarding CFPs is primarily to be found. This approach also builds upon the isomorphism, or correlativity, that exists between, on the one hand, the dynamic structure of human knowing and valuing, and, on the other, that which is to be known and valued—including future persons and the world, or worlds, they will possibly inhabit.

For two reasons at least, this essay is more suggestive than conclusive and detailed. There is no question, first of all, of exploring the range of Lonergan's thought that might be relevant to the discussion of CFPs. Lonergan never took up the issue as posed in the opening paragraph, so in looking to him for illumination we are necessarily engaged in inference or extrapolation [14]. But the essay remains suggestive for a more fundamental reason. I cannot overemphasize the fact that the inference or extrapolation that may aid our thinking about CFPs will not be from what Lonergan says to a problem he never directly addressed. Rather the decisive move will be back and forth between the reader's own intentional operations and the problem of CFPs. What Lonergan offers, through *Insight* and his several other writings, is a sophisticated aid to a personal appropriation of one's own knowing, evaluating, and decision-making that, in turn, becomes the basis for praxis: working collegially and collaboratively towards a human science designed to meet any number of practical and theoretical problems ([12], p. xxx), including those with future persons especially in view.

Lonergan's contribution to the discussion, in other words, carries the hope that we will better appreciate, possibly reconstrue, and seek to resolve the problem of CFPs not because we have overcome a logical conundrum (e.g., trying to compare a state of existence with previous state of non-existence) or moral quandary, but rather because we have better understood ourselves as questioning, attentive, intelligent, reasonable, responsible, loving human beings, and have chosen to live accordingly. One might say that the "generalized empirical method" ([12], p. 243), which Lonergan invites others to appropriate, provides the heuristic upper blade of a "scissors action" ([12], pp. 312-313, and passim) with which to begin severing the Gordian knot of the problem of CFPs. Our own involvement in situations that confront us—as prospective parents, or geneticists, or environmentalists, and so on—provides the necessary "lower blade."

I. CLUES FROM LONERGAN'S PREDECESSOR

It is appropriate to recall that Lonergan's thought is firmly rooted in, though by no means restricted to, the philosophy and theology of Thomas Aquinas. Elsewhere I have argued that one already finds in Aquinas a moral stance toward future persons [8], and here I wish to recall key elements of that stance because they anticipate and perhaps make more accessible Lonergan's own contribution to the discussion.

Aquinas's most explicit references to future persons occur in his treatment of fornication and adultery. Aquinas judged these acts to be morally illicit because they tend to injure the future child who might thereby be brought into a defective environment (*Summa theologica* II-II 154, 2, trans. Fathers of the English Dominican Province). Four features of Aquinas's thinking on the issues of fornication and adultery are worth noting. First, he seems to assume what recent authors call into question, namely, that it is eminently intelligible to think in terms of benefit and/or harm to future persons. Second is the moral weight he gives to the *conditions* under which children are conceived and which they are likely to encounter once they are born, primarily the lack of a stable marriage and a father's care.

Third is the simple but important point that the anticipated children and the anticipated conditions of their emergence and future existence *together* constitute the contingencies that enter into Aquinas's moral purview. Put in language familiar to contributors to this volume, for Aquinas, contingent future persons and contingent future states of affairs, while distinct, are not epistemologically or morally separable. This claim about inseparability will reemerge when we turn to Lonergan. Fourth is the central, albeit undeveloped, role that *probability* plays in Aquinas's dealing with future contingency. He bases his judgments regarding undesirable outcomes of fornication and adultery not on some unbending, absolute assumption about what is sure to follow from such acts, but rather on what occurs "in general" (*in pluribus*) (*Summa theologica*, II-II 154, 2). We shall see that probability, already a feature of Aquinas's world view [2], is central to Lonergan's moral epistemology as well.

Implicitly at least, Aquinas's concern about future persons extends beyond the issues of fornication and adultery. It is consistent with his general moral theology, as is evident from the privileged place he gives to prudence, that virtue which deals with future contingents (*Summa theologica* II-II 49, 6) and which explores the means for attaining justice, temperance, and so on. Given my concern about a latent individualistic bias in the way the problem of CFPs is sometimes presented, it is crucial to emphasize the inherently social dimension of prudence. For example, prudence requires that we learn from the past [*memoria*] and from others [*docilitas*] (*Summa theologica* II-II 49, 1 and 3). But it is equally crucial to stress that, while prudence concerns itself with future contingents, the focus remains the present moral agent and his or her decisions. For prudence "considers things afar off, in so far as they tend to be a help or a hindrance to that which has to be done at the present time" (*Summa theologica* II-II 47, 1 ad. 2). This link in moral consciousness between future contingents, on the one hand, and present understanding and decision, on the other, is something to which I alluded above under the Lonerganian heading of "norms immanent to conscious intentionality." It also suggests that thoughtful and affectively rich considerations of the future—of persons and states of affairs—can serve a crucial heuristic function in helping moral agents to make good decisions in the present.

Another critical point to be made is that neither prudence itself, nor Aquinas's theoretical discussion of this virtue, constitutes any sort of moral mega-theory or conceptual master plan (deontology, teleology, etc.). Rather, as Aquinas points out, prudence functions concretely and, one might say, in various "spheres" (the home, the city, the nation, etc) (*Summa theologica* II-II, 47, 10-12; 50, 1-4). It is rooted in one's openness and desire, one's striving for the good in concrete circumstances. Individual moral agents and communities must begin where they find themselves and then operate morally in limited, though often expanding, spheres of responsibility.

I mention this because if, in what follows, it seems as though I am drawing on Lonergan in order to construct an air-tight conceptual master-plan, some logic or meta-logic designed to unravel the riddle of CFPs or to handle, by way of logical deduction, every conceivable problem or "case" regarding CFPs, then I have led the reader astray. In the end, Lonergan does not take his stand on a particular conceptual system. Rather he brings into relief the shared capacity that persons across cultures and across time have for experiencing, understanding, affirming and choosing to act in accord not with some external substantive or even procedural norm, but rather with precepts immanent to their own consciousness. Aquinas sought to explain what prudence is and how it relates to future contingency, as well as to any number of other matters, such as the other virtues. But the lucidity of Aquinas's explanation did not absolve his readers from developing this virtue and hence actual attention to future contingents. Similarly, Lonergan points us towards the dynamics of our own conscious intentionality as a potential basis for dealing with issues surrounding CFPs, particularly the question of whether, and the manner in which, we might reasonably speak of benefit and harm to future persons. But he does not relieve us of the immensely difficult task of self appropriation—that is, of attending to, understanding, and affirming the dynamics of our own intelligent striving and responsible living, and of deciding to act in accord with those dynamics ([12], [13], chap. 1).

II. LONERGAN'S CONTRIBUTION

At the risk of over simplifying certain aspects of Lonergan's thought, I now turn there for further clues regarding the problem of CFPs

1. The Anticipatory Character of Intellectual and Moral Consciousness

The first thing to understand about Lonergan's moral epistemology is its heuristic character. I mean this in at least two distinct but related senses. First, through questioning, through openness or wonder, we are oriented to the world as the *to be known and valued*. As human subjects, we seek to know the real and to do the good. This searching or questioning attitude (which must not be confused with knowledge actually achieved or goodness actually realized) is unrestricted in extent and comprehensive in scope ([12], xi, xiv, 4, 9, 220-222 and passim). Human knowing and valuing are heuristic, or anticipatory, in this primary sense. But cognitive and affective operations are heuristic in a derivative sense as well. At various stages of the knowing and decision process, particular images, concepts, hypotheses, paradigms, feelings and so on aid the subject in his or her search for truth and value ([12], 36-7). Think, for example, of the "X" in an algebraic equation, a simple but important heuristic device or concept that stands for the "unknown"— or, more properly, for that which, it is hoped, is "to be known." As I will suggest below, the problem of CFPs may itself constitute an important heuristic device designed to generate new insights and better judgments and policy decisions with reference to future persons. I will also suggest that what we already know about benefit and harm can serve as critical heuristic aids in our efforts to make intelligent and responsible decisions with regard to persons yet to exist, with regard to persons *to be* helped or harmed.

The heuristic character of knowing and valuing, as Lonergan articulates it, also means that these concepts are not reducible to a single operation. Knowing, for instance, is not a matter of "taking a look," as though knowing could be reduced to sensation. Nor is it reducible to the act of conceiving or to building conceptual systems, as crucial to the overall knowing process as concepts or paradigms might be. On the contrary, propelled by questioning, knowing is a "formally dynamic" process that successively calls forth its own components" ([13], p. 16; cf. [11], [12], passim). Experience, the encounter with data of sense or consciousness, gives rise to questions for *understanding*, which seeks intelligibility in the data: What is it? How does it work? What makes it do that? How can we achieve that? Etc. Insights emerge ("Aha! I think I've got it!") and concepts, hypotheses, theories, expressive of the insights, are formulated. But these must be tested. For insights are "a dime a dozen" and so the mind spontaneously raises further questions of a *critical* nature: Is it so? Is my/our hypothesis correct? Is that *really* the way it is? The mind is properly satisfied only when, through an act of reflective insight, or judgment, it grasps a "virtually unconditioned"—that is, the fact that all questions relevant to *this* line of inquiry have have been satisfied ([12], pp. 279-318).

Anyone who has successfully completed a crossword puzzle knows, tacitly at least, what is at stake. Insights emerge ("Maybe it's this. . ."), squares are filled in, then sometimes erased ("No, because 7 Down *has* to be . . ."). Finally, no more *relevant* questions arise (we're not trying to solve the riddle of the universe, or even some *other* crossword puzzle—just this one) and the puzzle is completed. Or, one acknowledges that all the conditions have not been met ("I still can't get 28 Across and 13 Down. Maybe I'll try later.").

I cannot overstress the importance of distinguishing the act of judgment (reflective insight) from acts that occur at the level of understanding (imagination, insights, formulating hypotheses, etc.). For only with judgment, wherein one grasps whether or not the conditions set by the initial question(s) have been fulfilled, does one reach the existent, the actual, the real—for example, the actual solution to the crossword puzzle (or to any piece of the puzzle) as opposed to a clever, but unsatisfactory, attempt. This distinction, I believe, is key to getting to the roots of the problem of CFPs. One reason the problem of CFPs, as presently formulated, is so bedeviling is that the mind flits back and forth: "But if we had acted otherwise...." I would challenge recourse to "what might have been" as a way of invalidating benefit or harm conditioned, in part, by accentuating *actual* choices. Once one has come to the point of judgment, of affirmation that a particular set of conditions has in fact been met, one can no longer pretend that one is still on the level of hypothesis. There is no parity between what is and what might be or might have been. Unless one distinguishes clearly between the hypothetical and the actual, between the level of insight or understanding and the level of judgment, there seems no way to resolve the problem of CFPs on its own stated terms. When I say that the problem of CFPs may be like a puzzle with no solution, this is what I have in mind.

Questions for intelligence (or understanding) and questions for judgment are not the only ones that people ask. They also ask, spontaneously, "Is it good?" "Should I do the crossword puzzle or complete my report for tomorrow?" In other words, questions of the good, of value, arise. Again the anticipatory, or heuristic, character of decision-making is stressed. It is highlighted by the emphasis that Lonergan places on those intentional feelings that *apprehend* values, which in his view occupy an ascending and interlocking scale: vital, social, cultural, personal, transcendent ([13], 31, 37, 67). It is also highlighted by Lonergan's *notional* definition of the good as that which is implicitly sought in questions for deliberation ([13], 36). And again, when it comes to the level of decision, there is all the difference in the world between deliberating—considering alternatives—and actually making a decision. The road actually taken ("We decided to start a family right after we got married.") must not be confused with any or all of the roads that might have been pursued ("What if we had waited a few years?").

The mind's spontaneous questioning, its seeking the true and the good, gives rise to the mind's immanent norms or precepts, mentioned above. Although preconceptual in their operation, these norms may be thematized as: Be attentive (to data); be intelligent (seek intelligibility in the data); be reasonable (be critical of your insights, hypotheses, theories); be responsible (make decisions based on the apprehension of value rather than on that which merely satisfies) ([13], p. 53). The precepts are transcendental in that they move beyond the boundaries of particular spheres of meaning and value. Mathematics and science, the interpretation of texts and works of art, health care and genetic research—as well as, most problematically, the world of common sense invariably mixed with common nonsense—all of these are arenas wherein the precepts are implicitly observed or implicitly ignored.

But the precepts are transcendental in another sense. The mind is provisionally satisfied insofar as one gets insights, moves on to sound judgments, arrives at good decisions in this case or that. But insofar as the transcendental precepts are constitutive of the subject's basic openness to the real and to the good, they are never completely satisfied. For what is implicitly sought is *complete* intelligibility, the *ground* of truth, the *foundation* of value. In short, the transcendental precepts point the questioning subject towards God. As Lonergan puts it, the question of God is implicit in all our questioning (including our questions about future persons), for the question of God is the "question that questions questioning itself" ([13], 103; cf. [12], chpt. 19).[1]

Nor should it be supposed that these precepts are imposed, for they arise spontaneously. If, for example, the reader questions whether what has been said thus far makes sense, or whether it is correct, if he or she wonders whether the writer is irresponsibly riding roughshod over the data, then this indicates nicely that the reader's own spontaneous desire for intelligibility, for truth, for goodness is in working order. Unless the reader wants to contend that someone, or something, is forcing him or her to be attentive, to be intelligent, to be critical, to be responsible, in this as in so many other cases, then he or she can hardly protest that the precepts are imposed.

Of course, knowing and deciding are not so simple as all of that. Much can go awry. Not only is knowing and decision-making an arduous affair (even certain crossword puzzles may prove beyond one's reach, and something like the Human Genome Project is a massive, collaborative process of knowing and deciding), but human beings are also subject to bias: individual bias, or egoism; group bias (racism, nationalism, etc.); the "general bias of common sense" (the refusal to go to the heart of things, to think beyond expediency, to seek a theoretical explanation that relates things to one another rather than a common sense description that refers things always immediatly to "me" or "us"). For Lonergan, the problem of bias is massive. It blocks the emergence and communication of insights, of sound judgments, of good decisions, and it can operate on a widespread, institutionalized scale. Bias does not invite insight but rather oversight. Its fruit is not greater intelligibility, but, on the contrary, an absence of intelligibility and operative intelligence—a "social surd." It is, in theological terms, the problem of moral evil, or sin ([12], pp. 191-241).

What has this to do with the problem of CFPs? A few preliminary comments are appropriate. First, the heuristic character of human knowing suggests that, if we are to approach the problem of future persons intelligently and responsibly, then we must approach it heuristically. The key question regarding CFPs is whether it makes sense to speak of benefit or harm to future persons. On Lonergan's account of knowing and deciding, "good" (or benefit) with regard to future persons is intelligible, but as a heuristic notion, as that which is *to be* known through intelligent inquiry and *to be* further realized through deliberation and decision. Even as restricted categories (as distinct from open-ended notions), particular construals of "benefit," "burden," "harm," and so on, may aid us and carry us forward in our search for intelligibility and goodness. Just as we quite rightly use schematic images on our way to insight ("Let's see if a diagram helps . . ."); just as, following upon insight, we develop concepts and formulate hypotheses on our way to judgments ("Yeah, that *seems* to be the answer. Now let's make sure we've covered all the bases. . ."); just as we consider alternatives and scenarios on our way to decisions ("But if we use *that* grade of paint rather than *this*, it won't last more than a few years. . ."); so we can capitalize on what we already know about "benefit" and "harm" as we seek intelligent and worthy decisions regarding the future.

Third, if the problem of CFPs is to be met, it must be met wherever bias is to be found. In other words, the problem of future persons is not just a theoretical problem, much less a conundrum, but a very practical problem. It is analogous to the manner in which "therapy," if it is to get to the root of patient's problem, must be a practical, and not just theoretical, matter. The problem of CFPs cannot be met if egoism, if racism, sexism, and other forms of deeply ingrained "group-think," if short-term thinking and expedience, are not met as well. But to deal effectively with bias is an enormously practical task. Those troubled about questions of benefit or harm to future persons, arising from present cases (embryo transfer, population control programs, environmental strategies, etc.), need to ask, as surely they often do, such questions as these: As we face these situations, whose egos are at stake and how? Are narrow group interests dominant in the decision-making processes? Where do race and gender fit into the equation? Who in this generation stands to profit financially from decisions about the future, and at whose expense? What fundamental questions about the long term are being encouraged or, on the contrary, conveniently suppressed?

2. Isomorphism Between Knowing and Valuing, and World Processes

From a Lonerganian perspective, the starting point for addressing, in large part by reconstruing, the problem of CFPs is the composite process of knowing and deciding, with its linked and complementary levels. But consideration of cognitional structure, begun in the previous section, leads to epistemological and metaphysical positions. Key here is the notion that there is an isomorphism, or correlativity, between the knower and the known, between the one who values and the values sought.[2] In other words, the linked and ascending levels of conscious intentionality match the linked and ascending levels of world processes ([12] pp. 115, 399-400, 444-448, and passim).

One way of discussing this isomorphism is in the classical terms of potency, form, existence, and good. Just as the knower moves from data (the *potentially* intelligible), to understanding (a grasp of intelligibility or *form*), to judgment (an affirmation of *existence*), to decision (a realization of the *good* in this particular situation), so world processes may be understood under the categories of potency, form, existence ([12], pp. 486, 511-512), and goodness. But this isomorphism may also be expressed in the more contemporary terms of what Lonergan calls "emergent probability" ([12], pp. 123-128, 209-211; [16]; [6]; [18]). According to this world view, both on the side of the subject and on the side of the world to be known, higher schemes of occurrence emerge from lower schemes, rendering intelligible that which is left unaccounted for on previous levels.

This emergence of higher or later schemes is not governed by classical laws alone, but, living as we do in a universe with non-systematic features, is governed also by probabilities. Think, for example, of the manner in which a science laboratory, and all that it entails, is set up in a school to increase the *probability* that insights will emerge and accumulate among the students. Think of the way in which the Human Genome Project (with its enormously elaborate, collaborative processes) is organized to increase the probability of "breakthroughs" in knowledge, breakthroughs that makes sense of data that previously were only potentially intelligible (level of understanding), breakthroughs that may be confirmed through tests of various kinds (level of judgment). The emergence of knowing on the side of subjects is matched by emergent probability on the side of the world processes to be known. So, for example, physical processes condition and give rise to chemical processes; chemical processes condition and give rise to biological processes; biological processes condition and give rise to psychological processes. The origin and development of species, studied by Darwin and many others since, offers key examples of emergent probability.

Several aspects of this world view, which is necessarily overly simplified here, are pertinent to the problem of CFPs. First, on this view, lower level processes condition but do not determine the emergence of higher level processes (e.g., adequate funding for the Human Genome Project arguably conditions but does not ensure the emergence of a finished "map"). Nor does the emergence of later processes negate the intelligibility of the earlier schemes of recurrence (securing adequate funding for the Genome Project is itself a matter of intelligent activity, and grant writing is a specialized skill). Thus world processes are intelligible both at their own level (what Lonergan calls "horizontal finality") and in terms of their relation to the levels from which they emerge and to those levels whose emergence they in turn condition ("vertical finality") ([14], pp. 447-451).

Second, this twofold finality is important for our understanding of persons as intelligible beings. Persons cannot be understood with any degree of sophistication if we neglect their relationship to those processes (genetic, biological, economic, etc.) which condition, but do not determine, their emergence. This is a more sophisticated way of affirming Aquinas's conviction that, in thinking about future neighbors, we cannot ignore the manifold conditions of their conception, birth, and nurturance. But the notions of horizontal and vertical finality also urge that we understand the human in terms of that which, at any point, it conditions. Frederick Crowe (the "dean" of Lonergan scholars) has, for example, discussed fetal life in these terms [5]. One of Crowe's main points is that human fetuses may be understood, at various stages of development, not only as intelligible at their own level (horizontal finality), but also in terms of setting the conditions for the emergence of higher levels of integration (vertical finality). For instance, the disproportionate size of the brain at early stages of development anticipates the cognitive operations—the spiritual activity—that will regularly occur only much later.

This understanding of prenatal life may have normative relevance to embryo transfer and related issues often discussed in relation to the problem of CFPs. Precisely what the revelance is in any particular case, I am unprepared to say. But at the very least acceptance of this world view may alter one's way of regarding embryos. For if they possess vertical as well as horizontal finality, if they have an orientation beyond themselves, if their present state conditions the emergence of higher levels of organization, including the emergence of an intelligibility that is also an intelligence (i.e., a person), then they cannot be "just embryos."

A third point of significance is the fact that human beings both *participate* in world processes and *affect* those processes. As intelligible, human beings are as subject to classical laws (e.g., gravity) and statistical laws (e.g., games of chance, including such things as getting killed by a drunk driver, or contracting Lyme disease) as are any other finite existents. But human beings, as intelligent and responsible, can, within the limits of those laws, shift the probabilities that new schemes of recurrence will emerge. So, for example, the passage and enforcement of (or voluntary compliance with) seat belt laws may shift the probabilities regarding highway fatalities: conditioned by these laws and their compliance, a safer highway system may emerge. Outlawing landmines today may shift the probability that, several years from now, children will be a bit safer as they cross a tract of land [cf. 1].

This, of course, brings us back to the problem of CFPs, for at issue here is fact that we often *can* affect the emergence of new human beings (how many, of what genetic structure, etc.), and thus the question of whether or not we *ought* so affect their emergence. To begin a course of fertility drugs, for example, is an implicit attempt to shift the probabilities in favor of the emergence of a new person. The main observation I would make at this point is to reemphasize the isomorphism between the knower and valuer, and that which is to be known and valued. If there is a genuine question of "how many" or "what kind of" human beings will emerge as a result of our choices, there is simultaneously the question of how intelligently, how reasonably, how responsibly we are acting now. In other words, we are brought back to the fundamental question of whether we are abiding by the immanent norms of conscious intentionality, or whether we are allowing bias to have its sway. Put yet another way, the issue is not simply whether or not CFPs can be benefited or harmed; the issue is just as surely the moral quality of our own lives.

3. Centrality of Emergence

This brings us to closer consideration of emergence in relation to the problem of CFPs. Persons do not pre-exist, as though they were lined up in some cosmic bull-pen, waiting for us *randomly* to call one them into our world, and into our game, through our choices. On the contrary, prior to their emergence, people simply do not exist, for the conditions of their emergence have not been fulfilled (this, I take it, is in keeping with the truly radical Christian doctrines of *creatio ex nihilo* and *concursus*). There is no "cosmic bull-pen." I assume that no one engaged with the problem of CFPs is claiming otherwise—namely, that future persons do pre-exist. Yet it worth pursuing this issue briefly from a Lonerganian perspective because it helps to clarify why, if persons do not exist prior to their emergence, it still makes sense to speak of future persons, as well as of future harm or benefit.

To understand what is at stake, let us return to emergence as we experience it in our knowing. For if there is an isomorphism between knowing and valuing, on the one hand, and the world to be known and valued, on the other, then our knowing and deciding provide an apt and accurate analogy for that which we would like better to understand—in this case what we mean by "future persons." The notion of emergence is central to Lonergan's epistemology. Indeed, one might say that his massive book *Insight* is an *étude* on that theme: the act of insight, he says, is the prototype of emergence ([12], p. 481). Judgments and decisions have their emergent qualities as well. This is not some esoteric notion. The reader need only recall some past experience of being stumped by a problem and then—Aha!—the answer came; finally, everything fit. In such cases, the answer is not there and then it is; it is not yet found and then it is found; suddenly, or slowly, it emerges.

Very much to the point of our consideration of future persons, prior to judgment—the reflective insight that grasps that all the relevant questions have been answered, that all the relevant *conditions* have been met—we do not have knowledge, but only its partial components. Knowledge of the real has yet to fully emerge. This is the difference between thinking we *might* have the answer we are seeking and being able to say, "Yes, that's it," "No, that's not it," or "That's *probably* it (or not it)" (as is frequently the case, e.g., in science). It is the difference between what might be, or what might have been, and what is in fact the case.

A focus on emergence, with respect to future persons, steers us between two errors. One error would be a radical separation of the emergent person from the conditions giving rise to his or her emergence when those conditions are fulfilled. Just as insight grasps an intelligible pattern in *this* data, so to begin to grasp the meaning of a new person is to begin to understand fully the convergence of fulfilled conditions that gave rise to the emergence of that person. To give a homely analogy, the clues in a mystery provide the conditions for the emergence of an answer to the question "whodunit." But only when the sleuth "gets it" (usually about 45 minutes into "Murder She Wrote") do the clues come together in an intelligent pattern. So too, persons begin to understand themselves and others as they grasp the convergence and interrelationship of the conditions of their emergence and development. It is not for nothing that, in trying to understand themselves, individuals scour baptismal records and visit remote villages in search of their "roots."

One way of talking about this convergence and fulfillment of conditions is to speak about humanity as a "concrete universal" ([12], p. 743). Humanity is a comprehensive notion: it is that which is *to be* known and valued, not once and for all (e.g., through some a particular ethical theory) but progressively, through the accumulation of insights and correct judgments and responsible acts. One thinks, for example, of the efforts of historians to aid us in our search for knowing who we are. The basis for coming to know and value the human, including future persons, is itself concrete and comprehensive in intent. It is the virtually unrestricted capacity to raise and answer specific questions in any number of contexts—What is it? Is it so? Is it good? It is the capacity that serves as the creative impulse of every culture. It is the capacity to correct one's errors and false beliefs, to confront bias. It is the capacity, when necessary, to change one's mind.

In trying to understand the meaning of "persons" (including future persons) we cannot prescind from conditions giving rise to their emergence (just as, analogously, when doing a particular crossword puzzle we cannot prescind from these particular questions that must be answered). But neither can (or should) we *reduce* persons to the conditions of their emergence. This is the second error to be avoided. For just as, by analogy, there is all the difference in the world between getting the meaning of a joke and not getting it, between actually lighting upon a cure for AIDS and just wishing for a cure, between progressively cracking the genetic code and not cracking it at all, so is the emergent person truly "new." In terms of normative guidance, individual human beings are thus to be regarded as human—for their meaning is to be grasped precisely in their relationship to other human beings and to the rest of reality. But emergent persons are at the same time irreducible to any abstract or hypothetical notion of humanity. For unlike hypothetical persons, actual persons have the conditions of their emergence fulfilled.

To fail to grasp the significance of emergence, exemplified most clearly in the act of insight, is to fall prey to what Lonergan calls the errors of essentialism and conceptualism. Essentialism is the mistaken notion that "individual finite natures are logically and ontologically prior to the world orders that relate them to one another." Conceptualism is a misunderstanding of understanding. It views understanding as a grasping of discrete terms, perhaps piling one upon another as knowledge grows, rather than as grasping unified sets of terms ([19], pp. 172 ff.). If one is not careful, the formulation of the problem of CFPs found in the opening paragraph of this essay can lead to these errors. In that formulation, people are referred to apart from the *actual* fulfillment of conditions that give rise to their emergence: "If we had acted otherwise, some *other* person would have come into existence." Put otherwise, the *hypothetical* (the "other person" that might have been had we acted otherwise) is put on the same level as the *actual* convergence of fulfilled conditions and the emergence of new beings.

When conceptualism influences the manner in which we understand God, it results in the mistaken notion that future contingent persons are in God's mind "pretty much as the animals were in Noah's ark," rather than as derivative of the world orders God understands perfectly, dynamically, and in every detail ([15]; [19], p. 175). To make a theological point, if we think that "doing God's will" has anything at all to do with decisions affecting the emergence of new persons, we are mistaken if we regard those persons as somehow "free floating" in the mind of God, totally detached from the world order in which we human beings actually participate—an order which is governed by classical and statistical laws and which includes the vertical finality that relates world processes to God as source and end.

The understanding of human knowing and decision-making as anticipatory or heuristic, and the notion of emergence key to that understanding, does, however, indicate why we can rightly refer in our decision-making to "future persons" in the first place, as well to "benefit" and "harm." If we try to pin benefit or harm onto future persons as though they already somehow existed, then, of course, we are running down a *cul de sac*. But as heuristic categories which arise out of our present best individual and collective understanding of what it means to be human, harm and benefit and similar categories can be enormously significant. Just as scientists and scholars and people of common sense invoke or construct all sorts of images, scenarios, heuristic frameworks, models, and narratives to aid them in their quest to make sense of the world, so it is no waste of time and effort to use accumulated understandings of the human, and of benefit and harm, as heuristic devices when faced with decisions that may affect the emergence (number, physical make-up, etc.) of new human beings.

If the algebraist is not wasting his or her time by naming the unknown "X"—a heuristic device designed to guide inquiry prior to the emergence of insight—then neither is it a waste of time to think about future persons and their good prior to their emergence. When considering questions regarding future persons, it seems quite appropriate, for example, to recall our growing body of human rights law. Human rights covenants surely express some articulation of benefit and harm, and at least some human rights lawyers assume that such articulations may serve as heuristic means of guiding decisons affecting the emergence of new persons [20]. Or, to go back to the example given by Aquinas, it is quite reasonable to draw on present knowledge of what constitutes harm to children (and we know a great deal about risk factors today) as heuristic aids in our decision-making about bringing new children into the world under such and such a set of conditions.

There are two more things to be said about future persons and future benefit and harm, understood heuristically. First, by saying that present understandings of benefit and harm have their rightful place in our decision-making process, I am not saying that we already know, or can always agree on, what constitutes the good, and what might count for benefit and harm. That, of course, is a huge topic and I am not goint to discuss it here. Moral discourse in a variety of forms must continue. All I claim is that our best present understandings of and achievement of the good (e.g., the best collective wisdom of our religious traditions) are in no way beside the point as we make decisions affecting the emergence of new persons—any more than what scientists know about life on earth is beside the point as they seek to determine if there was ever life on Mars, or any more than the knowledge of genetic structure painstakingly won over the years is beside the point when seeking a complete map of the human genome, a map that has yet fully to emerge. Such a claim may seem minimal, but since the problem of CFPs as stated calls into question the meaningfulness of harm and benefit when future persons are at issue, the claim is nonetheless worth making.

Second, the problem of CFPs, as explored in this volume, is *itself* a powerful heuristic device that may further our understanding and aid us in our decision-making. But it might not function in quite the way we expect. Sometimes images, models, cases, etc., can obscure as well as enlighten. Sometimes the wrong questions are asked and we beat our heads against the wall seeking intelligibility until finally, through "inverse insight" ([12], pp. 19-25) we get the point that this precise line of inquiry is leading nowhere, that there is no way out, that no intelligibility is there to be found. Above I suggested that the problem of CFPs, as stated in the opening paragraph, may fit into that category: as long as the problem is stated such that the rules of the game put the *hypothetical* ("But if we had done otherwise. . .") on a par with *actually* emergent persons, no solution will be found and the inquirer does best to back up and approach the matter of future persons from another angle. I leave it to the reader to judge whether his or her own process of attending, understanding, judging and deciding might offer a more adequate ground, than does the currently stated problem of CFPs, for thinking about the emergence of new persons in our highly technologized age.

4. Reappraising Contingency

Finally, a few words must be said about contingency, perhaps simply by way of emphasis. If, as Louis Dupré has argued, the meaning of contingency and necessity is open to profound questioning today ([7], pp. 252-253), then we should be very slow to put intellectual clamps on that meaning. But that, I am afraid, may happen if we leave the problem of CFPs in its initially stated form.

First, we should be very clear that "contingent"—as in contingent future persons—is too narrowly understood if it refers only to those persons whose existence is *intentionally* altered through the timing of conception, etc. This would be to regard human beings as highly intelligent and responsible, but perhaps to downplay the fundamental fact that human beings share in the intelligibility of the universe, with its systematic and non-systematic features. Rather, as should be clear by now, I would understand contingency to have the more general meaning of *conditioned*. On this understanding, *all* persons, regardless of level or degree of human intentionality involved in their emergence, are contingent in the sense that *all* are conditioned in countless ways. This fact should not be downplayed, much less ignored.

Second, I am concerned that a more fundamental understanding of contingency not be lost, namely, the conviction that the world is not its own final explanation and ultimate ground. Such forgetfulness may be a function of a growing awareness today of the many ways human beings can, and do, intervene to shape the future. I want to keep in view the fact that human beings cannot *fully* explain and ground themselves, regardless of when and where they exist. Individual human beings, future or not, are not contingent simply in the sense that their existence is in part a statistical matter, and in that sense a matter of "chance" ([9], p. 6, n.20). For statistical laws, along with classical laws, are simply part and parcel of the universe in which we happen to dwell, and it is that universe as a whole that requires a complete explanation, a grounding, a foundation. Human beings are not contingent simply because, by someone else's choice, they were conceived in February rather than March. Human beings, as all other finite beings, as the universe itself with both its systematic and nonsystematic features, are contingent in the fundamental sense that they depend for their existence on God. *Pace* David Heyd [10] and others, on the view espoused here, through our choices we do not, *strictly speaking*, "create" anybody—or any thing, for that matter. Strictly speaking, only God creates.

III. CONCLUSION: THE CHALLENGES OF FUTURE CONTINGENT PERSONS

Let me now summarize a few of the points made here so that the "normative payoff" of Lonergan's contribution might be more apparent. First of all, Lonergan's moral epistemology renders suspect approaches to the problem of CFPs that would reduce it to a conundrum that is a trap for endless hypothesizing. Rather, the resolution of the problem is rooted in the dynamics of conscious intentionality—the potentially infinite capacity to raise and answer questions for intelligence, for judgment (which moves beyond hypothesis to affirmation of existence), for decision (which moves beyond considerations of alternatives to realization of some greater or lesser good). The good of future persons is a heuristic notion. Strictly speaking, of course, future persons cannot be benefited or harmed because they do not yet exist. But future persons can be anticipated by the insights, judgments, and decisions that, in part, condition their emergence. Benefit or harm to future persons may be anticipated, and actively sought or avoided, as well.

Second, when considering the good of persons, or benefit and harm, we do not need to start from scratch, as though each emergent person were totally isolated, with a "good" totally his or her own. Just as, by analogy, science proceeds towards the "unknown," towards the "to be discovered," by building on the accumulation of data, of insights into that data, of verification of hypotheses, and so on, so too in considering harm or benefit to future persons, and thus looking for moral constraints, we are by no means helpless. We can and ought to build on what we already know harm and benefit to be. If we find we cannot do that, then it may be that we are not so sure about what counts for the good life even for existing persons. At this point we need to be careful not to let the intellectual difficulties inherent in the problem of CFPs steer us away from the task of discovering the good to be done here and now, for the good done here and now conditions the emergence of future good.

Third, if the key to resolving the problem of CFPs (mainly by reconstruing it) is to be found not in some hypothetical world ("But if we had chosen otherwise...") but rather in the concrete and comprehensive human desire for intelligibility and value, then we need to attend to that which promotes or blocks this desire. More specifically, we need to be attentive to the manner in which biases—individual, group, and general—impede human living. From a prescriptive point of view, the need here is at least for better communication and collaboration on issues affecting the emergence of new persons. In that way, the biases might be more easily exposed and, in accord with the notion of emergent probability, possibly reversed ([17], pp. 332-333). If the problem of CFPs is to be met, then the problem of bias must be addressed.

The reader may be disappointed that I have not, with the help of Lonergan, resolved one or more very specific cases ordinarily connected to the problem of CFPs. I have tried to suggest some "normative payoff" of Lonergan's thinking along the way, but the real point is that the relevant norms are already available to the reader: Be attentive, be intelligent, be reasonable, be responsible. The challenge is for us to come to grips with those norms (i.e., to come to grips with ourselves) in a myriad of contexts (family life, genetic research, politics, etc.), and to work to condition widespread compliance with these norms and to counter their widespread denial. Also to the point perhaps, so far as normative payoff goes, is the following: If, for the reasons given throughout this essay, the problem of CFPs as formulated in the opening paragraph is in fact akin to a puzzle with no answer, then the challenge will be to leave the problem aside and focus attention elsewhere—beginning, I suggest, with the great deal we already know about what constitutes benefit and harm. If one has already expended enormous time and energy trying to solve a puzzle with no answer, giving it up may, for the moment, be challenge enough.

The reader may also be disappointed that I have not tried to show how Lonergan's theory of value might respond to the insistence that, in approaching the problem of CFPs one must opt for either a "person-affecting" or an "impersonal" theory of value ([9], pp. 8-9). Very briefly, from a Lonerganian perspective the alternatives seem too restrictive, or rooted in a failure to distinguish and relate, within interiority, two complementary (rather than mutually exclusive) realms of meaning: the realm of common sense (relating things to us) and the realm of theory (relating things to one another) ([12], pp. 417-21). Nor, finally, have I addressed, except in passing, any of the pressing theological questions raised by consideration of future persons. None of this did I set out to do. Rather, with Lonergan's aid, I have tried to do some "spadework" that, I hope, might prepare the way for further reflection, theological and otherwise, on the problem of future persons. If the reader has, through greater attention to the dynamics of his or her own attending, understanding, judging and deciding, begun to consider the problem of CFPs from a new angle, then this essay will have achieved its purpose.

NOTES

[1] This is not to say that the question of God overwhelms particular questions of fact or value. On the contrary, particular questions are significant precisely because they may be grounded in the subject's own desire for meaning, truth, and value, which reaches its term only in God. Thus in seeking to answer particular questions (What's wrong with this car? What is this patient's history? What are the actual causes of poverty in the United States?) whether or not a person or community "gets it right," or admits to ignorance when appropriate, is no small matter. Attentiveness, intelligence, reasonableness, and responsibility pertain not to some ethereal world, but to the universe in which we dwell.

[2] The reader should understand that, without attempting to defend the move, I am extending Lonergan's notion of an isomorphism between knower and known, which he discussed at length in *Insight*, to the fourth level of conscious intentionality (decision), which in his later writings he distinguished more clearly from the earlier three. See [3].

BIBLIOGRAPHY

1. Byrne, P.H.: 1981, "On Taking Responsibility for the Indeterminate Future," in S. Skousgaard (ed.), *Phenomenology and the Understanding of Human Destiny*, Landham, MD., The University Press of America, pp. 229-237.
2. Byrne, P.H.: 1982, "The Thomist Sources of Lonergan's Dynamic World View," *The Thomist*, 46, pp. 108-145.
3. Crowe, F.E.: 1989, "An Exploration of Lonergan's New Notion of Value," in F.E. Crowe, *Appropriating the Lonergan Idea* (ed.) M. Vertin, Washington, DC, The Catholic University of America Press, pp. 51-70.
4. Crowe, F.E.: 1994, "The Genus 'Lonergan and' . . . and Feminism, in C.S.W. Crysdale (ed.), *Lonergan and Feminism*, University of Toronto Press, Toronto, pp. 13-32.
5. Crowe, F. E.: 1989, "The Life of the Unborn: Notions from Bernard Lonergan," in F. E. Crowe, *Appropriating the Lonergan Idea* (ed.) M. Vertin, Washington, DC, The Catholic University of America Press, pp. 360-369.
6. Crysdale, C.: 1995: "Revisioning Natural Law: From a Classicist Paradigm to Emergent Probability," *Theological Studies* 56/3, pp. 464-484.
7. Dupré, L.: 1993, *Passage to Modernity: An Essay in the Hermeneutics of Nature and Culture*, Yale University Press, New Haven.
8. George, W. P.: 1992, "Regarding Future Neighbours: Thomas Aquinas and Concern for Posterity," *The Heythrop Journal* 33, pp. 283-306.
9. Heller, J. C.: 1996, "The Challenge of Contingent Future Persons," paper delivered at the 1996 Annual Meeting of the Society of Christian Ethics, Albuquerque, NM., Jan. 5-7.
10. Heyd, D.: 1992, *Genethics: Moral Issues in the Creation of People*, University of California Press, Berkeley, CA.
11. Lonergan, B. J. F.: 1967, "Cognitional Structure," in F.E. Crowe (ed.), *Collection: Papers by Bernard Lonergan*, Herder and Herder, New York, pp. 221-239.
12. Lonergan, B. J. F.: 1970, *Insight: A Study in Human Understanding*, 3rd. ed., Philosophical Library, New York.
13. Lonergan, B. J. F.: 1972, *Method in Theology*, 1973, 2d ed., Herder and Herder, New York.
14. Lonergan, B. J. F.: 1985, "Mission and the Spirit," in F.E. Crowe (ed.), *A Third Collection: Papers by Bernard J. F. Lonergan*, Paulist Press, New York, pp. 221-239.

15. Lonergan, B. J. F.: 1967, "The Natural Desire to See God," in F.E. Crowe (ed.), *Collection: Papers by Bernard Lonergan*, Herder and Herder, New York, pp. 84-95.
16. Melchin, K. R.: 1987, *History, Ethics and Emergent Probability: Ethics, Society and History in the Work of Bernard Lonergan*, University Press of America, Lanham, MD.
17. Roy, J. D.: 1981, "Bioethics as Anamnesis: What Lonergan has Understood and Others Have Overlooked," in M.L. Lamb (ed.), *Creativity and Method: Essays in Honor of Bernard Lonergan, S.J.*, Marquette University Press, Milwaukee, pp. 325-38.
18. Schute, M.: 1994, "Emergent Probability and the Ecomfeminist Critique of Hierarchy," in C.S.W. Crysdale (ed.), *Lonergan and Feminism*, University of Toronto Press, pp. 146-174.
19. Stebbins, J. M.: 1995, *The Divine Initiative: Grace, World-Order and Human Freedom in the Early Writings of Bernard Lonergan*, University of Toronto Press, Toronto.
20. Weis., E.B.: 1989, *In Fairness to Future Generations: International Law, Common Patrimony, and Intergenerational Justice*, Transnational Publishers, Inc., Dobbs Ferry, NY.

NOTES ON CONTRIBUTORS

Cynthia B. Cohen, Ph.D., J.D., is Senior Research Fellow, Kennedy Institute of Ethics, Georgetown University, Washington, D.C., U.S.A.

Avner de-Shalit is Senior Lecturer, Department of Political Science, The Hebrew University, Jerusalem, Israel.

Robert Elliot is Professor of Philosophy and Dean of Arts, Sunshine Coast University College, Queensland, Australia.

Nick Fotion is Professor of Philosophy, Department of Philosophy, Emory University, Atlanta, Georgia, U.S.A.

William P. George is Assistant Professor of Religious Studies, Dominican University, River Forest, Illinois, U.S.A.

R. M. Hare, is White's Professor of Moral Philosophy Emeritus, Corpus Christi College, Oxford, U.K.

Jan C. Heller, Ph.D., is Director, Center for Ethics in Health Care, Saint Joseph's Health System, Atlanta, Georgia, U.S.A.

David Heyd is Professor of Philosophy, Department of Philosophy, The Hebrew University, Jerusalem, Israel.

Michael Lockwood is University Lecturer in Philosophy (Continuing Education), Fellow of Green College, University of Oxford, U.K.

Lukas H. Meyer is 'Wissenschaftlicher Assistent' for Political Theory, Institute for International and Intercultural Studies, Universitat Bremen, Bremen, Germany.

Ingmar Persson is Professor of Philosophy, Department of Philosophy, Lund University, Lund, Sweden.

Carol A. Tauer is Professor of Philosophy, College of St. Catherine, St. Paul, Minnesota, U.S.A.

Clark Wolf is Assistant Professor, Department of Philosophy, University of Georgia, Athens, Georgia, U.S.A.